—

Andrew
Lloyd Webber

Gerald McKnight

—

Andrew
Lloyd Webber

GRANADA
London Toronto Sydney New York

Granada Publishing Limited
8 Grafton Street, London W1X 3LA

Published by Granada Publishing 1984

British Library Cataloguing in Publication Data

McKnight, Gerald
   Andrew Lloyd Webber.
   1. Lloyd Webber, Andrew   2. Composers—
   England—Biography
   I. Title
   782.81'092'4   ML410.L7/

ISBN 0-246-12093-2

Printed in Great Britain by
Richard Clay (The Chaucer Press) Ltd,
Bungay, Suffolk

Contents

Illustrations

Cameron Mackintosh, producer of *Cats*
  JOHN HAYNES

With Elaine Paige at the *Cats* opening in London
  EXPRESS NEWSPAPERS

The Broadway cast of *Cats*
  MARTHA SWOPE

Bonnie Langford, Elaine Paige and Finola Hughes in the London show
  DEWYNTERS LTD.

In rehearsal for *Song and Dance*, starring Wayne Sleep and Marti Webb
  ZOË DOMINIC

Andrew cuts his 34th-birthday cake, watched by first wife Sarah and Marti Webb
  EXPRESS NEWSPAPERS

Andrew and Julian with the Everly Brothers
  PHOTO: ALAN GRISBROOK, COURTESY OF JULIAN LLOYD WEBBER

Andrew buys the Palace Theatre, London
  EXPRESS NEWSPAPERS

Andrew with Sarah Brightman
  PRESS ASSOCIATION

Andrew enjoys a ragging from the cast of *Daisy Pulls It Off*
  EXPRESS NEWSPAPERS

THE PHOTOS OF ANDREW LLOYD WEBBER AS A CHILD ARE COURTESY OF JEAN LLOYD WEBBER

Acknowledgements

I should like to express my thanks to Andrew Lloyd Webber for granting me extensive and invaluable interviews during the writing of this book. Without his help the work would have been far less well informed and true to the facts.

Through Andrew, too, I was able to reach those loyal friends and family who would never speak about him without his consent. I am no less grateful to them.

Sadly, Tim Rice alone declined to be interviewed.

My personal thanks are more than due to many others: to Mimi Wise in New York for kind hospitality and help; to Paul Rossiter (once again) for his painstaking research; to Merrilyn Cook for expert typing; and to all who kindly assisted me.

Gerald McKnight

1

Cats on the Rooftops

AT ten in the morning the New York day under a hazy sky is already warm for October. Two technicians are wiring a magnified model of a cracked teapot on the sidewalk at the back of the Winter Garden Theater in full view of passersby. The men are wearing sweat-stained tee-shirts over jeans rumpled as if they've been fitfully slept in. Probably they have. These are the last tense days before Broadway and the American public will see the show everyone's been talking about for weeks, Andrew Lloyd Webber's *Cats*. For those working on or in the show sleep is already a rationed commodity.

This is no orthodox production. Lloyd Webber uses a theatrical interior like wet clay, forcing it to his design. Eighteen months from now, his *Starlight Express* will draw gasps in London for its astonishing transformation of a musical stage into a roller-skating spectacular. Here in Manhattan his *Cats* is straining every fibre of the old Winter Garden's frame. Even the roof has been desecrated – chopped open to allow a gigantic elevator to rise heavenwards from the stage, where John Napier's set is taking shape.

The two electricians have fixed the teapot. Their tee-shirts carry the emblem which has become a familiar sight in New York newspapers and on the city's hoardings for weeks past, a pair of slanting cat's eyes against a jet-black background. Giant replicas are being lofted into place over the marquee of the theatre's front on Broadway. Back here, the pavement is cluttered with last-minute preparation.

The big backstage doors are open. Inside, on props and trestles, is what looks like a huge, semi-circular junkyard. The objects decorating it are battered, larger than life, slightly crazy. Passers-by stare and grin. An oversize bottle of Japanese 'Kirin' beer leans its papier-mâché weight against a workbench. For these few hours Seventh Avenue has become an annexe of Wonderland, but instead of Alice the whole neighbourhood is given over to strange, prowling, four-legged beasts in human form . . . the cast of *Cats*, psyching themselves into feeling and acting like cats. The director, Trevor Nunn, has demanded no less.

'He suggested we should all have an individual cat in mind,' Anna McNeely, playing Jennyanydots, says. 'Well, I don't particularly care about cats, but we've all had to do it. "Be a cat, don't act one," Trevor told us. It's hard sometimes. You have to give yourself a lot to get up and do silly little cat things without feeling embarrassed or intimidated. But everyone is involved on the same level of giving. And at the end, when they giggle and address you as a cat, it's fun to see the reaction from people who've seen the show. It's as if they've spent the evening with a lot of cats.'

A slim, lithe girl, one of the dancers, walks up with two excited friends. They whisper and she goes inside, returning with spread hands. 'They won't give us *any*,' she explains, meaning house seats. The friends ebb away and the dancer enters the stage door. A messenger delivers a package, then comments to anyone who'll listen: 'I hear it's a *great* show.'

Activity on the street is growing. A larger-than-lifesize standard lamp, rusty and tattered, is balanced against empty cartons overprinted 'three-speed whisper-quiet fans' made by a firm called Lasko. Three red trucks have pulled up to remove some of the mounting debris; their sides carry the legend 'Manhattan Demolition Co Inc'. Rubbish already fills two of them. Ahead is another small van belonging to John T. Smith, massage therapist. Mr Smith has his hands full today.

A prowling security man grows edgy. 'Can I help you?' His eyes are suspiciously unassisting. If you have business here, they seem to say, do it and go. If not, clear out. There are still days to go to the Broadway premiere, but already the show is breaking records for pre-opening bookings.

How much of this stems from the expensive publicity and advertising campaign, the 'hype' being given the show by press representative Fred Nathan and the show's general manager, R. Tyler Gatchel Jr, and how much from reports of its London success nobody knows. Bernie Jacobs, who operates the Winter Garden as president of the owners, the Shubert Organization, is too busy counting to care. The show's English producer, Cameron Mackintosh, is joyously 'up' on the favourable bookings. He can hardly sit still in his office two blocks away. Everyone seems to smell a hit brewing, even the famed Broadway composer Marvin Hamlisch who caught the show in London and says, with understandable professional envy, 'I didn't like it, but it'll be a smash.'

It will if the critics don't pan it. Or perhaps even if they do. Hedging bets, Clive Barnes, who'll review it for the *New York Post*, admits that earlier Lloyd Webber shows have been successful in spite of bad or lukewarm notices in the American press. But before seeing *Cats*, Barnes is sceptical: 'Consider that Lloyd Webber is asking Americans to come and listen to child poems by an obscure poet, T. S. Eliot. OK they're set to his, Lloyd Webber's music. But few will have ever read a line of Eliot in print.' Bernie Jacobs admits he has booked the show in spite of the difficulty he had with the poems. 'I was on my way to

London to take a look at the play to decide if we wanted to do it here,' he explains. 'I bought a copy of the poems to read on the plane, and said to myself, "How can you make a musical out of this?"'

How indeed?

Yet if it does romp home a winner – and this is the really extraordinary and exciting thing about the looming pre-miere – *Cats* will make theatrical history for its 34-year-old composer. New Yorkers calling up for seats don't know it, don't care much. Many couldn't tell you who Andrew Lloyd Webber is, though his and Tim Rice's *Evita* has been packing them in across the way at the Broadway Theater for four straight years, collecting a galaxy of awards – including one in abject recantation from the very drama critics who'd panned it at birth. Nonetheless, it is a startling fact.

If *Cats* lands on its feet on Broadway this will mean that for the first time a composer – and an English one at that – has succeeded in providing both the West End London stage and Broadway with three hit musicals simultaneously. In London, there is *Cats*, booked seemingly endlessly solid for the coming months. *Evita* doing capacity business. And *Song and Dance*, among the city's most popular shows. Here in Manhattan *Evita* is one of Broadway's longest runners, with *Joseph and the Amazing Technicolor Dream-coat* already established round the corner at the Royale.

And now *Cats*.

That this has been achieved during a massive slump in theatre box-office takings, a recession which has closed several famous halls both in Britain and the United States, is remarkable. That it has been accomplished by a young man who came to New York almost penniless less than twelve years before, with only a recording of his and Rice's unknown rock-opera, *Jesus Christ Superstar*, to speak for his talent is even more astonishing. Nobody, not even

America's own acclaimed geniuses of musical theatre, from Jerome Kern and Richard Rodgers to Stephen Sondheim, has done as much.

And the historical significance is reluctantly admitted. Americans of course would far rather see their own composers triumph, at the very least in their home arena. But Lloyd Webber has been unstoppable. In New York now, he quietly reveals his own feelings on reaching the summit. 'I feel,' he says, 'like an outsider. In London, I'm the only fish in a very small pond.' Feel like an outsider, he may. But with *Cats* he will gain access, however much he is envied for doing so, to that coveted circle of America's highest order: the successful. 'I think,' he admits diffidently, 'that *Cats* will make people in New York take a lot more notice of me than before.' Well, understatement is recognized here as an unconsciously British art.

In fact, with Lloyd Webber it is a calculated reading of the professional yardstick. He assumes nothing until it is hard fact. His capacity for distancing himself from everyone he works with, other than the élite band of his inner circle, is marked. To the lead players he seems 'shy, very, very shy. He'll say "hi" in passing, but you don't get very close to him.' An American backstage dresser who's worked on several of Andrew's earlier shows, Pixie Esmond, comments: 'He's very weird. We always thought he was a bit peculiar, wearing that same velvet coat which made me think of Carnaby Street.' A Broadway veteran stresses the same impression: Andrew, he says, 'looks such a sweet little boy'. The same man adds: 'Lloyd Webber? He's this English guy with funny-looking eyes and a fancy taste in patterned shirts and velvet, old-fashioned jackets.'

To a lot of Americans, he is an alien odd-ball at best, a raving English eccentric at worst.

In the profession, though, it is intuitively accepted that Andrew is anything but soft to work with. One week before *Cats* is due to open on Broadway, the experienced sound director Abe Jacob quits, reportedly in fury after a bitter row with Andrew. Others have gone the same way. While his erstwhile lyric-writing partner, Tim Rice, is universally popular (to Pixie, 'cute, wonderful and charmingly friendly') especially with girls in the cast, Andrew's abrupt, sometimes distant manner and breathtaking ruthlessness with his own and everyone else's work has won more admirers than friends. Even fewer are those who try to get closer to him during rehearsals than is absolutely necessary.

Everyone, of course, wants to be *in* a Lloyd Webber show. For *Cats* the company auditioned scores of dancers, singers and actors before Trevor Nunn (widely respected in New York as director of the running hit, *Nicholas Nickleby* and of the Royal Shakespeare Company in England) made his selection. Those who keep up with Broadway 'dish' (gossip) know at least this about Andrew: he is a success in a profession where there are many more snakes than ladders. He has flopped only once, and then valiantly, trying to bring P. G. Wodehouse to theatrical life in 1975 with his musical *Jeeves.* But to work with him, or for him, is to be tested to the ultimate.

'There's no "that'll do" with him,' Anna McNeely says. 'No half measures. He puts demands on you that really surprise me.' A lyric soprano turned dancer who used to teach music, she finds *Cats* one of the most difficult scores of her career to sing. 'There are high Ds in it!' she exclaims. 'We're just very lucky to have dancers who can reach such high notes.'

Andrew's standards come as a total surprise to the Americans. 'It really astonishes me,' a dancer says. 'I'd thought an English show would be much easier for our dancers, who are used to very demanding roles. Because I'd always heard that over there [in Britain] they don't have the same calibre of dancers. But, on the contrary!'

The other dancers in *Cats* agree. One has already had to leave with a strained tendon. Choreographer ex-ballerina Gillian Lynne is stretching them, they say, to the limit.

'It hurts,' Anna declares. 'It's harder than *Chorus Line* or *Dancin'*, which a lot of us have been in. It's so fast, and just doesn't stop. We come off, change our clothes and run right back into it. The non-stopness is what gets you, because we're hardly ever off-stage.'

It's the same, she says, with Andrew's music. 'It's *very* difficult. Because it, too, is non-stop, and you have to sing it moving all the time. A dancer's breathing isn't the same as that of a singer. This really is, I think, one of the most difficult scores to sing. But the stamina is growing.'

So too is the show. A convincing answer to those, like Barnes, who doubt if New Yorkers will be attracted by Eliot's lines set to rock-style music: the box office of the Winter Garden is constantly busy. All through this unusually warm and sticky late summer the phones seldom rest. To the Shuberts, the theatre owners and managers handling this live-or-die business barometer, it's prodigiously heart-warming. It means that the public is gambling, sight-unseen, on Eliot's 'book of poems'.

On opening night four starry-eyed women from New Jersey will try to explain why this is. Asked 'what makes you stand out here, risking the trampling hooves of police horses, when you haven't any idea what the show's about?' they'll answer in unison 'That's just it. We *don't* know, but it sounds exciting *because it's so different!*'

And by then, as the *New York Post* and others will shrewdly have figured, more than five and a half million dollars' worth of advance bookings to see this 'so different' show will have come in, pledging up to forty dollars apiece (soon to rise to sixty dollars) for seats in the 1,400 capacity theatre, expensively converted into a junk yard and rubbish-dump playground for Lloyd Webber's cat dancers and singers. By then, too, Andrew Lloyd Webber himself will have realized that he has pulled off the greatest gamble of his soaring development.

The downside risk has been unnerving. 'Now, it all seems so easy,' he told a reporter soon after the triumphant launch in London. 'But then? I was terrified. Just think what people were saying: "Andrew Lloyd Webber working on a whole series of poems about cats! And without Tim Rice! And after he's left Robert Stigwood [on expiration of a ten-year contract with the great Beatles' agent and manager]! Oh, and with Cameron Mackintosh, who's done nothing but a few, you know, revivals like *Oklahoma* and *My Fair Lady*! He'll never pull this together. Never!"'

Well, they've been proved wrong. And are to be proved wrong again, here in the hardest city in the world to win with a musical show. But Andrew isn't counting chickens, even though the golden eggs are dropping hourly into his till. As he recalls: 'For six months, I was scratching around London for the money. Everyone in the profession was showing a complete lack of confidence by their closed chequebooks. Rubbing their hands, too, in the belief that I couldn't possibly pull it off.'

How nearly they had been right. 'At the very eleventh hour, the one theatre we'd found suitable, the New London, told us, "Listen, we prefer to be a conference centre [which they'd been before]. We don't want you in." We had to go and get Bernie Delfont to do us (and incidentally them, as things turned out) a great favour, and talk them into letting us go in there in the spring of 1981.'

Meanwhile the profession just sat on its motheaten velvet stall-seats and passed up one of the best investment opportunities ever offered in show business. Before the first three months of the run were over, the few who'd risked a stake in *Cats* were getting their whole investment back, plus handsome interest and the sure prospect of golden profits to come. Since then small fortunes have been made on the show on both sides of the Atlantic. Andrew can enjoy wry satisfaction as he looks back.

He can also enjoy the gambler's conceit of having risked all on an outside chance and won. His own guarantee was a note-of-hand which almost nobody would have under-witten. And even that has not been enough. A close friend in London, the antique furniture dealer David Crewe-Read, remembers: 'It was an amazing thing. Andrew was still £80,000 short when, out of the blue, a very substantial businessman came in like a good fairy and put it up for him!'

Andrew is the first to admit that it was the riskiest moment of his professional life.

'The final thing which everyone thought was sure to mean the knackering of *Cats* was that we were going into the New London, of all places,' he explains. 'You see, historically nothing has ever worked there. It's regarded as the unluckiest theatre in London.'

It took his own guarantees, underwriting more than half the formidable enterprise, to swing the thing. 'If that show had gone down the pan on the opening night,' he says, 'I should have been, if not actually bankrupted, as near it as meets the . . . I *would* have been bankrupted! I'd have lost over a quarter of a million!'

By now, more than a highly successful year later, he relishes the memory, the experience it gave of the fragility with which theatrical backers, angels, risk their wings. With the subsequent success of *Evita* in the States, and other profitable projects, his confidence has been supremely vindicated. But in 1981, as that first *Cats* launch approached, he was in no position to meet the guarantees. 'Even if I hadn't gone bust,' he admits, 'I'd have had to sell my house.' And still, as the great Broadway premiere creeps up on him, the risk is there. A really appalling bunch of reviews from the New York critics, and the word-of-mouth of people who like Hamlisch have seen the show and disliked it, are capable in this fickle city of ruining him. As Bernie Jacobs says: 'no show is critic proof'.

Cameron Mackintosh has only a small financial stake in the show. But his reputation is in the firing line with his composer friend, and he knows it. Trapped in his office for a few still moments, this active young producer expands on Andrew's phlegm in the teeth of the approaching test. 'He's what the Americans call a terrific guy,' he says admiringly. '*Cats* here in New York is carrying about five million dollars' worth of backers' money, yet Andrew can still laugh at it all!'

Others feel less sure that the composer is so untroubled by the approaching verdict. 'Andrew is paranoid about losing his money,' a British PR executive remarks bitchily (and ungenerously, since the composer has donated half the proceeds of one of his premieres to a charity which the PR man represents).

Andrew himself admits that he more than once seriously decided to leave England to live and work in America, in order to avoid the crippling taxation imposed by the last Labour government. Only Margaret Thatcher's victory at the polls prevented him. 'It may not be obvious to a lot of people,' he says, 'but the climate the Conservatives brought in with them in 1979 (and I'm not talking as a political bod) has kept a phenomenal number of creative people in this country. I mean, *Cats* would never have been done first in Britain if it hadn't been for that change of government. It would have just been done in New York and I'd be living in New York.'

Nevertheless, he insists: 'Money is not of vast import-ance to me.' To many who know and work with him, this apparent contradiction can only be weighed as an interesting reflection on Andrew Lloyd Webber's need for more than artistic acclaim.

Yet on the morning of 7 October 1982 here he is, peacefully asleep. As undisturbed by spectres of tonight's opening as if his own fortune is not involved. In his hotel suite at the old Mayflower Hotel overlooking Central Park he lies more like a becalmed sailor than a man facing an approaching storm. The frustration is that there is so little now that he *can* do. It's all done.

Far from pacing the room in a chainsmoking replica of the stereotyped first-night showman, and as unlike as possible his illustrious predecessor Arthur Sullivan (who required morphine and a four A.M. breakfast to brace himself for the torture of facing his and W. S. Gilbert's Broadway premiere of *HMS Pinafore* almost exactly a century before), Andrew is to spend most of the morning, indeed the better part of the day, dawdling.

When he wakes up the sole distraction to the breakfast in his room which Sarah, his wife, has ordered from Room Service is a succession of calls and messengers announcing and bearing gifts. 'All those presents!' Andrew writhes in recollection. 'We spent most of the morning opening them. But there was little else we could do.'

Unless an explosion is to wreck the theatre, or a plague decimate the cast, Andrew's fate eleven hours hence is already set in type in the composing rooms of New York's three leading daily newspapers. Their reviewers have been in to see one of the previews, which have been usefully polishing this American, and much-altered, version of the musical. It is this advance invasion by the Broadway critics which is robbing Andrew's first-night gingerbread of much of its lustre.

'Understand,' he says, 'Broadway first nights aren't the same any more. The critics there have got the managements to let them come in and see shows ahead of time, so that they can have more time to write their notices. It reduces premieres to nothing, to limbo-land.' His irritation gives way to a flash of anger. 'From now on,' he declares, 'I'm going to make it a kind of crusade. I want to stop this thing the journalists like so much, if I can. It makes an opening night a fake.'

It must indeed be galling to the showman who has been wrapped in the show for weeks past. An intense anti-climax on a day when, traditionally, all theatreland is on tiptoes to see the creation unveiled. For today's Broadway impresarios, composers, directors and artists, the premiere can be no more than a performance before an invited audience of friends and celebrities. And, of course, a time to exchange those gift-wrapped presents and goodwill messages which Andrew finds so inappropriate, with their curiously inverted terms of encouragement (to 'break a leg' is recognized in the profession as cheering, for reasons which might baffle a psychiatrist).

The Mayflower is a nice hotel, as unlike an airport lounge as others resemble one. Andrew and Sarah are sharing the suite with Cameron Mackintosh, who has gone down to take breakfast in the coffee-room and to mull over the morning newspapers. Tomorrow, the notices will be in, available around midnight in the city. Certainly on hand at the Waldorf Astoria, where Andrew is giving a party for friends, family and cast – amongst others his parents, his brother Julian and his wife and several other loyal supportive chums. What he likes about the Mayflower, apart from its solid comfort and unostentatious decor, is that Sarah has got them into it cheaply.

'She discovered that it was going to be pulled down,' he announces happily. 'So they let us have the suite at the top of the building for much reduced prices. As foreigners, there was no danger of us establishing squatters' rights.'

Their children, Imogen seven and Nicholas four, have flown home to Berkshire, where Andrew spends what time he can in his country place. Equipped with all the music-making machinery a high-tech age can provide, Sydmonton Court is, in fact, a splendid studio besides being a residence. In the grounds, the small and ancient chapel serves as a hall in which nearly all the Rice–Webber, and Webber solo, works have been tried out. The audiences are either invited, or pay to come and see them each summer. Now the children are there, safe from whatever is to come of Andrew's New York gamble. While here, they have enjoyed daily walks in Central Park, as well as privileged peeps into Daddy's theatre. Staring wide-eyed at the prowling, rehearsing cats they have been joyously deafened by the amplified music swelling from a dozen enormous speakers under the control of a disco-like console.

Without the children Andrew and Sarah are suddenly in a void. They plan a quiet day. 'Lunch with my parents and friends,' Andrew says. 'A quiet lunch, at that place on 62nd Street, the Veau d'Or.' He speaks as if everyone must know such places. An epicure, he recognizes only those restaurants where, in his considered judgement, the cooking excels and the wine is eminently drinkable. The Veau d'Or, one may be sure, lacks neither of these qualifications.

And at lunch, with Cameron and the others, there seem to be no frayed ends to his nerves, no anxious forecasts of what the next twelve or fourteen hours (until the reviews appear) will bring. Surprisingly, he has managed to avoid even the clutching hands of the media on this auspicious day. His explanation for this sounds quaint:

'You see, I don't *do* publicity about myself. I'm not interested in doing it. Of course, if I have to for the sake of a show I will, but I don't regard it as central to my work. My role, my real role, is in the rehearsal room wondering about musical values. Listening and observing.'

Well, some have such things thrust upon them. Andrew has suffered nearly a hundred TV and radio interviews and programmes on BBC alone. If he has seriously tried to dodge the limelight of notoriety he hasn't been all that successful in doing so. 'Andrew doesn't exactly seek publicity,' an experienced publicist of his London shows confirms, 'but he definitely attracts it.' On this October day in New York he could be enjoying the lull before a tornado.

The afternoon passes in lazy, uneasy chat. Professor William ('Billy') Lloyd Webber is curious about some aspects of New York musical life. As the eminent director of the London College of Music, the glittering programme of concerts and events at the Juilliard and other Manhattan music centres fascinates him. His wife Jean, Andrew's mother, is concerned about the stories in the newspapers of crime and poverty in the city. A music teacher, who gave Andrew his first lessons in playing the piano and is a teacher at Andrew's first pre-preparatory school in London (where she once taught both her talented sons), Mrs Lloyd Webber cares deeply about the underprivileged. New York, for her, is harsh and dangerous.

Andrew's brother, Julian, talks quietly with his wife. Three years younger, and with a growing world reputation as a cellist of distinction, he knows what the day means to Andrew as well as anyone, and keeps quietly in the background. This has long been his role in their relationship. 'Andrew does what he wants to do best on his own,' he tells a friend in New York. He would not deny that he is defining genius.

When the time comes to dress, Sarah takes over. Andrew is rested, has had an unusually trim haircut for the young virtuoso whose eccentric clothes and shoulder-length locks have raised conventional New York eyebrows on earlier visits. He dons a black double-breasted dinner jacket of impeccably sedate cut over a soft white shirt with turn-down collar and wide butterfly black bowtie. Sarah, the soft curls of her golden blond hair charmingly casual, is wearing an eye- and camera-catching long-sleeved silk dress of zebra-style vertical stripes, giving height to her petite figure. Neither goes in for jewellery, though Sarah's neck and the square-cut, open front of her dress support a solid gold name tag on its chain, a present from Andrew. They leave for the theatre in the limousine without coats, Sarah having added a new white satin scarf as a final touch to the ensemble. Together, they might be any young married pair of means, going out on the town.

Broadway premieres may have lost their zest. But to the Manhattan public they remain sparkling events. Put up police barriers here, and a crowd will gather. On the occasion of the first full-dress opening of a musical which has commanded headlines and TV coverage over past weeks, there may well be a stampede. By seven the *paparazzi* photographers and TV cameramen denied official entrance are taking up and disputing rights to favourable positions. Outside the stage door they snatch pictures, which will never be published, of the cast as they come to work. In front, on Broadway, a few stragglers and a small posse of blue-uniformed police – their holsters tactfully empty of guns – patrol under the wide apron of the Winter Garden. It's a warm, sticky night. And the lights make it hotter.

An old Broadway actor, out of work for years, shambles by. 'It's always the same in this city,' he barks. 'They come to see the matadors gored by the bull! Don't make any mistake, that's what they're here for. To see all these famous nobodies arrive for the wedding, then go home and read that the show has flopped and it was really a funeral!'

His is the only bitter face. The crowd is thick as the Lloyd Webbers arrive. Three specially hired extras, girls with lithe figures, are prowling sinuously in and out of the crowd, the police and the cameramen. Wearing fishnet black bodystockings and cats' ears, their faces hidden behind made-up cat-noses and whiskers, their fingers taloned, they hiss and sway in feline chorus. The crowd, mostly women, loves it.

'Excuse me, please!' A burly policeman pushes, but with studied politeness. 'Move back now. Let the folks get in.'

Arlene Francis, Neil Simon, Marty Gable and other stage, film and television players arrive, pretending non-chalance as the crowd salutes with excited oohs and aahs. No doubt for the reasons Andrew pinpoints, the turnout is anything but star-studded, but it is still fairyland for some. 'I've been coming to premieres for five years, whenever I can,' a woman in a red hat breathes. 'My friend and I have just been to see *Joseph* and we liked it *so very much*. It makes you feel lighthearted! And isn't this by the same people?'

No, it isn't. Tim Rice is a notable absentee from *Cats*, his place having been usurped by the late great man of poetry, Thomas Stearns Eliot. And by the distinguished Royal Shakespeare director ('Additional material and the song "Memory" written by Trevor Nunn,' the programme affirms). Tim is in England, busy with television hosting, book publishing and the search for a new partner. It is said that his own lyrics for 'Memory' have been rejected by Andrew.

Inside, with the first blare of the overture music crashing round the walls, the rustle of 'darling, darling!' greetings and social stall-hopping is drowned out. The claws come out, with shafts of light from the spots swinging like alarmed searchlights. Where possible they hit the dancers, who leap barriers, prowl aisles and weave, jump and snake their ways through and in-and-out of the delighted audience. A sea of cats is literally insinuating itself among these well-dressed, pampered people, hissing and purring at them with catty disdain. They're loving it. And the singing of the prologue, 'Jellicle Songs for Jellicle Cats', is enormous, a feast of voice and verve. The whole company giving it every tonsil-quivering decibel as they crawl from old cars, garbage cans and rubble on to the moonlit stage. Suddenly, and really, the night belongs to cats. As with thousands of audiences elsewhere, Broadway falls at their furry feet.

Afterwards, New York comes out rubbing its eyes, like children wishing the story didn't have to come to an end. 'I'll come and see it *again and again*!' a woman says. Her husband smiles indulgently. 'It takes a little time to warm up,' he says, 'and the first act was a little slow. But it's very good, and the audience loved it.' From the happy glaze of his eyes, so did he.

An elderly woman sums it up. 'I like Eliot's cat poems, so I was already . . .' She interrupts herself, anxious to get to the point. 'They were so like *real* cats,' she exclaims. 'It's such a technical production! And New York people love that. I'm sure it'll run very well.' The man with her nods. 'Yeah,' he says. 'Good theatre.'

It's the same all round. '*Like it?*' 'Fabulous! Every single minute was fabulous!' '*No complaints at all?*' 'No, roses all the way.' '*For Mr Eliot, or Mr Lloyd Webber?*' 'For everyone involved.' '*Did you feel you were among cats?*' 'Yeah, and the audience appreciated the whole evening.'

Absolutely. They give it a standing ovation.

Outside the unarmed police are sweating to clear a path. Official politeness is wearing thin. An over-persistent, middle-aged *paparazzo* who has ducked under the crush barrier is manhandled roughly by five cops. A mounted officer rides through the crowd, parting them in alarm. The photographer is arrested, dragged away, charged with 'disorderly conduct'.

Eve Krisokowski, a CBS news reporter, gathers her team for a late-night assault on the Lloyd Webber parents and party at the Waldorf. Mrs Valerie Eliot, sitting with Andrew (who owes much to her for unpublished material of her husband's which has given the show its main theme, the poignant tragedy and romantic renaissance of Grizabella the Glamour Cat), gives the interviewer her verdict: 'I was very pleased.' Valerie Eliot has seen the show eleven times. Her husband would, she says, 'have been very moved'. Others agree, for the record. Neil Simon declares the show 'terrific. A smash!' His actress wife, Marcia Mason, raves. 'We heard nothing but good reaction,' she says. 'All round.'

The praise sits like a halo on the young English head which has given it life and meaning. Andrew can go now to his party, to the bargain of his suite on the park, knowing that he has done it. 'Guts as well as flair,' reports *Newsweek*, adding in mock astonishment: 'The most extravagant musical ever to hit Broadway from a foreign shore. A *foreign* musical – and from blimpy old England at that – on Broadway? Yes, and welcome too. *Cats* is the biggest London stage hit of the modern era, and only catastrophe or catatonia will bar an even greater success here.'

After which, who cares about the critics? Bernie Jacobs, for one. As the sleek Cadillac hirecars crawl to a halt outside the Waldorf, the reviews are already soothing his last doubts. Clive Barnes has described *Cats* as: 'A shattering triumph . . . a deserved box-office hit . . . a phenomenon in New York . . . I don't think I have ever seen such decorative virtuosity on the stage.' Even his glancing side-blow at Lloyd Webber's score, 'breathtakingly unoriginal yet superbly professional' can do no damage to that. As Barnes concludes, 'It, *Cats*, is a statement of the musical theater that cannot be ignored, should prove controversial and will never be forgotten. Thanks to Nunn and Napier [John Napier, the designer] – and to Lloyd Webber, who has enabled them to start their miracles – this is theatrical wizardry at a compromised level of genius.'

The influential *New York Times* man has found *Cats*' success equally assured, if unidentifiable. 'It's not that this collection of anthropomorphic variety turns is a brilliant musical,' Frank Rich writes, 'or that it powerfully stirs the emotions, or that it has an idea in its head. Nor is the probable appeal of *Cats* a function of the publicity that has accompanied the show's every purr since it first stalked London seventeen months ago. No, the reason why people will hunger to see *Cats* is far more simple and primal than that: it's a musical that transports the audience into a complete fantasy world that could only exist in the theater and yet, these days, only rarely does. Whatever the other failings and excesses even banalities of *Cats*, it believes in purely theatrical magic, and on that faith it unquestionably delivers.'

As Cameron Mackintosh says, rubbing tired eyes the following morning, 'that may not be a great review but it will sell seats. Andrew, I think, is very happy.'

Andrew may be. Nobody knows, because nobody sees much of him. The composer is being left to enjoy his saucer of cream, with Sarah and the memory of another great milestone passed. Once again he has demonstrated that even a supercat has to lay all nine lives on the line to prove – to himself and his muse if to nobody else – that he can do it, and do it again and again.

Just as he has more than once proved that his journey through life will be at his own and nobody else's direction.

2

Nursery in Bohemia

IN London, meanwhile, *Cats* has been running for well over a year and bookings seem to guarantee it eternity. There is an attraction in the joint forces of Eliot's child-*like* (though never child-*ish*) poetry and Andrew's rooftop-prancing music which enthral the sophisticated as readily as the innocent, the British as readily as the Americans, and the young in heart mind and soul wherever. What has taken root in the universal consciousness, it seems, is an appetite for magic.

As both the magician and the architect of this Andrew is regarded with fresh interest. He has confounded those who said he could not succeed without his old lyric-writing partner, Tim Rice. The pundits who sneered, however diplomatically, at his 'angular rhythms' and 'derivative' themes fall silent. If it could be said that setting Eliot's cat poems to music is not entirely original (Humphrey Searle's 'Cat Variations' on a theme from Prokofiev's *Peter and the Wolf* come to mind), the success of the show effaces such carping. The only ground left to the sceptical is Voltaire's consolation to mediocrity: 'the reflection that genius so often comes to a bad end'.

Yet there are those who resolutely refuse to believe that such a triumph can be deserved by one so young. And one – when early in 1983 news of his entanglement with a talented dancer from the London production of *Cats*, Sarah Brightman, brings his astonishing announcement of coming divorce from his wife Sarah – so apparently flighty. It is certainly true that Andrew is astonishingly young for such events. He was born on 22 March 1948, six years after the wartime marriage of his parents, Jean and William Lloyd Webber. He was the first of their two sons, both of whom were to be acclaimed in their different musical careers. He and his brother Julian, three years younger, came into the world in the maternity wing of the Westminster Hospital, no more than a decent stroll away from the flat in Harrington Road where the family lived.

This was where Andrew's parents first set up home together. Jean Hermione Johnstone was already living in the flat, which was owned by her mother, when as a 20-year-old bride she married William Southcombe Lloyd Webber (at the time a serving soldier of twenty-eight in the Royal Army Pay Corps) in Chelsea. William – or 'Billy' as he was familiarly known – was the musically-gifted son of a local tradesman, a plumber in the King's Road (who was also serving the war effort, as a Public Assistance Officer). In that mansion flat in Harrington Court provided by Jean's widowed mother, Molly Johnsone, Andrew and Julian were to take their first steps, and many succeeding ones, in the world.

The Lloyd Webbers have had a long association with Chelsea. As the son of a master plumber, Andrew's paternal grandfather, William Charles Henry Webber, was a journey-man plumber there himself when he married Andrew's grandmother, Mary Winifred Gittins, in 1913. Southcombe was one of his father's forenames, though their choice of the name Lloyd for their son William (born shortly before the outbreak of the First World War in 1914) is more likely to have been for convenience than due to any imagined pride in Celtic origins, a hark-back to ancestral links with the Welsh valleys. If a Welsh connection did exist, it had been entirely obliterated by time. William baptized both his sons, Andrew and Julian, 'Lloyd Webber', though without the hyphen sometimes ascribed to their names.

Andrew's own recollections of these early years ('I'm afraid I have an appalling lack of memory for everything except what really interested me'), are sometimes unhelpful, occasionally faulty. 'The first thing I do remember,' he apologizes, 'is being in hospital when I was about three, having had my appendix removed.' He laughs, explosively. 'I was told afterwards by my mother that I made so much fuss and noise that they got me out of the place in about three days, when I should have stayed a week!' The following year he was photographed making presumably less disturbing sounds on a violin.

Two years before his death in October 1982, Andrew's greatly loved and understanding father explained on the television show *This is Your Life* why he and his wife had given their unruly son 'a special nickname'. 'When he [Andrew] was little, he was for ever jumping and bumping around the place, making a dreadful din and disturbing all the neighbours at three o'clock in the morning,' Jean said. But Dr Lloyd Webber wouldn't say what the nickname was, which in fact caused last-minute concern to the show's presenter Eamonn Andrews and the Thames Television team. On the air at least, dignity was preserved. However, Billy and Jean had talked frankly to the programme's diligent researcher, Vivien Lind. 'He was always a mass of energy and even when very small would create lots of noise,' Billy Lloyd Webber exclaimed. 'He just wouldn't go to sleep at night, but wanted to jump around screaming the whole time, which obviously disturbed the neighbours.' The nickname was 'Bumper'!

'We discovered Andrew loved Latin American music,' Billy said, 'and he'd sit for hours as good as gold listening with rapt attention to the music of Edmundo Ros.' Was it true? Let us say it *might* have been so, once or twice; though the desire of the programme producer to have the colourful Mr Ros as an additional personality in his show may perhaps have made more of this than it deserved.

Certainly Vivien's research notes confirm that it *was* a Ros record which put Andrew the Unruly to sleep. '"The Wedding Samba" would play all night long if necessary,' his mother told her. 'It was the only thing that would keep him quiet.' And later, 'It was essential to keep Andrew occupied,' his mother said. 'Otherwise he drove everyone mad.' 'We'd spend our summer holidays touring ancient monuments so that he could look at heaps of old stones,' his father recalled.

One particularly unfortunate holiday was described by Jean Lloyd Webber as 'disastrous'. Indeed Billy's moods could descend from riotous mirth to tearful self-pity, while Andrew was not only inclined to be noisy and bumptious as a child, but in the grip of his worst and blackest humours would rage like a demon.

Jean had ample opportunity at that time to study her unusually gifted son, since she taught music and piano at his first school, Wetherby in South Kensington (now removed to Notting Hill Gate and numbering Prince Michael of Kent's son Lord Frederick Windsor, among its pupils). Andrew (to be followed one day by Andrew's son Nicholas) was sent to this popular and well-run academy at the age of three and a half.

The school building continues as a private tutorial establishment for A-level crammers at No 36a Rosary Gardens, on the corner of Wetherby Place, SW7. It is a mildly curious fact of Andrew's life that, apart from Broadway, all his main activities have been contained within a short London bus ride. His birth, upbringing and schooling were relatively adjacent. His own small bachelor flat in the basement of No 10 Gledhow Gardens, SW5, from which he was first married, and his later London homes in West Eaton Place and Eaton Place equally so.

The area possesses a faintly shabby chic, a suggestion of cosmopolitan and cultural vitality which comes close to being theatrical in its own right. It is, of course, the same neighbourhood in which Arthur Seymour Sullivan lived and worked a century earlier. He, too, was London born (in 1842) and went to school in the West End of the city. Whether or not the dusty, dormitory roads and squares of South Ken can claim to have influenced either is a moot point, but the analogy is both fascinating and inescapable.

It was certainly in Harrington Gardens, at No 39, that Sir Arthur's librettist-partner (or, as his idolators prefer, 'dramatist') W. S. Gilbert was inspired to write their masterpiece musical, *The Mikado*. The story goes that Gilbert (like so many other lyricists, Tim Rice included) suffered moments of acute anger at the refusal of his composer-partner to embrace one of his favourite notions. Gilbert had twice had this particular idea rejected, and in thumping his infuriated way about the room overlooking the lovely gardens of his magnificently-appointed home (now the Central Midwives Board) he brought down a fine ornamental Japanese sword from the wall. With it in his hands, Gilbert saw the possibilities of the Orient open before him, and *The Mikado* was born.

Remarkably similar in terms of the unexpected was Andrew's flash of inspiration one evening in 1969 while walking down the Fulham Road. 'I started getting a melody,' he has since explained, 'and when I got to the restaurant (Carlo's Place) I wrote it down on a napkin.' Both he and his then new partner, Rice, recognized that he had jotted a perfect theme for their first full-scale rock-opera, *Jesus Christ Superstar*.

'Often, Sullivan would refuse to set much of the stuff Gilbert would write,' Ian Bradley says in *The Annotated Gilbert and Sullivan* (Penguin, 1982). 'Theirs was an incredible combination. They didn't like each other, but it worked.' In Andrew's case, there has been no suggestion of his having had to put up with partners he has not liked as people. But with Rice, then Alan Ayckbourn and Don Black, and now Trevor Nunn and Richard Stilgoe, there is a common and most noticeable denominator: Andrew's complete control over his own creative forces and his disinclination to listen to any voice but his own.

If this suggests that as a child his parents allowed him too much of his own way – indeed, that they spoiled him – this may be so. Yet at school Andrew behaved well. From first going there, in the same year in which Julian was born, 1951, until he moved on to the Westminster Underschool, he showed himself to be a serious and reasonable little boy to teach.

True, there were occasional outbursts of uncontrolled wilfulness. His temper and the black moods which could stir it to its fiercest depths were already familiar to the family. 'Andrew,' his father told a sympathetic interviewer some years before his death, 'was a terror. There was never any pressure on him to do anything he didn't want to do.' To some who knew him at the time he seemed to have become headstrong in the extreme.

Yet firm enough in his conviction that he alone could, and would, dictate his own future. Up to the age of eleven, Andrew was unshakeably convinced that this would lie in the preservation of ancient buildings, with no thought of music at all. 'When I was seven or eight all I wanted to be was Chief Inspector of Ancient Monuments to the Ministry of Works,' he remembers now. 'It started off by my being interested in ruined and medieval buildings. I wrote books about them. I've got stacks of them somewhere. Oh yes, I wrote learned dissertations on them. Truly, it never occurred to me at that age that I was going to be interested in music.' Indeed when he was about nine he asked his mother to write and find out the qualifications to set about this career. It was a sudden flare-up of interest that followed the departure of Andrew's first girlfriend, Barbara Beskin. 'She was at Wetherby with him, and they used to hold hands and so on,' Jean remembered. 'I think they just lost touch when Andrew was about eight and went to the Underschool. He was doing much more with music by then, having played the violin since he was about four, and later the French horn.' Mrs Lloyd Webber laughs at a mental picture she has of her son at that time. 'He always played his instruments in a *completely* unorthodox manner!' she says. 'All the pieces he was supposed to play, he wouldn't touch. He wanted to play his own tunes, and no others.'

3

Cats on the Tiles

AT home in Harrington Road, cats were sacrosanct. The Lloyd Webbers had several, and one who became a treasured member of the family was Perseus, a most aristocratic Burmese beauty of such intelligence and perception that he could and did find his own way home from many a farflung nocturnal prowl. The embarrassment was that Percy would frequently be brought back to the flat (its address inscribed on his collar) by concerned people who knew nothing of his remarkable powers. Andrew's mother finally decided to have the wording changed. Where before it was: 'My name is Perseus, and I live at . . .' with the address following, it now read 'My name is Perseus. Please don't bother, I know my own way home.'

Percy used to be taken everywhere with the family, even to visit Andrew at school in due course. But he was left in London when Andrew went away. It was on one of these visits, to share a holiday in a rented dower-house on Lord de l'Isle's estate at Penshurst with a friend of his aunt's, the actress Joan Colmore, that he discovered the awful truth: not everybody loved, or even valued, cats.

Mrs Colmore now lives in the South of France. She recalls the day when a very diminutive Andrew took a stroll with her and two of her favourite cats, to be pounced on by her landlord and one of his keepers. 'He was furious,' she says. 'Lord de l'Isle had no idea I was his tenant. And he obviously didn't care for the two cats sitting on my shoulders. 'Got you on two counts,' he cried triumphantly. 'One, you're trespassing! And two, you're accompanied by cats! I warn you, Madam, that if you come here again my keepers will shoot your cats!'

Mrs Colmore was still recovering from this unwarranted attack – his Lordship apologized as soon as it was explained to him that she was entitled to be on his land – when an eight-year-old Sir Galahad stepped chivalrously forward. 'Lord *Ass*,' Andrew said boldly, 'if your keepers shoot Mrs Colmore's cats, *Mr* Colmore will shoot your keepers!'

On the same holiday Andrew showed how deeply interested he was in historical architecture. There was a strange, shrine-like place on the estate which immediately drew his attention. At that time he had a lisp. 'You know, that is a Druid pla*the* of worship,' he said. Mrs Colmore checked up and found that it was so indeed. 'He had worked it out by the way the oak and elm trees were planted,' she remembers. 'To let the shadows cast by the sun point the way to it. Amazing!'

His knowledge astonished her. But so it did everyone who discovered his encyclopaedic grasp of historical architecture. His mother believes it started with a picture book of ancient castles taken to him in hospital after the disturbing appendicitis operation. It is also probable that it developed largely from the amount of time he spent on his own in those precocious early years.

'It's a funny thing,' he reflects. 'I really didn't know my parents well when I was small. I really didn't. My father was very much wrapped up in his own world, the academic world, and my mother was always busy. Her whole interest was – has always been – in finding people who are interested in music, and then in trying to make their careers possible.'

In search of such under-privileged talent, Jean Lloyd Webber and her mother, Molly Johnstone, would make regular forays away from genteel South Ken and into the meaner, hungrier ways of London's East End. 'Our life was consequently very very bohemian,' Andrew says. 'There was no money at all. No money in the family, except for my grandmother, who had divorced my grandfather before he died. My father didn't earn much, and although we lived well enough in that old-fashioned mansion-house flat, it wasn't at all grand. My grandmother lived with us until much later, when somehow we took on the smaller flat next door and she moved in there.'

Their talent-searches into dockland and the poorer districts involved Jean and her mother in the support of many less-endowed tyros. 'My mother had a young opera singer, a tenor, whom she'd discovered,' Andrew recalls. 'And later, in the junior department of the Royal College of Music – which is sadly not in the same form as it was – she discovered John Lill.'

Lill, today one of England's most distinguished and internationally known concert pianists, became 'almost like an elder brother' to Andrew. 'He moved into my grand-mother's flat when I was fourteen, and there was an interconnecting balcony we used to jump over, so we were always in and out. I suppose John came to live with us because it was close to the Royal College. And we had pianos and so forth. The flat was full of music, all sorts of music. And at holiday time he used to come with us, as one of the family.' This Victorian ethic of charitable help 'for the less fortunate' was deeply embedded. 'All of my mother's side of the family share a very real interest in developing people,' Andrew says. 'It's a very Left-wing interest, of course. In fact, my grandmother was a founder member of something called the Christian Communist Party – which I must say sounds rather incongruous. I've never been able to understand its logic!'

Andrew is far from being tarred with a red, or even faintly pink, brush, and his childhood pursuits, under his father's tolerant direction, were taking him out of range of any connection with the noble endeavours of his mother. Their lives tended to run on largely parallel lines, meeting mainly in the classrooms of Wetherby School or at home for often hurried meals. Indeed Andrew has no clear recollection of his mother teaching him to play the piano. 'I suppose she must have done so. Yes, of course she *must*,' he says. Plainly his appetite for five-finger exercises was not enormous in those days.

'I was much more interested in wandering around, looking at buildings,' he explains. 'The earliest dream I can recall was of being taken one day to Fountain's Abbey which was a tremendous ambition of mine at the time. I mean, I really was wrapped up in the history and architecture of old places.'

Nevertheless in 1980, on the occasion of his receiving the CBE in the New Year's Honours List, Dr Lloyd Webber commented, 'Andrew was always interested in music although we thought he'd probably become an historian. He sketched out his first piece when he was about nine, and studied the violin and the horn.'

'I now learn, after his death, that my father was very much more interested in me than I imagined at the time,' Andrew says. 'But our musical tastes were so completely different. He did, very kindly, help me to get that first suite of mine published when I was nine, and I do think he may have come to like my things much more later on. But while I was very young I can't remember him sharing my passions for pop music and so on at all.'

Yet a deep and understanding tolerance was the Lloyd Webber keynote. 'They never opposed me in anything,' Andrew declares. 'They were perfectly liberal parents. And, in my mother's case, very much persuaded by Left-wing Socialist ideals. You've got to remember that Julian's best friend at school was Stephen Wedgwood Benn, and my parents undoubtedly admired the Wedgwood Benn set-up, or my mother did. Perhaps my father had reservations.'

Jean Lloyd Webber has retained many of her humanitarian interests, and she still rides off from her South Kensington flat on a bicycle twice weekly in term-time to teach music at Wetherby's new premises. Her clothes, which a friend declares are sometimes obtained at jumble sales, speak loudly of her refusal of ostentation.

'And she was most desperately ambitious for both Julian and me,' Andrew says. 'I'm not quite sure how to put this, but she probably fastened on to the fact that I had an unusual interest in history and architecture. Thus she may have thought it best to push me through, rather than Julian. I was expected to concentrate on the academic side more. Which, unfortunately, was not the side I wanted; and when I was about eleven or twelve I just decided I couldn't go on doing it.'

That was also the time when Andrew first made up his mind, as he says, 'that I would go and play my own music rather than the violin, or the French horn, or whatever it was.' To an extent it was the pull of the sounds he was hearing on record and radio that governed this important turning-point. But theatre was also part of the chemistry of his change.

'I was never going to be a performer, I mean not in the sense that Julian was going to be,' Andrew declares now. 'There was that on my mother's side, but it didn't come down to me. What I did get was an interest in how theatre works, how it is put together. My mother's sister, Aunt Vi, was a terrific encouragement.'

Viola Johnstone was an actress who had retired from the stage when she married a London doctor, George Crosby. They lived 'over the shop' in Weymouth Street, W1, where Dr Crosby ran a moderately successful practice. Andrew became a regular visitor.

'Vi was a great friend of mine,' he says of his late aunt. 'She helped me with a lot of my early ideas; for instance, when I was building a model theatre at home. And, later, when I was about fifteen and they retired to live in Ventimiglia, I used to go and stay. She was always a wonderful companion who really loved the theatre.'

Those who knew both sisters were impressed by Viola Crosby's gaiety, somewhat in contrast to Jean Lloyd Webber's serious, intense manner. Friends of Andrew, who enjoyed her hospitality in Italy with him, were particularly struck by Aunt Vi's enthusiasm for everything theatrical, and by her *rapport* with her young nephew. 'They were very close,' one of them remembers, 'and Vi always seemed to lighten his heart. She was relaxed and giggly, where Jean was inclined to fret about things and was always passionately concerned about the sick and the dying. Of course George and Vi did everything together, while Billy and Jean had so many separate interests.'

The model theatre which Aunt Vi encouraged Andrew to build was no simple toy. 'It was huge,' he says proudly. 'With a marvellous Victorian auditorium and a great stage. It even had a revolve and a sound system. It could actually do everything.' Talking about it earlier, he had remembered it as being 16 feet in length, but admits: 'Perhaps it was less. I haven't seen it for years, in fact I wish I knew where it's got to. But it was certainly very big.'

Julian, 'press-ganged into helping' with those nursery-floor productions, assisted his brother by performing musical sketches and shows which, Andrew recalls, 'were all heavily based on things going on at the time'. The revolve was an old gramophone turn-table, inspired by the London Palladium. Andrew built the entire model out of bits and pieces he collected from the neighbourhood. He also worked out, finally, a way of recording his earliest pieces of music. 'It was very primitive,' he says, 'but at least I managed to make it sound as if there was an orchestra in the pit.'

At the age of six or seven he had written down his first tune in note form on musically scored paper. By the age of nine, when his six-year-old brother was struggling with his first lessons in playing the violin and later the cello, Andrew was able to perform works from his first published suite on either French horn or violin. Sadly missing from his collection of those early pieces is a copy of the then-published music magazine, *Music Teacher*, which he remembers 'picked up half a dozen of my tunes and had them arranged and printed'.

Dr Lloyd Webber was observing this development with

interest. His father, though trained as a plumber, had been a chorister from the age of seven and possessed a most unusual voice, both tenor and alto in range. As a member of the Bach Choir and the Oriana Madrigal Society he sang professionally and had worked with the BBC Chorus and the George Mitchell Choir on radio. 'He was one of the original members of the Black and White Minstrels,' Andrew has explained. 'And my father hadn't any highbrow notions about music, you know. He came from a very ordinary background. He too had sung in choirs and played the organ for years before he became the distinguished director of the London College of Music, and so on. I mean, to a lot of musicians, a job is a job. If you'd asked my father to accompany the Black and White Minstrels one day and play in Westminster Abbey the next, he'd have been quite happy doing both.'

Happier, no doubt, than in having the flat filled with the musical sounds which Andrew was buying on record and playing at full volume in the room reserved for music. 'The decibellage was ear-shattering on occasion,' an early visitor remembers with a shudder. 'But somehow his father never seemed to object. And I believe Billy's own musical tastes were never very far from the romantic. The many pieces he composed for the organ were all stamped with a simple, sensuous – I'm afraid you could say sentimental – style, though they were always highly expressive. He was a wonderfully kind man.'

One who, nevertheless, must have been happy to see his over-active and at times uncontrollable son reach the age when his serious schooling, at the Underschool of Westminster, could give him less acoustically disturbing work to sharpen his teeth on. The year was 1956. Nobody had yet heard of the Mersey Sound, or of those responsible for it, the Beatles. Nobody had yet heard of Andrew Lloyd Webber, but soon they would.

4

Boredom in Eccleston Square

ANDREW has little recollection of the morning when he first crossed the threshold of Westminster Underschool. One of the more exclusive (and expensive) London preparatory schools, this academy endeavours to shape small, well-bred boys from the middle and upper classes for that summit of British social fitness, the public school. Moreover, the Underschool offered in Andrew's time (and still does offer) the best-known and well-trodden route to the great, ancient Westminster School itself.

But after the warmer red brick of Wetherby, the two tall houses on the south side of Eccleston Square behind Victoria coach station extended a daunting and chilly welcome. Within lay convincing proof that here was a fearsomely adult world. Boys twice his size were surging along corridors, barging into noisy classrooms from which masters' commands rang out imperiously. At Wetherby it had been mainly lady teachers. Here only the lowest form, Petty B, enjoyed such mollycoddling.

Patrick ('Pat') Campbell was a popular head. To his eyes Andrew, in uniform grey sweater and knee-length grey shorts, looked little different from the seventy or so other small boys in his care. 'I remember him as a rather unusual-looking little chap,' Campbell says, 'but I can't say I recall anything about him very particularly. We had quite a few boys who later left their mark in the world.'

It was Pat Campbell's wife, Camilla, who saw into the

inner soul and nature of the boy. 'Andrew was a boy who did not need the company of others,' she recalls. 'I don't mean to say he was unpopular. He just got along perfectly well on his own.'

'Perfectly well' is a pardonable exaggeration, because Andrew himself would far rather have been elsewhere. The school and its hearty 'play up and play the game' spirit proved uncongenial to him. His introduction to Algebra, Latin and Geometry created no real problems for, as Pat Campbell says, 'He was among our brighter pupils, certainly'. But the boredom of routine lessons, of enforced sports in the Square gardens or on the Big School playing fields at Vincent Square, restricted his energies and cramped his spirit.

'I was being pushed through the forms because of my mother's belief that my unusual interest in historical architecture was a sign of academic brilliance,' he explains. 'She'd convinced the school of this, so I was marked out for special "encouragement".

'My main difficulty was that I gave the impression of being vaguer than really I was. It was just that I had no memory of what had sometimes led up to what was going on.' The effect was best summed up by his future housemaster at Westminster, Frank Kilvington, who has a clear recollection of Pat Campbell discussing Andrew with him at some length and in some perplexity.

'He told me his staff were entirely divided about Andrew's intellectual ability,' Kilvington says. 'One half was inclined to think that he was simply precocious, and not very clever intellectually. This they put down to his rapid development and the upbringing he'd had at home, in a family of unusual cultural distinction. The other half believed he was really extremely able, an outstanding person intellectually. I personally found him to be a naturally precocious boy with a great facility for words as well as music. Enormously gifted, of course.'

The question nobody at the Underschool seemed able to answer was how best to develop and channel these gifts. Andrew was inclined to succeed or disappoint at his lessons with the unpredictability of April sunshine.

In Andrew's time at the Underschool music was in the hands of a teacher called Clive Chapman. He too seems to have noticed nothing very special in his precocious young pupil, although Andrew did put together a musical parody of each of his teachers before he left. His father helped him to edit it into shape, and it was performed at the end-of-year Underschool concert, of which no record exists: a pity, since it would certainly point up Andrew's critical judgement of the men who were entrusted with his development. The *Underschool Magazine* merely records that 'A Lloyd Webber and B. M. J. Cruft gave their first [violin] solo' while in the school's lowest form.

Campbell has what he believes to be 'one important recollection of Andrew: that he failed to gain our Internal Scholarship to the Great School, when everyone expected him to.' Andrew recalls no such thing. 'I did not even enter it. I refused to, because I knew I wouldn't get it,' he declares. 'I got the ordinary entrance exam to Westminster. The scholarship I *did* get was the one I entered myself for, two years after I'd been at Westminster proper.'

Could this be a fault of his admittedly sketchy memory? Camilla Campbell supports her husband's account of the examination and its resultant disappointment. 'I remember it well,' she says. 'Pat announced the results after Prayers that morning, and quite a few of the boys were surprised that Andrew hadn't won. But, you know how these things are, boys soon forget. So I was rather touched when I happened to walk along the corridor afterwards, where the boys hung their coats and things, and saw a small figure – Julian Lloyd Webber – with his head buried in a mack hanging on a peg. I put my arm round him, and tried to comfort him, and he told me he was crying for his brother – because he hadn't won. I found that *very* moving.'

The Internal Scholarship, as Pat Campbell explains, was for the outstanding boy of the Underschool year going on to Westminster School. It was quite apart from 'the Challenge' scholarship, offered by Westminster itself to all boys of under fourteen years. Westminster scholars became Queen's Scholars and entered a separate house, College House. They had no connection with Campbell's Internal Scholarship, which he had persuaded Westminster to let him bestow annually on an exceptional pupil who might otherwise have been unable to go on to the Great School. The *Underschool Magazine* covering the years 1959 to 1962 shows that in 1960, when Andrew left to go to Westminster, the Internal Scholarship was shared between A. R. Starling and A. F. K. Monkman.

But by then Andrew knew that his future *had* to be in music. The difficulty was to see how his liking for popular melodies and rhythms could serve this bent. 'I knew I wanted to make my *own* music. I knew it had to be in the theatre, which had become my main interest, with architecture and history now in second place. But I wasn't at all sure about what kind of music it was going to be, except that it was definitely going to be my own and not the kind that was being conventionally taught.'

The idea of 'adapting' popular music to theatrical production was as yet unrecognized in respectable musical circles. Gilbert and Sullivan had, via the Savoy Operas of d'Oyly Carte, succeeded in mollifying all but the most entrenched classicists, and their work was universally popular. But between the true theatre and the syrupy musical fantasies of Ivor Novello and Vivienne Ellis existed as large a gap as it is possible to imagine. As one musical critic snorted in a monthly music magazine: 'While a case might possibly be presented for jazzing up a solemn piece of classical music, there can be no valid reason for ruining a tuneful segment of Opera-bouffe . . . but thus do the awful hacks of Tin Pan Alley sit in their grimy basements (or sumptuous offices) and plot how to undo the good work of their forefathers. We have travelled a strange road since the Strauss era!'

Andrew refused to accept this barrier from the start. He was 'very bitten by opera', but fascinated and excited by the contemporary 'pop' of his day. The point was that he was letting every existing musical form play on his ears and senses. 'I mean,' he says, 'it was quite natural for me to hear Rock and Roll alongside Prokofiev. And, because my family were very catholic, with a small 'c', in their musical tastes, they never had any particular wish to force any kind of music on me, really.'

Also, much of his pleasure at this time came from being taken to London theatres with and by the family. 'I used to see quite a lot of things, because they took me. And I also used to go to shows with my aunt Vi quite a bit. Sometimes on my own, as well. We weren't gallery-squatters or anything like that, so I usually had a pretty good view of whatever we were seeing. And sometimes I'd just drop in if something appealed to me on the spur of the moment. I remember going to see the final show at the Chelsea Palace just before it closed, almost by accident.'

The music of his generation was more forceful in its approach. There was nothing accidental about its effect on him. 'It was an enormously creative time,' he says, 'and when you're about twelve that makes a tremendous impression on you. I was a bit on the young side for Elvis. But I sort of caught the tail-end of him, and of the Rock 'n Roll era in general. That, and the arrival of the Beatles in the early 'sixties, were really my main influences.'

Against this trend, Andrew *did* go to see the musical

shows of the period. 'They weren't, and still aren't, really fashionable among kids,' he says. 'But I wanted to see them, and I loved some of them. You see, I saw music in a much wider context. I thought the Beatles were superb, and I particularly liked the Everly Brothers who were extremely clever in their use of harmony. You know, the earliest memories I have are nearly all about the theatre.'

He was soon writing down his own melodies and discussing harmonics and orchestration with his father. 'By then most of the people of my sort of vintage were trying to *be* Beatles,' he explains, 'while I found it almost impossible to write music which didn't have a theatrical basis on which to do it. I still find it hard if there isn't a theatrical *raison d'être*. At that time I suppose it seemed a little odd.'

Mainly so because the musical theatre was almost entirely in the grip of the Americans. Hit shows such as *Oklahoma*, *Annie Get Your Gun*, and *South Pacific* were storming over from Broadway to enthral the entire Western world, which, in the middle 'fifties, was still shaking itself free of wartime gloom. 'We in Britain had very little going on,' Andrew says. 'And what we had was mainly American.'

He himself was passionately sure that he could change that.

'My ideal, really, was Richard Rodgers,' he says. 'And then, subsequently, it grew into musicals in general, by all the best writers and composers. I remember I was able to play some of the tunes from them on the French horn, which I was rather better at than the violin. I suppose I was being influnced to compose my own tunes in roughly their style. Though I must say that, when I think back to those days, I remember almost nothing to do with music at all. It was all prep, prep, prep, and being made to learn this and that.'

The impression left at the Underschool was of a boy

whose parents, and in particular his mother, insisted on the most determined stretching of his academic talents possible. 'They were very nice people,' Pat Campbell recalls, 'but with an extremely high regard for their sons, that I do remember. Not,' he adds, 'that that is an uncommon trait in parents.' Less common was the suppression in Andrew of his natural gifts, because his mother was understandably striving to make him into what he never intended to be, a successful scholar.

Campbell recognized this sooner than she. 'I taught him maths and scripture,' the ex-headmaster says, 'and maths was *certainly* not his best subject; probably his worst! I can't say I remember him being particularly interested in scripture either. But I did always make a point of trying to make the Bible stories live for the boys. I told all the stories, including the one of Joseph of course, as if I'd known the characters in them personally. I hope that may have given Andrew more interest in the subject than he showed at the time.'

Sport was a cherished aspect of Underschool life but Andrew was a reluctant performer in almost all physical activities, as his old headmaster rather sadly recalls. 'I'd say he was probably unsuccessful at all sports,' Campbell says. 'Most probably because he didn't give a damn for any of them!'

There is also a belief, supported by his mother, that Andrew had suffered in early infancy from a mild bout of poliomyelitis which may have affected slightly the muscles in his legs. He was not a robust boy, certainly. And childhood illnesses of whatever sort took their toll.

Andrew's parents naturally attended the shows he put on in his model theatre. 'Julian was allowed to move the characters around to their correct places,' their mother remembers, 'but Andrew would be furious if anything went wrong.' As she says, 'Friends, too, had sometimes to be subjected to these plays although normally, it was just us. I

believe he has since used quite a few of the tunes he wrote
for those early shows in his musicals, but I can't swear to
it.'

There was also a noticeable budding of commercial
interest (foreshadowing his recent extension into the role
of theatrical impresario). Sarah, his ex-wife, has revealed in
an interview that Andrew tried to sell the books and
pamphlets he wrote when he was about twelve. 'They were
about ancient buildings in Britain and British history,' she
said. 'They were just one-off projects, but Andrew had the
cheek to price them and make his relatives buy them from
him!'

Nevertheless Andrew's decision to devote his life to
music, to composing for the stage, showed that he was
governed by considerations other than merely trying to
make his fortune. 'You're very lucky in life,' he says, 'if you
know what you want to do and are able to do it. And it
doesn't really matter if you succeed all the time or not.'

5

Up Rigaud's

TWICE during the war Westminster School had been moved to places of safety. When it returned to the hallowed stone of Dean's Yard, in the shadow of the Abbey, it was much depleted. Andrew's headmaster, the late John Carleton, shared in the invigorating task of rebuilding Westminster into one of the finest teaching academies in the world.

Underwriting the school's Latin motto, *Dat Deus Incrementum* (God Gives Increase), was the noble aim of supreme quality: excellence. In this, Andrew had shown potential in at least one field. 'He produced for me, when he first came to Rigaud's, something he'd done on English castles, a most ambitious thing,' his first housemaster, Frank Kilvington, remembers. 'I rather gathered that he'd completed the whole project, with drawings and diagrams and so on, at home in his spare time.'

The school had three 'sides'; classics, history and science. Andrew's greatest good fortune, in the view of everyone who knew or was taught by Charles Keeley, was that history in his time was in this inspired teacher's hands, and that Andrew was marked out for his 'history sixth'. Keeley, now retired and reticent, was by all accounts an extraordinarily gifted master.

There were many other advantages to Westminster, and even Andrew's indifference to conventional schooling could not altogether ignore their influence. 'In my opinion,'

Frank Kilvington says, 'it was an absolutely ideal school for a person like him. Boys were left free to develop their own interests, far more so than at most schools. I personally always thought that those who did best, in fact, were the intellectually able rather than the scholars. Boys who had, as Andrew had, interests of their own which they wanted to get on with.'

Andrew agrees. 'But it was the flat and the family and everything which were much closer to me than the school,' he insists. 'I learned a great deal more *outside* the school, you see, than in it. And, quite honestly, great place though it unquestionably was, Westminster's real value to me was in being situated in the heart of London. And in allowing me to get out on my own enough to use that to advantage.'

Remembering Camilla Campbell's view that here was a boy who had little need of companionship, one can see how Andrew would relish these solitary excursions into the outside world. Also there was little alternative to seeking his own company. 'I didn't have too many friends in that first year,' he recalls. 'None at all really. You see, I got in when I was very young, younger than most.'

And Westminster's musical tradition was hardly to his taste. Andrew belonged to the 'new wave', the group who were cultivating an interest and absorption in meticulously selected pop-music, playing it wherever and whenever possible at ear-shattering volume.

He and the few like him at the school who collected records of their favourite pop-stars were given every freedom, even to playing their music in common rooms. But as dayboys most of this activity went on at their homes, and ranged against them in strength was the solid teaching at Westminster of classical music, led by the school's distinguished Director of Music, Arnold Foster.

'Foster was a tremendous character,' Kilvington remembers. 'Everybody had a great affection for him as a real northcountryman *dedicated* to serious music – and it had to be serious! He wouldn't have taken to Andrew's style of music at all, I'm quite sure of that.'

But in 1963 Foster's place was most fortunately taken by David Byrt, a young and enthusiastic music master who had been taught harmonics by Andrew's father at the Royal College of Music. According to Kilvington, Byrt was a very different type, a teacher who tried to lead rather than rule. 'He was very much broader in his musical outlook,' Kilvington says, 'altogether more catholic in his tastes.'

In the Westminster School magazine, the *Elizabethan*, issue of March 1963, an article signed by the new Director of Music states that 'the Director has no patience with the juvenile sophistication which pretends to despise enthusiasm'. Andrew would have agreed with that.

Byrt, now teaching music at the famous Dragon School in Oxford, was to spend the next seventeen years at Westminster. His recollections of Andrew and his musical ability are overshadowed to an extent by the isolation with which Andrew shrouded himself. 'Alas, he played very little part in the music of the school,' Byrt says. 'I do just remember him in one of my classes; fairly well on, when he was in the Sixth. But he wasn't really interested in the general classical theme which predominated in the school.'

Byrt recalls Andrew's being given lessons in playing the French horn by his predecessor. He himself failed to recognize any quality in his pupil during the early stages which would have merited special attention. 'Really, he was a dark horse,' he says. 'Andrew didn't show his style until very late on in his school career, when he wrote and produced a musical show. That I do remember. It was entirely his own production, and I'm pretty sure he didn't ask for any staff help at all.'

As David Byrt wisely surmises: 'It may well be that he had reacted *against* traditional classical music, like a number of other boys at that time. His family had rooted him in the classics. He went the other way. And at Westminster, where the tradition was certainly classical, he just didn't fit in.'

Byrt, of course, was well aware of Andrew's background, and of his father's position in the world of music, and he makes an interesting comparison between them. 'It seems curious to me,' he says, 'that Dr Lloyd Webber chose to write so many pieces which were rather frowned on by the musical establishment, so to speak. Now that I come to think of it, I suppose both he and Andrew were alike in that: they wrote the music they wanted to write, rather than anything expected of them.'

Two years passed before Andrew showed, by a remarkable flash of scholastic flair, how determined he could be when he set his mind on getting something he really wanted. 'I entered myself for "the Challenge",' he says. 'I don't know that Charles Keeley would have thought I should do so, when I was still just under fourteen (one had to be to win the scholarship – it was one of the basic rules). I did it on my own, because I suppose I realized that I ought to do something with all the stuff I was having to learn. And of course I could manage the papers quite easily, once I'd decided I'd do it.'

Kilvington's recollection is of a boy who 'might well have surprised himself' by getting the scholarship. 'But I can also believe that he was very determined and sure of where he was going.' To win the award, which was unusual but not unknown for a boy already in the school, each candidate had to complete satisfactorily two Maths papers, one French, one English, one Latin and one History. An old school-friend, now a Westminster master, Tristram Jones-Parry, says: 'The way things were done, and still are, was to add up the marks, giving rather less for history as a rule (which makes one wonder how Andrew managed, since this

was the one subject in which he was known to excel), then
award the scholarship to the top six or seven.'

Andrew's award must again go to the credit of the
school's unconventional approach, its search for 'excellence'.
As Jones-Parry explains: 'People's hunches are backed
quite often. You see, there may be twenty or so from
various schools in the original list; but if any boy shows
excellence in one or two subjects, he may be given a
scholarship irrespective of his poor showing in the others.
That could well have been why Andrew, with no great
grasp of the other subjects, was given one.'

'The Challenge' was worth the total cost of the fees, in
those days some £400 a year for boarders. (In the case of
Scholars entering College House, boarding was obligatory.)
To a musical professor earning less then £3,000 a year, it
was a welcome relief, and all the better for being
unexpected. But Andrew's mother was not in the least
surprised. 'The night I won it,' Andrew remembers, 'my
aunt Vi was the only one who seemed to realize that I'd
done anything very much. She rang up and asked my
parents "Isn't anybody going to take Andrew out to dinner
to celebrate?" Nobody had even thought of it!'

When Andrew first went to Westminster, housemaster
Frank Kilvington was encouraging senior boys in his house
to get up concerts and engage in creative activities. Other
houses in the school had long outshone Rigaud's, and
Kilvington, who had come to Westminster from Repton
and was hankering after his old school's Gilbert and
Sullivan Society, was keen to change this. 'I wanted our
house to rival Busby's, which was where things were always
being done in that way, and very well done,' he says.

Kilvington called on the talents and enthusiasm of his
headboy, Robin St Clare Barrow, whose ambition was to
become a writer of plays and lyrics. Everyone with acting or
dramatic ability was roped in to help. The first production,

which Barrow wrote, was a mild spoof on the life of Bishop Rigaud, founder of their house. 'I'd really brought the idea with me from Repton,' Kilvington says. 'There was a master there in my last days who'd been teaching in Switzerland. He'd introduced the notion of writing one's own witty verses to Gilbert and Sullivan tunes. Very clever it was, and I tried to launch the same thing at Rigaud's.'

In Kilvington's recollection the Barrow show, entitled *Three Little Boys*, 'went quite well.' But a review in the rival Busby's journal, the *College Street Clarion*, scorned its lack of originality. Undeterred, Robin Barrow set about writing the lyrics for the following Christmas show, and this time went in search of a composer. He discovered (probably via Kilvington who, having founded his beloved G & S Society, vaguely remembers Andrew accompanying on the piano on occasion) the still extremely young Andrew, in his second year.

If a three years age gap and the relative difference in status between a head of house and a second-year student put strains on their collaboration, fusion was inevitable, since both were inspired by the same love of popular music, though Andrew had little time for Gilbert and Sullivan. Each had suffered from the classical tradition of Westminster's musical side, and felt it to be both antiquated and inflexible. What they wrote together was largely in joyous reaction to this, expressing mutual anarchy. It became the second of Kilvington's Rigaud pantomimes, under the satirical title of *Cinderella Up the Beanstalk and Most Everywhere Else*.

To the older boy, nonetheless, Andrew's ability was slow in showing itself. 'I underestimated him,' Barrow says. 'To be absolutely honest, I was dewy-eyed. I saw myself as an accomplished lyric writer and only thought of Andrew as a useful piano-player. He was so young, and ever so shy. I remember that when he wanted to write a series of related tunes for the show with one common theme we wouldn't let him do it. Being so senior to him, we were pretty ruthless, and the fact that he had much more talent and determination than any of us was overlooked.'

Some of Andrew's tunes which did win approval and were included in the *Cinderella* bill with Barrow's lyrics were graced with such titles as 'Greater Men Than I', 'Foolish Tears', and 'I Continually Reflect on My Present State of Mind'. The titles suggest a streak of mawkish sentimentality in the lyrics.

The second piece he and Barrow wrote together demonstrated how much Andrew had gained from the *Cinderella* experience. The show, entitled *Lovers and Friends* or *Socrates Swings*, was based on a classical story in literature, the theme of A. C. Malcolm's O *Men of Athens*. It is doubtful that it would have been recognized by the Greeks, but in Barrow's view it was 'the best of our joint work, and favourably received'.

Andrew had also managed to overcome native shyness sufficiently to attempt a live performance at the school. On the makeshift stage of Rigaud's house he had taken part in what he recalls as 'a sort of concert, in which I came on and just did one piece, playing a number'. The performance appears to have brought him to the notice of the school as something of a rebel, but one worth listening to. 'It was when Russ Conway was all the rage,' he explains. 'Everyone said when they saw me "My goodness! He can do popular music!" They hadn't known that.'

Robin Barrow, of course, did know it. His belief is that Andrew not only played that particular number but also sang – at least in rehearsal. 'I've still got a tape of it, with Andrew I think singing the lyrics which I'd written, but which Tim Rice adapted and changed later,' Barrow declares. The song, *Too Young to Understand*, is recorded in the *Rigaudite Review* issue of Winter 1962 as having been 'first performed last term', so it could well have been the 'piece' Andrew remembers doing. The words in the 'improved' Rice–Lloyd Webber version suggest a budding sophistication:

> The things I do from time to time
> They say the law has banned
> When I ask why, I'm told that I'm
> Too young to understand.

A second chorus echoes the same adolescent frustration:

> Should I come home at half past four
> In handcuffs, stoned or canned,
> Don't blame me, I don't know the score,
> Too young to understand.

And the verse confirms the sentiment:

> I'm far too young to understand
> The girls I should avoid,
> I don't know when I'm out of hand
> Though I know what I've enjoyed.

All good, rollicking, youthful stuff. As the final chorus sums up:

> How could they think the state I'm in
> Is something I had planned?
> I'm far too young to know my sin,
> Too young to understand.

In the new school show, a 'follow-up' to this spirited appeal was given fresh music by Andrew, with plaintive lyrics by Robin Barrow. It was entitled 'Too Shy'. The producers announced 'ambitious schemes of production . . . for instance . . . three sets of scenery on two flaps that, when draped over the corner of the flap, produces an indoor effect and when draped over the centre represents a garden.' But they had been unable to find anyone capable of or willing to paint the scenery.

Andrew's music was well received, and Robin was coming to realize that his young recruit's talent exceeded the merely useful. 'All I'd wanted at first was that he should sit down at the piano and play tunes,' he admits. 'You just had to have somebody who could do that – somebody who could make up a melody for a lyric I'd only written about five minutes before. He was very good at that . . . In the pop songs, he was very adaptable and amenable even, but he could be stubborn. Very stubborn.'

Being himself 'Not a very musical person – ironically, with a very catholic taste, but not really caring for show tunes, *except* for G & S—' Robin Barrow looks back on the early days of the collaboration with some regret. 'I don't think, deep in my heart, that I really believed either of us was going anywhere, because I knew nothing about the world of getting things accepted, which Andrew did know a little about through his family.'

On the other hand, as he says, there was a sense in which he, so much older and more mature, seemed to be taking the whole thing more seriously. Andrew's sense of humour was still essentially immature, bursting out in schoolboy jokes and japes. John Lill was particularly struck by this, but nobody who had known him will deny it. 'He loved anything ridiculous and childishly embarrassing,' Lill says. 'A "whoopee cushion" would send him into hysterics.' Robin may have misjudged Andrew for this reason alone.

John Lill was now an important part of Andrew's life at home with the family, and his recollections of those days suggest a more personal reason why Andrew prefers to forget some of the happenings at that time. 'It really surprises me that Andrew can't remember if his mother taught him piano,' he says. 'My impression always was that she did a tremendous amount for everyone. But then, she did an *extreme* amount for me, I'd say dangerously close to overdoing it.'

Lill is no doubt thinking of his own mother when he says this. 'She was very grateful for the help I got, but I must stress and underline the fact that, despite all that the Lloyd Webbers did for me, and all their tremendous help and kindness, it was my mother who was the one saviour of my life. Because I was almost a finished product, artistically, by the time they met me. And I feel rather sorry now for my mother, because she had had a terribly hard life, doing three vicious factory jobs a day to pay off our debts and help my career.'

The Lills lived in a small terraced house in Leyton, one of the poorer districts of the East End of London. John's father had incurred debts from which, from his wages as a common worker in a wire factory, he was unable to free himself. His wife took on the task, at the same time insisting that John should have every possible opportunity to study and improve his natural talent. 'So I was a perfect object for Jean's kindness. She had, I think, a *need* to help people. I dare say she still has it. In those days it was a force second to none. Nothing could stand against it.'

And inevitably it cut across the grain of much that Mrs Lill had done and was doing to help her gifted son. 'My mother liked Jean and was very grateful, but I think she must slightly have resented her,' John says. 'Jean could be so very domineering, introducing electric fires and so on into our home, and doing such a lot for me in every way. After all my mother had done for me it can only have seemed that Jean's great kindness was almost a way of buying her way in. My mother died six years ago and I know Jean had been very fond of her; but she never realized, I think, how she had affected my mother's life.'

The visits to Leyton, to the Lills' humble home, became almost weekly rituals. Andrew and Julian were taken by their mother to experience a very different sort of life there from the comfortable security of South Ken. 'We used to bait my mother hugely about all her good works,' Andrew remembers. 'Nothing would keep her away from the East End when she felt the call. She went every time. And it was because she used to take us down there with her, to John Lill's house, that Julian and I got to be interested in, and became supporters of, Leyton Orient football team.'

Andrew says that it had never occurred to him to take an interest in football before this, but both boys became keen fans, following every match and player. Once this interest rooted itself Jean no longer had to drag her sons to Leyton with her. 'We wanted to go,' Andrew says. 'We wanted to see the games, and Julian and I still support Orient, you know. We have long and usually highly disturbing conversations about what we're going to be able to do for them. They're in bad trouble, I'm afraid.' He shakes his head. 'Yes, it has to be said that the "Os" are not in great shape.'

In one of these sorrowing talks, Andrew and Julian reached the conclusion that financial support for the troubled club was not what they wanted to provide. 'It's just the wrong place for us,' Andrew explains. 'In fact, we even got round to wondering if perhaps we shouldn't support a similar establishment nearer at home, like Brentford. In the end we decided it just wouldn't be the same.'

Lill reluctantly went with them to the matches, being the least enthusiastic of the three about the game. They would tramp the distance to the ground, standing among the crush of spectators in the stand or under a grey London sky. Julian's voice, which John Lill had first heard as 'a high, squeaky little sound' when they had met at the Royal College, was now booming out with the others. 'O – O – O' they shouted, with no noticeable attempt at harmony. All three remember the afternoons with a certain primeval joy, despite John Lill's faint heart about football.

Meanwhile he was winning the affection and regard of both his mentor and her family and also gaining an insight into the family's ways, which, as he says, were 'anything but ordinary'. 'Dr Lloyd Webber, Bill, was fairly orthodox,' John recalls. 'Very kind and introverted, but where Jean was inclined to be mystic and had a strong belief in life after death I think he fought shy of admitting any such thing. Even if, inwardly, he knew it was so.'

Andrew's father also taught John Lill composition. 'And he did it very well indeed,' John says. 'He was a delightfully modest man, liked by everybody, and we had a tremendous amount of fun with him on occasion. But, like Andrew – and indeed, his mother – he could have black moods. The difference was that in Billy Lloyd Webber's case they usually became tearful and self-pitying, while both Andrew and his mother had fierce tempers.'

John Lill saw both the dark and the light side of the family. 'Jean laughed with me over several of Billy's funnier ways,' he says. 'She tried once to give me driving lessons in Billy's car. It was a black Ford Consul. I'm afraid I wrecked the gearbox by running it up a steep gradient, which can hardly have amused him. But she thought it very funny.'

There were many times when the whole family, plus John, would enjoy a joke at the expense of others. 'Billy's sense of humour was colossal,' John says. 'We were always laughing. Quite often at the behaviour of others, which struck us as hilarious. Jean, too – though at times she would find it harder to join in. Get her in the right mood and she'd be giggling non-stop.'

John believes that Billy, whom he grew very close to, would have liked a daughter. 'More than once he told me how he'd wanted one. I suppose he would have enjoyed the warmth a girl would have brought into the family, though she could hardly have added to the fun.'

Life at No 10 Harrington Court was full of humour. 'I was doing a lot of tape recording while I was there,' John Lill recalls. 'Very keen on it. I used to steal in and record Billy snoring after lunch on Sundays, when he took a nap.'

Andrew was just as much of a prankster, John says. 'He loved practical jokes, and I often couldn't look at him without starting to laugh.' There were times when the two youths would find themselves in an underground train convulsed with laughter. 'One of us would spot some amusingly dour, or sober, face opposite and it would strike us as funny. We'd start giggling, and end in fits of laughter.'

On one famous occasion, which both remember with the glee of naughty boys, John and Andrew were actually ejected from a concert. As Jean Lloyd Webber tells the story, 'This wasn't the only time they got into trouble, but it was probably the only time they had to be forcibly removed.' The performance was a recital of obscure concertos for 'unusual instruments' such as the sopranino, which has the highest pitch of any orchestral instrument. John Lill takes up the story with relish:

'We went along together to St Pancras Arts Centre, where the concert was being held, with no intention of playing the fool. It sounded like an interesting and out-of-the-ordinary sort of evening's entertainment, and we both wondered, I think, what was in store. But when a fellow came on with a great huge tuba, and another with a tin penny whistle, it was fatal! Then, when they produced a tympani concerto, it was altogether too much. We couldn't control our hysterics.'

Andrew's humour can be extremely contagious, as all close friends know to their cost. Lill says it stems from 'his curious keenness for funny, odd sounds'. In those early days conversation between them, he remembers, was usually about such things rather than any other aspect of music.

'I think I introduced Prokofiev to him,' Lill says. 'Either that, or he introduced him to me. I forget which. The point is that he caught on to what I was finding enjoyable in it: that it was very outrageous, without being a severance of the classical tradition. The composer had built on classical foundations while giving his music vast, imaginative flair and depth. I think Andrew not only grew to like this enormously, I believe the style affected his composition.'

John Lill echoes others in suggesting that the Russian composer – of the orchestral fairytale, *Peter and the Wolf*; the opera, *The Love of Three Oranges*; and three symphonies – had a recognizable influence on Andrew's music. Sergei Prokofiev, dead less than ten years, was then winning mass acclaim particularly from the young. 'We were both tremendously influenced by him,' Lill declares. 'We used to talk about very little else. Whenever we were together in the flat, Prokofiev was one of our prime subjects. Or tubas, because these also fascinated Andrew. He just liked anything that made a peculiar noise; any instrument in an orchestra which suggested something new and different to his ear.'

'New and different' sums up Andrew's musical taste at that time, and it also explains why traditionalists at Westminster found him unacceptable. There was no obvious show of opposition or distaste, but he was made to feel less a part of the school than many more conventional boys. Ivan Asquith, a contemporary who shared his interest in history and architecture and got to know him fairly well in later school years, says, 'He was quite eccentric, which I found amusing, but I think the "hearties" didn't get on too well with him. He was among the more precocious, sophisticated and intellectual types: essentially an original. And there were people at Westminster who didn't much care for that.'

Asquith was one of the companions from school who

went abroad with Andrew to explore old castles and churches. 'In the 'sixties, I suppose, there was a general spirit of rational and enlightened progressive thought,' he explains. 'This showed itself mainly among the educated middle classes, of which Andrew was a member. The new faith was in the progress of science, the general belief that Society could be improved by social engineering. Well, Andrew was one of the people who would question that. He was both capable and clever enough to be independent and to some extent original in his thinking, though one has to bear in mind that he was still very young.'

Another drawback to his becoming a popular schoolboy was Andrew's hatred of organized activities such as the compulsory cadet corps. 'It was the thing I loathed most about Westminster,' he says. 'I was absolutely . . . I mean I always have had a mental block about things to do with games and all those sort of things. The corps was the worst. I was actually nearly thrown out of it, which would have been something of a feat – the only person ever to be thrown out of something that was compulsory!'

On more considered reflection, he wonders if the fault was all his. 'I think at that time the whole of that side of school life was pretty poorly represented. To someone like myself, who was afraid of making a fool of myself, it was made very unsympathetic, which is silly really. Because if some of the games and so on had been less aggressively taught I think probably I would have got over my hatred of them.'

In a school where a number of boys habitually aspired to become academics and artists, a reluctance to join in the heartier side of life – the rowing, football, cricket and athletics in which Westminster also excelled – was no bar to popularity. Among Andrew's contemporaries were such future luminaries as the concert pianist Anthony Peebles; consultant psychiatrist David Cook; the chief editor of

Humanities at Oxford University Press, Ivan Asquith; and the entertainers Peter and Gordon (Peter Asher, Jane Asher's brother, and Gordon Waller). Talking to them now, it is clear that Andrew was not alone in feeling irked by the school's antiquated curriculum.

Ivan Asquith describes Andrew's attitude to the school as his 'eccentric sophistication', but he shares the view that little tolerance existed in their day for the non-conformist. 'The school was changing,' he says, 'but such tastes as Andrew elected to prefer, such as the music of his time, the musical theatre, and the abstractions of conservationism and exploration, were still very far from being embraced.'

It does seem that those first two years as a day boy 'up Rigaud's' had scarcely marked Andrew with the stamp of the school. Yet if he stood aside from its mainstream he managed to do so without arousing hostility. Westminster may have been slow in moving from a rather rigid intellectual conservatism, but it rose above petty chauvinism. Andrew was left to his own caprices. His old housemaster, Frank Kilvington, puts it rather well. 'Andrew,' he says, 'was a rather nervous boy who was very determined about where he was going, and also where he was *not* going.'

To Kilvington Andrew was 'a rather vague sort of chap. Fairly law-abiding and so on, but not always knowing what the rules *were*, so that if he disobeyed it wouldn't have been deliberate. I really remember his parents rather better . . . and I do have a mental picture of his father standing in our drawing-room; and of his mother too. They struck me as very intellectual people, who took education seriously and were ambitious for their boys. I was told that one of the reasons they sent Julian to UCS [University College School] and not to Westminster was that they wanted him to study music on Saturday mornings, which wasn't possible because we had Saturday school.'

In Jones-Parry's recollection, 'Andrew, I think, *did* enjoy

Westminster, at least the stimulus of the place. He may have hated games, but he played squash with me sometimes. And after his first year he could get away with doing very little. We used to spend an enormous amount of time just sitting around, drinking cups of coffee. Conversation was highly pretentious; thirteen-year-olds talking learnedly about Goethe and so on. The idea was to outscore people by sheer intellectual brilliance, however little one really knew. I'd say he was pretty good at that.'

And Robin Barrow misjudged his young friend completely.

'I once told him that he'd never make a success as a composer,' he admits, 'which shows how little I really understood him or his talent. I'm delighted I was so hugely wrong.'

Andrew seems to have shown no better knowledge of his proper purpose. 'I just entered myself for the Challenge because I knew I'd have a good chance on the history paper,' he says, suggesting that he was still less decided to make music and theatre his joint future interests than he now believes. It would have been a difficult decision for anybody. But for a boy of less than fourteen with the capability to succeed academically, perhaps even to achieve brilliant results in those subjects which interested him, it was a major problem. To go all out for the 'profession of vagabonds', depending entirely on his eccentric ear and an as yet-untried talent, was a gambler's throw.

Fortunately, he backed both horses; won the Challenge to College, ensuring himself of the best education Westminster or probably any other school could have offered, and at the same time found his way into a freedom to develop his theatrical and musical interests at will. The road ahead was clearly signposted: with or without the reluctant drill of the school corps.

6

Vivat,Vivat

ANDREW'S first housemaster in College, the man who had sat on the board with the headmaster to award the Challenge scholarship to him, was Henry Christie. A bluff and hearty six-footer, Christie was only in charge of the Queen's Scholars of College House for the first year of Andrew's residence, but his recollection is of an amusing eccentric rather than a musical genius-in-the-making.

'He came to me one day and asked if he could go, with a friend of his, Gray Watson, to take part in some demonstration. I asked what they intended to do there, and Andrew said they were going to carry a banner. It was in support of some peace movement or other, perhaps an anti-nuclear or CND march, I can't recall exactly. Anyway, I saw nothing wrong with it. "All right," I told them. "Well, behave yourselves." And off they went.'

But that was not the end of it. 'I happened to be coming back to the school later that same day, along Great College Street, and there they were. The demo or whatever was all over, and I saw two small boys – Andrew at that time was rather smaller than average, I'd say – with a banner drooping miserably to the roadway, staring entranced at a magnificent military parade which was passing along – the very thing they'd been demonstrating against!'

The irony of the situation was lost on Andrew and his friend until Christie put it to them both. 'Then, I must say, they saw the funny side,' he says. 'It tickled all of us that they'd been fascinated by the very militaryness that they wanted to abolish. And, of course, they were so young that they could hardly have escaped being fascinated by the pomp and ceremony of a military band, soldiers on horseback, all that sort of thing.'

Was Andrew really so small, or did he just give an impression of smallness? Christie says: 'Small physically, yes. Not outstandingly so, but I do think of him as a *small* boy. The funny thing is that, unlike many small men, and small children certainly, who tend to try to make up for their lack of stature by being a bit more pushing, he wasn't at all like that.'

There was no need for him to push. 'College House,' says John Field, then a teacher trainee at the school, 'was always very sociable and easy-going; in the nineteenth-century tradition. Nobody cared much what the forty or so scholars did when they went outside the school.' Henry Christie agrees. 'One did tend not to mind where they were all the time,' he says. 'Or want to know exactly what they were up to. Occasionally the housemaster or the master in College would whip round and see where they all were. And, oh, in ninety-nine cases out of hundred they'd be doing something completely virtuous. Very occasionally one might find a boy doing something silly, but you reckoned that was the penalty you had to pay, as housemaster, for the ninety-nine others who were exploring London's Wren churches, going to the Science Museum, and so on. You gave them a great degree of freedom to live their own lives because that, you see, really *is* Westminster.'

It was an aspect of the great school which would appeal mainly to someone with clear-cut interests. But as Christie says of his scholars: 'They were, and probably still are, highly intelligent young men. I believed they'd make much better use of their time if left alone than if they had been dragooned around by a lot of schoolmasters.'

A highly privileged group then, in which Andrew's natural ability and intelligence was by no means unique. But his sense of the bizarre was perhaps more exceptional. 'Matron told me she was delighted by him, I remember,' Henry Christie says. 'You see, he and Gray Watson wrote up their laundry lists every week, but in picture form! They did hilarious drawings of dirty rugger socks, and school underwear, which amused her tremendously.' A keen musician himself, Henry Christie finds it odd, looking back, that he was almost wholly oblivious of Andrew's musical potential at the time. 'Don't get me wrong,' he cautions. 'College was a very musical place, if not successfully so. And by then, in the early 'sixties, guitars were of course very popular. So there was no shortage of musical appreciation, and a fair amount of talent.'

Yet Andrew's style found little favour, as he sadly admits. 'Yes, I think that is true,' he says. 'He, I think, was probably feeling himself to be a sort of modern-music rebel. His father had let him get on with it, and he may well have been reacting against the music he'd been brought up with. Only natural really. At Westminster, anyone who wanted to be modern found himself slightly *out*. Mind you, I don't think Andrew really suffered; but it's probably true that the school was a mixed blessing for him. Rather sad, I think.'

Christie had come up against Andrew's mother, Jean, at a very early stage. No sooner had Andrew been packed off to his new abode, complete with regulation clothing, pocket money, sports gear and books than she was calling on the housemaster. Jean had nothing against the school or its academic teachings, but her strong views about sports were well known. Henry Christie and his wife were certainly left in no ignorance of them.

'I shan't ever forget her telling me one day,' Mrs Christie says, 'how wrong it was that boys like Andrew should have to "waste their time playing games". She told me this very firmly. "He doesn't like them, and it's perfectly obvious that he isn't going to need them, because he's cut out to be a musician. So why force him?" I said something to the effect that "Well, if he's going to spend the rest of his life doing music, surely this is the one time when he can enjoy the chance to play games?" But it was a losing battle. Mrs Lloyd Webber was really quite indignant about it.'

Her husband adds: 'I think we as schoolmasters played down the fact that he was going to be a professional musician, however much his mum and dad wanted us to take it into account. We didn't actively discourage him, but neither did we help him in that direction. And, you know, Andrew didn't have the reputation in my time of being noticeably "un-trad" or "mod". He may have thought he was, but to us he seemed no more eccentric in that way than any other boy at the school.'

And the master who succeeded Henry Christie as housemaster, Jim Woodhouse, agrees. Having gone to the school as a house tutor, or assistant housemaster, he was appointed to take over the prestigious College House in September 1963, when Andrew was beginning his second year as a gowned and privileged scholar. 'My main impresion was that I never knew where he was,' Woodhouse, now headmaster of Lancing and an amiable and popular teacher, remembers. 'He was always at home when he should have been at school, and at school when he should have been at home, or elsewhere.'

Woodhouse tried, he says, 'to cope with this in various ways, but eventually I decided that "dignified acceptance" was probably the best answer!' He laughs. 'Westminster was rather like that. And it was quite clear that Andrew was educating himself perfectly well. That was particularly true, you see, of boys in College. In fact, I encouraged them to take advantage of being in a capital city, where they could

get out to lectures and museums and all the rest of it.
Andrew certainly rushed about the place.'

Didn't this ever worry those in charge of him? After all,
an English public school housemaster is very much *in loco
parentis*. Was Jim Woodhouse, or his wife Sarah, who
shared his interest in the boys fully with him, never
seriously alarmed by Andrew's mercurial absences? Not
overmuch, it seems. 'Well, certainly I was both concerned
and curious at times,' he says. 'But I knew he mostly went
home. And knowing his parents – his father a distinguished
classical musician – and the general atmosphere of his
home, I realized that he was learning a great deal there
which perhaps one wouldn't have been able to teach him at
school. Also, you know, I was greatly in favour of boys not
treating school and home as two different worlds.'

Sarah Woodhouse's view of Andrew was similar to her
husband's but she saw Andrew with a warm and motherly
eye. 'The boys were always in and out of our house, our
private rooms,' she says. 'Our kitchen door opened on to
their stairs, and it was always open. It was really rather like
having your own sons rushing about, which was lovely.'

Sarah Woodhouse remembers Andrew particularly well.
'He was scatty!' She smiles broadly. 'He sort of willowed
around. Always friendly. His friend Andrew Manderstam
(the television reporter) was exactly the same, a boy in
another house who actually had a job while he was still at
school, with Radio Luxembourg. Used to say things like:
"I must just slip off to Paris for the weekend, but I'll be
back for my maths period on Monday morning"; that sort
of thing. Quite mad, really.'

Being thus encouraged to go his own way, there appears
to have been no stopping Andrew. Jim Woodhouse kept
what he called his 'signing-out book' in which boys in the
house who were allowed to go out beyond the normal
hours were required to enter their destinations or reasons

of absence. Andrew's occasional entries (the book-rule was not always obeyed) suggest a whimsical sense of enjoyment and radical chic. On 23 October 1964, for example, his entry reads: 'Out with French girlfriend.' The following month he rather pompously wrote 'Lloyd Webber – out to dinner with Lord Harmsworth.' Other entries refer mainly to theatres and concerts, including one given by John Lill; but on 10 June 1965 he was ostensibly to be found at a Young Conservatives meeting – an interesting reflection on his growing political awareness; and very different, if not diametrically opposed, to the Fabian-style Socialism of his mother's family.

And Andrew, in his old housemaster's opinion, did contribute 'a great deal' to the school, whatever he himself may believe. 'I don't know why he feels that,' Woodhouse says. 'He produced his tunes. I can't remember now what form they took, but I have a rather hazy impression that in his last year or two he was beginning to produce tunes which combined jazz and the classics. This, you know, was a time when a lot of schools were finding a rather distressing gap opening up between the two, and I should have thought Andrew was another quite considerable influence of that kind. The more established set probably thought very little of it at that time, and that is perhaps why he found so little encouragement, musically, in the school itself.'

Meanwhile Andrew was managing to score successfully enough in normal schooling to gain entry to a major Oxford college, Magdalen, even to win an Exhibition scholarship there. Jim Woodhouse sees nothing strange in this fact. Even though (as Andrew freely admits) he hardly knows why they gave it to him. 'It was quite surprising,' he told an interviewer recently. 'I'd done so badly in A-levels that they told me not to bother to enter it! I mean, I actually ended up with one D and an E, for history and

English!' So his getting into Oxford at all was totally unexpected. 'My parents hadn't even given notice to the school that I was going to leave, or anything. I'd had no idea, you see, that I was going to win the Exhibition. It was only after other people had gone in for the Christchurch one, which I didn't get, that I thought, "Well, I'll just do the Open one." I must admit I was quite pleased when I got that, having failed the other.'

He had entered *himself* for the Oxford examination, and claimed to be 'completely staggered' by the successful result. 'I still don't understand how it could possibly have been,' he says. 'All I can attribute it to is that the person who interviewed me kept Siamese cats, and I was talking to one at the time of the interview.' He chuckles. 'Not that I believe in the "cat mafia" going that deep!' Anyway, he got in.

But sadly it was – as he also remembers – 'quite the wrong move for me to take'. In view of what happened when he got there it would indeed seem to have been kinder of the fates if they had kept cats out of it.

Nevertheless, Jim Woodhouse sees nothing odd in Andrew's elevation to the ranks of old Westminster scholars who have won laurels at the great universities. 'Andrew was known to be inconsistent. He could shine one day and not another, depending on the questions and whether he was interested in the aspect of the subject under review. He was much better in history than English, of course. And Charles Keeley was teaching him. Charles was a wonderful teacher – he had the gift of creating an atmosphere among his boys which made them feel intellectually enriched. He created a silence around himself, almost an aura. And that room in Ashburnham House, where the Upper History Seventh met, was a great place. Andrew certainly benefited from that in his final year.'

In fact Andrew was showing once again that he could do better on his own, and when he had set the course himself. 'Charles Keeley, who my mother thought was doing so much for me on the history side - and who was in fact a marvellous teacher - hadn't had anything to do with my getting the Exhibition. I mean, he wouldn't have *prevented* me from doing it. But I don't think he'd have remotely believed I could have got it.'

His own explanation of how he managed it is almost as curious as the result itself, and suggests a dubious quality in the system by which prizewinners are selected for and by our major universities: 'Something I'd learned very early is that if an examiner is going through thousands of exam papers, what he wants to find is the one that's a little bit "off the wall".' He laughs. 'I remember my Magdalen paper was great fun. I think I proved all kinds of highly improbable historical theories. Because, I mean, I do adore medieval history. I certainly did then. And particularly I was interested in anything that was or could be related to architecture.'

Unfortunately, Oxford did not satisfy the great musical urge in him. Musically, Andrew found the university extremely disappointing. He went for his interview on 9 December 1964, trusting - indeed believing - that Oxford, and more especially the college which he had chosen, would provide a framework for the creative energies he now knew to be seeking both outlet and encouragement. It failed him, as Westminster had in his final year.

'I'd ended up doing a show to celebrate the fact that the school had produced two artists, Peter and Gordon, whose record had gone to Number One,' he recalls. 'But that was all I could do, because nobody there would put their talents into running a musical, which is what I should have liked to do if I'd got any support. It was all rather frustrating, really. You see, I couldn't do in it what I'd done with Robin [Barrow] because he'd left by then and I didn't have a lyricist.'

The show was, as he says, 'quite slickly done. Technically it wasn't at all bad. But my contribution as a composer was really negligible. I just put it together vaguely, while other people who wrote the words were allowed to take the limelight.'

This, had he known it, was the dilemma of any composer of theatrical music, and Andrew was consciously modelling himself on theatre as opposed to music in isolation. 'Yes, that was my interest, that and what was going on in the background – the new works coming from Richard Rodgers, Leonard Bernstein and Irving Berlin. Shows like *West Side Story* had broken new ground. I wanted to go farther in the same direction if I could. I cannot explain really why, but this motivated me.'

And Oxford seemed, in prospect, to offer a way. 'My whole interest, really, was how could I get on to actually doing music? Westminster had been very limited. The only good thing about it had been that, as a boarder, I'd been able to get out and see a lot of first nights. They were certainly very good about that. But it was a very unfashionable time for the kind of music I wanted to do, and I imagined Oxford would be more progressive.'

He was beginning to see that some of his energies had been misdirected. 'Charles Keeley, you see, obviously thought that I was good news and likely to be able to make it through on the history side. But I knew I'd fall down, because my problem always has been that I've never had a brilliant memory. Also, where my interest was in medieval history, Charles was not really a medieval historian. So the areas I was seriously interested in were not really ever taught to me.'

Nevertheless, it was one of Charles Keeley's 'topics' –

described by Andrew as 'subjects he handed out for us to choose one and go away and write an essay about in half an hour or so' – which prompted him to record the fascination he and John Lill had discovered in Puccini's *Tosca*, which he had just seen and been captivated by. 'It so happened that at the suggestion of various masters, of whom Charles was one, a few of us had been to see the Maria Callas performance at the Royal Opera House. I wrote a piece that was reasonably controversial about it, I think. I actually said that Puccini had not been a great love of mine up to then, but I'd never realized that the composer could be *made* to work; in other words, to *come over*. And I concluded in my piece – terribly arrogantly, the sort of thing that only a 15-year-old would do – "this therefore must have been because the standard of performances in his day (when he was writing the pop music of his time, equally unfashionably) had been so inadequate." And that therefore we had to examine whether or not popular composers are considered bad news purely *because* they are popular, and are given bad performances? Or whether or not what we had actually seen was a revelation?'

He had already answered the question for himself. But it made flowing rhetoric for the paper and was well received. 'In fact,' as Andrew says now, 'that wasn't a particularly original thought. At the time I think the critics were pretty much agreed that admiring Puccini meant sinking pretty low, and it was only the Callas performance of *Tosca* that had brought his name back. Most people thought that; I mean, my father thought Puccini was the greatest composer who ever lived. Neither he nor I were ever able to go to a performance of his music without being removed from the auditorium in total tears.'

In this Andrew had found a curious bond with his sentimental parent. 'It was the one thing that he and I had in common,' he says. 'He always told me that anybody who could write a great tune was all that he wanted to know about.'

Billy Lloyd Webber also told Andrew of how he had first heard the great sentimental ballad from *South Pacific*, 'Some Enchanted Evening', played to him by Teddy Holmes, the publisher of Chappell's. 'My father said it moved him so much he really wasn't able to go on listening to it. All Holmes replied was, "Well, at least, Bill, this'll send the birth-rate up!" You see, my old man was always of the view that melody was the most important thing.'

Andrew chuckles in rare self-deprecation as he recalls his father's actual words. 'He said several times to me that if I ever wrote anything as good as "Some Enchanted Evening" he'd tell me.' The smile turns a shade rueful. 'Well, he never did tell me,' he admits.

At least by the time he left Westminster, having completed the year there after gaining his Exhibition, Andrew was in pursuit of his father's ideal. It was during this waiting period that, in the month inappositely celebrated for fools, on 21 April 1965, a young and very junior assistant working in the offices of the EMI record firm, Timothy Rice, typed a short letter on one of the office machines inviting Andrew to get in touch if he was at all interested in teaming up with a lyricist.

Interested was hardly the word.

7

Enter Tim Rice

THE letter, characteristically mild and modest, arrived by
the first post. Whoever Tim Rice was he had managed to
convey just the right note to whet Andrew's appetite for an
accomplice. From an address in Barons Court, at No 11
Hunter Grove SW10, Tim had written: 'Dear Andrew, I
have been told that you "were looking for a 'with-it' writer
of lyrics for your songs", and as I have been writing pop
songs for a short while now and particularly enjoy writing
the lyrics I wondered if you considered it worth your while
meeting me?' There followed an even humbler self-
assessment: 'I may fall short of your requirements, but
anyway it would be interesting to meet up – I hope!'

Timothy Miles Bindon Rice had not the slightest need
for diffidence. Not only was he already working in the
music business which Andrew wanted to get into, but he
was three and a half years older and had been out in the
world for the greater part of these. He may have seen
himself as, he says, a mere 'bored and minor dogsbody' of
an assistant to the great Norrie Paramor of recording fame,
but to Andrew he was already an achiever, in close touch
with the music that mattered.

Their very first encounter seems to have convinced at
least one of them that their future lay together. Andrew
was utterly charmed by the tall, casual young man who
called on him at the Harrington Court flat. Tim's
recollection is less effusive, but there is no doubt that he

saw how lucky he was to have come across somebody sharing his enthusiasm and tastes. 'I went round to meet Andrew and we got on quite well,' he recalls rather lamely. In fact the meeting and the harmony which flowed from it was historically fruitful.

Tim, in a script written for a radio programme, vividly describes it: 'He played me some of his tunes, and said "I'm looking for *words*, man!" I thought the tunes were very good and told him I'd give it a go.'

From a comfortably middle-class background Tim had left school at Lancing College on the Sussex coast for a course at the Sorbonne in Paris. This, though short-lived, gave an opportunity to assess qualities in himself besides musicianship. He was an attractive young man, able to appeal to the young girl students at the university with his amusing, debonair good looks, light fair hair and blue eyes. By the time he came home to his parents in Hatfield he had sampled quite a large measure of what is loosely called 'life'. It was time to take on a career.

Unfortunately for anxious parents, these things do not always go according to plan. In Tim's case, odd juvenile jobs as a petrol pump attendant and similar had filled in the time until he was able to join a law firm. But after a painful year or two it became clear that this was not going to last.

An early and devoted pop-music fan, he applied for and got a job which, though he later described it as 'an EMI serf under the title of management trainee', did at least put him within touching distance of his idols. The great British recording firm was handling Elvis Presley, Cliff Richard and The Shadows and many of the emerging giants of Rock and Roll. Tim's contact with them was frustratingly slight, but being in the world of music made him think about his own capabilities and he began to seek an outlet for these.

'I was keen to make a record as a singer,' he remembers. 'I recorded some songs I'd written on tape, and they let me play them over to them. Amazingly they liked them, even though they didn't care for my way of singing. And they did actually record one of my songs by a group few people had ever heard of called Night Shift. It was a total flop, but it gave me confidence.'

The record, he admits, sold only about twenty copies. 'The point was that it was something I could talk rather grandly about to publishers,' he explains. 'This was a great advantage.'

And one day, when the notion came to him to write a book and he went to see a literary publisher with it, it was this qualified success which led him to Andrew. 'The man didn't really like my book idea,' he admits, 'but when he discovered I was in the music business he said I ought to meet this young fellow, Andrew Lloyd Webber, he knew was looking for a lyric writer. So I wrote the letter, simple as that.'

Not really so simple. Because, as Tim now admits, 'It wasn't until I met Andrew that I really became a writer.' And Andrew vividly remembers the first time Tim walked in through his parents' front door. 'I knew almost immediately that he was exactly right. As soon as we started to work together I saw how much better he was than all the people I was ever likely to meet at Oxford. In fact, he was the reason I left there after only one term. I didn't leave Oxford for anybody else. I left for Tim.'

And for the very sound, practical reason that, in the three years it would have taken Andrew to complete his university degree course, 'I'd most probably have lost him.'

As Andrew rightly realized, Tim Rice was on the brink of a career which could successfully have followed a number of directions. 'He was already out and working in the big wide world, and he was *that* talented: I mean, I thought if I don't hang on, he'll be gone when I finish up. I couldn't risk it,' Andrew explains. 'You see, apart from some help

I'd had from an actress friend of my aunt Vi's – Joan Colmore – who tried to write the lyrics for a couple of songs of mine while I was staying with them in Ventimiglia (more to keep me quiet than anything else), there had been nobody since 1962, three years before, when Robin Barrow left school.'

Tim's experience of the world outshone his own narrow sophistication completely, yet their fields of interest were sufficiently alike for this to add harmony rather than discord. They both shared a rapturous appreciation of the same idols of rock and pop. Tim's impression is that Andrew 'had this bursting ambition to be Richard Rodgers, while I sort of vaguely wanted to be Elvis'. In terms of musical theatre it was an ideal marriage, and Andrew makes the point strongly.

'We didn't write anything at all for the first six months,' he says, 'just kept up a sort of contact. But I knew when I did start to write with him that I'd found what, for me, is absolutely total: the other half of the whole. This is a very important thing to understand about musical theatre – that it is the *most collaborative* form of theatre, or show business, you can find. Musicals are the one thing nobody can do on their own. *All* the different links in the chain have to fall into place or it snaps. It just goes pfffffmp!'

From the experience he has since added he knows, too, that the producer of a musical show has to be the controller of all these highly individual strands, a veritable four-in-hand coachman. 'The only possible way to run this group is to have a feeling of total trust between everyone in it,' he says. 'Any weakness, and it isn't on. It won't work at all.'

With Tim Rice he felt instinctively that he had found the most vital link between his own creative music and the theatre. Like his, Tim's is a mind of restless originality, committed to expressing itself in lyric form of remarkable quality. Since Andrew could never hope to write the words he so badly needed, and is unable to describe in words what he can say in music, it was or seemed to be the perfect match.

He believes now that the meeting with Tim was the whole counterweight which swung him against continuing with Oxford and getting at least a Third-class degree while doing what he could in the music field. 'I was absolutely overjoyed to *leave* Oxford,' he says, 'but you have to realize that the decision to do that didn't come until later, after they'd been kind enough to let me take a couple of terms off as a kind of sabbatical after my first term. And by then I'd come to realize what working with Tim could mean to my work.'

The famous OUDS – Oxford University Dramatic Society – had nothing to offer him. Andrew's thirst was for musical theatre, not for the drama and revue on which the society under its president, Bob Scott, was concentrating. 'I knew Bob Scott very well and he's a great friend of mine, but quite honestly there was not a lot going on in my particular field. There was a good designer, Paul Beard, but you can't teach musical theatre to undergraduates.'

Also it was a time when his earlier decision to make his career in music and the theatre rather than architectural history was ripening. 'I realized that it was a waste of time for me to be doing history at all,' he explains. 'And knowing that Tim was there and available, and that I'd lose him if I didn't put everything into working with him, there really wasn't much choice.'

In an inconclusive talk to his parents during the 1965 Christmas vacation Andrew announced that he had been given leave to take at least the next two terms off from the university, and tried to explain what he was doing and what he hoped to attain. It is much to the late Dr Lloyd Webber's credit that, according to both Andrew and his mother, his father lent a sympathetic ear.

Nevertheless, it was a terrific decision for an extremely young and able student to take. His mother makes light of it now, but at the time she and his father must have been very worried. John Lill remembers Jean Lloyd Webber expressing great anxiety about Andrew's future.

'Naturally she was worried,' Lill says. 'She is a very sensitive person and his decision to leave must have come as a shock.'

John and Andrew's mother had found a shared interest in spiritualism. 'Jean is very psychic,' he says, 'very gifted as both a clairvoyant and clairaudient. At times she can both see and hear psychic phenomena, while in my case I am only able to "receive" when giving concerts sometimes; which, unfortunately, has been sensationalized in the press, but is absolutely genuine.'

His interpretation of these communications from the spirit world has, he says, enabled him to write and play in the manner of Beethoven. 'I discovered these powers in me more than twenty years ago,' he explains. 'Jean had told me of her own experiences, and I saw that she was far more developed than I was. But over the years I've had quite a struggle with her sometimes, because we've both experienced these things and they've been proven. And when you've been given direct evidence it makes a tremendous difference to your life.'

Lill does not explain what the struggles with Andrew's mother were, or what caused them. 'No, not now,' he says. 'In fifteen years or so I intend to publish it all, so let us leave it at that. Jean knows. I imagine, too, she has been in contact with Billy since he died in October 1982.'

Lill feels that Andrew's mother's anxiety about her son's future was more acutely felt because of her sensitivity. 'Jean is almost obsessed by darkness and disease,' he explains. 'She always seems to get the subject of any conversation round to it. When someone's ill, she'll try to ring them up for a chat. And it's not as if she's cast down by it, it seems to enliven her. In any emergency she'll be the first to rush in and visit whoever's involved.'

John Lill acknowledges that, of all the Lloyd Webber family, Andrew and he had been the least compatible. Indeed, he confesses to having found Andrew 'angular and awkward, difficult to get on with sometimes'. No doubt his own early struggles for survival had made him critical, if not envious, of a boy who was able to enjoy so many privileges.

'He was always very friendly, and most of the time we got on splendidly,' he says, 'and still do. But we have different ways. He seemed very spoilt, and I thought all the more so because I knew what a struggle could be about.'

One wonders whether, by the time he went up to Oxford in October 1965, Andrew had ever been in love. Lill does not think so. 'I didn't think of him as the romantic type,' he says. 'He never seemed very interested in girls. In fact, I never thought he would get married early.'

The contrast with Tim, who shortly afterwards accepted an offer from Andrew's grannie, Molly Johnstone, to come and live in her flat adjacent to her daughter's and become, as John Lill was, a very modestly-paying guest, was particularly marked. 'Tim was far more natural and predictable in every way,' Lill says. 'I warmed to his stability by comparison with Andrew's up-and-down moodiness.'

He reflects now on the growing suspicion that the collaboration between Andrew and Tim which brought them so much success may be unlikely to recur. 'I wish they'd go back,' he says. 'Because I always felt a lot of Tim's stability was needed to help Andrew.'

A bitter assessment? It is interesting to note that when Andrew was made the subject of the popular programme *This Is Your Life* on 4 November 1980, John Lill was not among those invited to share his public acclaim. 'I was there in the audience,' Lill says, 'and they had asked me to go on, but then changed their minds.' What decided this, and whether or not Andrew's mother had anything to do with the selection, is not known. It certainly cannot have been Andrew himself, since the identity of the subject is one of the best-kept secrets in entertainment.

Andrew's single abortive term at Oxford had come at a time in his adolescent development (he was seventeen) when many young men and women experience poignant feelings of futility and despair. It also seems that he was still torn by the change of heart over his earlier desire to spend his life in and around ancient buildings. During the year prior to his going up to Magdalen he and friends from school who shared this architectural interest went with him on holiday excursions. Tristram Jones-Parry, one of a party Andrew joined on a trip to the West Country, recalls Andrew's not inconsiderable value as a piano player. 'We'd go to pubs in the evening and Andrew was always able to strum any tune the locals wanted to hear on the piano,' he says. 'It made us very popular.'

Since their days at the Underschool together, Tristram and Andrew had shared a love of exploration and appreciation of great architecture. 'He knew a great deal about the churches and places we went to look at together,' he says of Andrew. 'He was particularly interested in the work of William Butterfield (a noted English Gothic architect of the late nineteenth century), but it was his piano-playing I will always remember from that holiday.'

Ivan Asquith had known Andrew in the history Sixth at Westminster. The holiday they went on together was more exotic, with no musical pub evenings, but it revealed another side of Andrew's developing tastes: a growing right-wing political slant tending towards 'Tory anarchism', despite what he now remembers as 'a strong Socialist

tendency - almost to the point where I joined the
Communist party' - at Oxford.

'We went to Italy together with three other friends in
the spring of 1965, the year Andrew went up to Oxford,'
Asquith recalls. 'The tour we mapped out took us to
Florence, Rome, Assisi and Ventimiglia on the way back,
where we stayed with Andrew's aunt. I remember flowers
all around the house, a wonderful place near the sea; and I
remember being greeted and treated with remarkable
hospitality. I think the others in the party were David
Carpenter, Gray Watson and somebody whose name I
can't recall. The interesting thing wasn't that we got
involved in heated political discussions - everybody of our
age did that. It was the way we all divided, rather sharply I
seem to recall.'

Asquith is guarded about his old school-friend's strength
of political feeling. 'I'll leave Andrew to explain how he
felt,' he says with understandable reserve. 'But in general I'd
say that he was rather Right in those days. And the thing
was that whenever we got into a lively discussion, about
Mussolini and so forth - and of course we were very
conscious of what the dictator had done in the way of
architecture - Andrew and Gray would take that side, and
Carpenter and the other chap would take the other, and I'd
be somewhere in the middle.'

Asked about this now, and whether his political opinions
have stuck, Andrew expresses a lightly mocking detach-
ment. 'You can't take these things too seriously,' he says. 'I
find politicians the most insulated beings there are. They
spend their time talking about themselves.'

To illustrate the point he quotes a notable recent
happening in his own life, at a party given by the Royal
College of Music of which he is an honoured patron. 'I was
chatting to Sir Keith Joseph, the then Secretary for Trade
and Industry. He absolutely astonished me by asking, "Tell

me about your musicals – *do they export at all?*" Well, as I had four separate productions of *Evita* running in the States at that moment, and various shows in other parts of the world, I really didn't quite know how to reply without offence. So I just said, "Oh, not terribly much," and walked away. It did occur to me afterwards that if somebody like that couldn't be briefed at least on the rudiments of his job, who could?'

And if politicians surprise him with their lack of insight into the delicate but far-reaching economics and values of show business, they are surpassed in his estimation by businessmen. 'The extraordinary fact is that almost nobody in industry knows the first thing about musical theatre,' he insists. 'Not so long ago I had an hysterical conversation with a very big industrialist indeed. When I told him I'd been working with the director of *Nicholas Nickleby*, he said: "Oh really? I didn't know they'd made that into a musical." And that chap runs one of our most successful public companies!'

Oxford, Andrew says, increased his interest in other aspects of life. 'I became slightly more taken by politics there,' he says. 'You see, I'd never really cared about them except in one degree; though at school everyone had a point of view. Mine was that I'd always believed, hugely, in the British liberal tradition with a small "l" (which is something I probably share with Tim Rice). But apart from what I've described about my mother, and her way of helping underprivileged musicians like John Lill, my political background had always been pretty conventional. I mean, my parents were the same. As a family, the only things we really felt very deeply about were the preservation and care of buildings, architecture, and music. And I really do care hugely about all those.'

Ivan Asquith 'bumped into Andrew' at Oxford, but can throw no light on his state of mind. 'He was up at

Magdalen while I was at Christchurch,' Asquith says. 'The one thing I'm pretty sure about is that Andrew didn't take to Oxford at all. I imagine he'd realized that what he wanted to do was music, and of course he'd gone up to read history. People like me, I think, were struck by the sheer boldness and rashness of it when he made the decision to leave – though I myself disliked my first terms at the university so much that I may even have encouraged him to do so. But I'm sure others tried to persuade him to stay on and get his degree.'

Robin Barrow, the ex head boy, was one of these. Andrew barely remembers any meeting with his old lyricist at Oxford, but Robin clearly recalls Andrew visiting him and telling him he was leaving. 'He'd been mixing mainly with other Westminster chaps,' he says, 'and I hadn't seen much of him. But when he told me he was giving it up and going to write music with some fellow he'd met I told him he was crazy to attempt it. I honestly believed he'd never make it, and I'm absolutely delighted I was so completely wrong.'

Barrow's impression of his old partner at that time suggests that Andrew was in unusually low spirits. 'He seemed healthy and cheerful enough,' he says, 'but he struck me as being somewhat insignificant in his appearance. I dare say he may have felt a bit out of things in the university, and that may have depressed him. It may also have been in reaction to that that he later adopted a flamboyant way of dressing.'

Strangely, Andrew revealed to Barrow nothing of the difficult decision he was having to make about his future, though he well knew that his friend had survived a far worse emotional crisis – a broken love-affair which had upset him deeply, and in which Andrew had shown sympathy and understanding. 'At a time when some people were not even speaking to me, he was always understanding,' Barrow says. 'He obviously didn't share the narrow, conventional view. He wasn't judgemental. He used to come round and cheer me up.'

'I really only came across [Robin] very occasionally in the Oxford days,' Andrew says, and he 'wasn't interested in writing any more. Like all composers I wanted to cling on to lyricists, but I think Robin had rather changed direction. At school he'd been a rather frivolous Rock and Roller. Then against all the odds he'd become a Classics don and gone to Canada. [Barrow later became a reader in philosophy in the Education Department of Leicester University]. So there wasn't very much contact, which was rather annoying.'

Either Andrew's memory of their relationship has faded, or Robin Barrow's is faulty. His differs considerably. 'I'd gone up to Oxford before him, of course,' he says. 'But he'd somewhat caught up on me, because I'd stayed at school very late for all sorts of personal reasons. We used to go back to his parents a lot – whom incidentally I liked very much; strict, but lovely people – and we both built up record collections together. I got married very young, and Andrew was at my wedding. So, while we were up at Oxford we naturally talked about ideas for musicals, and he wanted to do one of the Borgias. While I was on my honeymoon I wrote a script and sent it along to him, but I never heard what he thought of it.'

Robin added: 'Later, when I'd gone to Canada, a friend told me that Andrew was missing contact with some of his old Westminster friends, so I wrote to him. All I got in reply was a brief acknowledgement on a postcard. After that I sent him a Christmas card, but didn't get one from him. So I had no idea how much he really wanted to keep up his old friendships.'

Andrew doesn't remember any such script. 'Did he say that?' he asks. 'I really don't remember. My impression was that Robin no longer wanted to write lyrics. And, of course, by then I had met Tim.'

Today, Andrew looks back on the decision to leave
Oxford convinced that it was the right step. Yet he
wonders how he would have fared if he had stayed on. In
some ways he appears to regret, yet not to regret, the
decision. 'I often wonder,' he muses, 'if I'd been older,
perhaps? Would I have enjoyed it more? I was only
seventeen and a half . . .'

To an earlier interviewer, he complained: 'I was too
young to go really, only just seventeen when I went up
[actually, having taken his place in September, he was
halfway towards being eighteen]. And by that time I'd met
Tim Rice, you see. And, he was, for me, such an
extraordinary find! I mean if you don't write lyrics, and I
don't, then you get to realize jolly early on that lyric-
writers are extremely precious. They have to be treated like
very rare birds.'

As he recalls: 'The difference in Tim's and my ages meant
an awful lot to me at the time. When you're in your teens
and you meet someone who's twenty-one or two, that kind
of age gap really means something to you. Later on, of
course, it means nothing. But, at the time, I guess I must
have thought he was something very special indeed, as he
was. What he thought of me? Well, probably that I was a
sort of much younger long-shot.'

For both – the one gambling his whole career, the other
doing little more than accepting a sensible offer of
collaboration – there was then little in the future apart
from their own belief that their words and music could,
together, find a market. The odds were shorter for Tim
Rice, who still had his job. For Andrew, throwing up his
university course, they involved a plunge into the unknown
with almost no tried equipment.

8

Chasing Shadows

TO hear his mother talk about the gamble, Andrew's rejection of Oxford and his leap into musical and theatrical composition was a cool and considered step. 'He'd thought it would be a good place, because Oxford has a tradition in theatre, and to some extent in musical theatre,' she told Vivien Lind. 'But there was not much going on.' Jean Lloyd Webber allowed that the meeting with Tim ('four or five years older and already embarked on his career') had weighed with her son, but she gave no hint of how unexpected and disappointing a blow Andrew's return home after such a brief experience of university life had been. To a family steeped in scholarship, devoted to accomplishment, and aware of their special gifts in music and the arts, the sudden and apparently whimsical decision must have put a severe strain on the tolerance of his parents.

Jean's loyal claim that her husband 'realized that Andrew's style was unique and would be spoilt by formal musical training' suggests a barely credible flexibility in a man who was playing an increasingly distinguished part in the fabric of established academic music and was to be elevated to Honorary Academician of the Royal College of Music within the year.

Perhaps by way of compromise late in 1965 Andrew enrolled for a year's course in orchestration at the Guildhall School of Music. He had recognized the imperative need for at least this amount of professional equipment. Early the following year, 1966, he took an abbreviated course at the Royal College of Music, of which today he is an honoured and greatly valued patron (proceeds from one of the New York previews of *Cats* went entirely to the College) and of which his brother, Julian, is a part-time professor.

To these courses he gave a minimum of time, spending every possible hour at work on the projects which seemed to float into his mind like bubbles. He had learned to avoid counting on success while at school. 'A song of mine was recorded by a singer called Wes Sands, but it came to nothing,' he says shortly. Robin Barrow is more explicit. He is not altogether sure that this 'opus' ever got off the ground except in Andrew's lively imagination. 'I never knew quite how much to believe,' he says. 'At the time it seemed fantastic to me that he could be right in all the claims he made. But now I can see that I was a complete idiot! I mean, he used to tell me he'd got an enthusiastic response from some agent or other to one of the pop songs we were writing together. I never *wholly* believed him. And he did tell some tall stories, I'm pretty sure. For instance, but this is way back, he told me once we'd had a song recorded by Wes Sands, one of three pop singer brothers. I still think that may have been one of his more imaginative tales. But in those days we spent a lot of time – really, a *lot* of time – doing these pop songs without ever believing they'd be accepted. And it was probably for that reason I was so pessimistic about Andrew's chances in the music world. I really had no faith in myself.'

With Tim Rice, there was no such disbelief. No limit to the scope offered, if only he and Andrew could hit on the right subject, the right blend of originality. Talent was never in question, as they were equally sure of each other. Andrew was the driving force, the motor, but they were

both ambitious. If Tim veered, Andrew's laser-like concentration brought him back on course with little effort.
When he says of Andrew: 'He persuaded me to write some
lyrics for a musical he wanted to do on Dr Barnardo,' he is
merely reflecting this propulsion. His own enthusiasm was
no less keen.

Two years, though, is a testing time for any partnership
when nothing comes of it. Tim recalls: 'We had sold rights
to "Dr Barnardo" for £100 each, and that was all. For those
first two years we simply waited. It wasn't until the
summer of 1967 that we managed to get two songs
recorded by Ross Hanniman, the *Evening Standard* "Girl
of the Year".'

How they did so pays amusing tribute to their entre-
preneurial zeal. Roping in a few old friends, among them a
singer called David Ballantyne who was later to become
Julian Lloyd Webber's brother-in-law, they scoured London
for copies of the newspaper carrying entry coupons for the
annual contest. Ballantyne tells the story with relish:

'Nobody had ever heard of Ross Hanniman, which was
understandable because she'd never recorded anything at
that time,' he chuckles. 'But Tim and Andrew, for whom I
had been doing the singing on some of their demo discs,
wanted a girl singer to do this, so we filled in dozens of
these voting forms, and she won!'

Reporter Ray Connolly was in the newspaper's Fleet
Street offices when Andrew and Tim came in, flushed with
their achievement, from the recording. 'I'd come for an
interview for a job on the paper,' he later recalled. 'They'd
just offered it to me when these two blokes wandered in
with the record they'd made. I remember I didn't think
much of it, and as it turned out neither did they, or the
record-buying public!'

Rejection was something they were well used to.
Ballantyne, who had met Andrew through a girlfriend of

his, a model called Pamela Richards who lived in the same block of flats as the Lloyd Webbers, was singing a variety of Andrew's songs. As he recalls: 'He and Tim had some loose arrangement with Southern Music under which their demo discs were offered to singers and published in that sense. But as writers of one-off pop songs they were notoriously unsuccessful, and I don't expect they were paid more than a minute retainer.'

Yet, without their knowing it, the word was beginning to get round: that 'fairly bright, rather odd' chap, Lloyd Webber, had teamed up with a young writer in the music business; they were both writing fantastic musicals which, though nobody had heard a note of them, were 'going to set the Thames alight'. It was largely Westminster gossip, shop-talk among 'old Westminsters' as they like to be called. But it reached the ears of a schoolmaster who had taught at Westminster Underschool in Julian's time and was known to Andrew's parents.

Alan Doggett was a sad, pathetically mixed-up man in private life, but his passion for music endeared him to Dr and Mrs Lloyd Webber. By 1966 he had moved on from the Underschool and was teaching at the great choirschool, Colet Court, which bears the same relationship to St Paul's as the Underschool does to Westminster. It was in Hammersmith, opposite the public school, and very much part of it. The aim was to train Colet Court singers in the style of the Vienna Boys Choir, by the Continental method which differs so considerably from old, traditional English form in that it requires four-part voices. Doggett, as director of music, entered into this with his usual gusto.

Among the first things he did was to contact Andrew. He asked if he and his collaborator would care to write a brief cantata for the school's annual concert. He had the then headmaster's consent to this unusual request, although Henry Collis remembers being surprised that Doggett had persuaded him to agree. 'He came to me with the very remarkable notion that we should commission such a work,' he says. 'Well, I let him do it, but really only because I wanted to give him, the new director, every encouragement. Also, since I was not much of a scholar, I always tried to be innovative.'

Andrew and Tim seized on Doggett's proposal. They launched themselves into their first work to be guaranteed an audience, though consisting only, in Andrew's recollection, of 'bored parents'. And Collis, after a first meeting, was completely won over. 'They came to see me and asked very nicely if they could use the school music room for their work,' he remembers. 'Naturally, I gave consent. They were so very charming about it. As a matter of fact, I still have the letters they wrote to thank me afterwards. But I must say, when Doggett told me what the piece was to be – a Bible story set to modern pop music, or something of the sort – I had serious doubts whether I'd done the right thing. And some of my colleagues were incredulous. They'd never heard a noise like it!'

Sadly, Alan Doggett's remarkable vision was barely completed when he left the school. His successor, then his assistant (and the piano-playing accompanist of that first historic performance of *Joseph and the Amazing Technicolor Dreamcoat*), was Ian Hunter. As the present director of music recalls, Doggett's departure was a sad loss to the school.

'Alan was not very brilliant musically,' Hunter says, 'but his great gift was his ability to communicate with kids. He also knew the right people and could get things moving. I suppose his influence on Andrew and Tim was largely that. He pushed them when they needed a push to get them going. Without him, I wonder, would they ever have been given such a start? It's an interesting question.'

An even more interesting one is why Tim Rice and

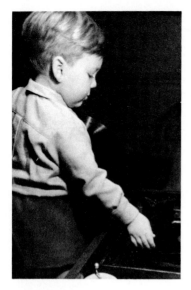

Only eighteen months old, but already
Andrew knows how to put on a record – and
look as if he can read the score

Both violin and piano have been added to his
accomplishments by the age of four and a half

Walking beside the river Avon on one of his many 'expeditions'

Now nearly seven, Andrew plays an early duet – his violin and three-year-old Julian's mini-cello

Andrew (far right, seated) at Westminster Underschool in the summer of 1960

Andrew in his teens, enjoying a rest during a walk with pianist John Lill

At his aunt Vi's Italian villa

With his beloved cat,
Perseus

With 'Percy', John Lill, his father Dr William
Lloyd Webber, and his brother Julian . . .

. . . and on a foray with
Julian, his parents – and his
cat

Recording *Joseph and the Amazing Technicolor Dreamcoat* at Colet Court (the St Paul's junior school): Andrew is attentive as his first cantata is brought to life

Tim Rice hears his lyrics and Andrew's musical score put on record for the first time

Alan Doggett directs

Thirteen Colet Court choirboys take part in this historic first recording

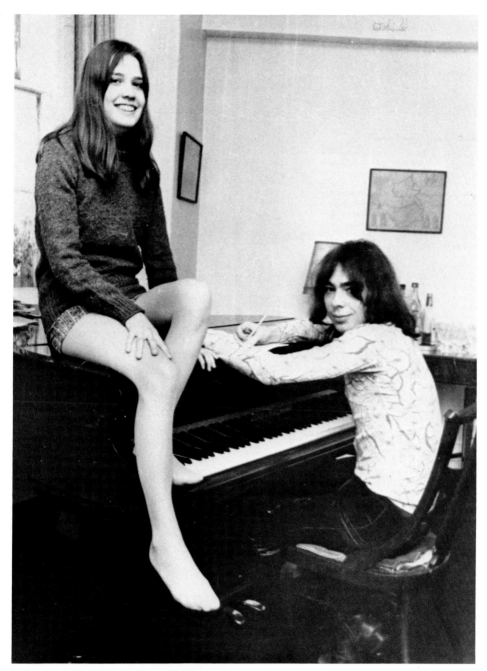

Andrew and Sarah Hugill (the girl he is to
marry) at the piano

In America David Cassidy plays Joseph in the
show; by then Andrew has become well-
known

Front-of-house display in London for Tim and Andrew's 'miraculously' successful *Jesus Christ Superstar*

The album of *Jesus Christ Superstar* proved a golden seller for Tim and Andrew. There were plenty more to follow

The result of a lost bet: Andrew honours his promise to his brother Julian by composing 'Variations' for him

Backed by Tim's collection of cricketing prints, Tim Rice – and Andrew – face an earnest interviewer

On a visit to P. G. Wodehouse's Long Island home (to discuss the ill-fated *Jeeves*) Andrew and Alan Ayckbourn play over ideas for the show – an atmospheric photograph

Andrew Lloyd Webber (the names at that time were habitually given in order of seniority) chose the subject they did choose. *Joseph* had obscure roots in both their minds.

For Tim, the Bible was unashamedly 'one of the greatest books ever written' despite his personal scepticism as to its truth. His years at Lancing, the school dominated by a towering chapel, and his conventional Anglican upbringing had brought him in close touch with its stories which, by their sheer magnificence, had seized his imagination. As he says: 'I suppose there's a basis of truth behind the story of Joseph, but I certainly don't for one moment believe that it's literally true. That's not the point; it's a wonderful story.'

He laughs if anyone suggests that he and Andrew pored over the Bible for long hours in search of story material. 'In fact I got most of it out of *The Wonder Book of Bible Stories*, which takes about four minutes to read!' he says.

Since Doggett's request had been confined to an end-of-term cantata for boys of thirteen and under, the theme of the piece had to be attractive to young minds and voices. 'We kept it to that,' Andrew says. 'Its level really is that of a show that is close to children, and I don't therefore believe its home is a West End theatre at peak times. But, having said that, it has certainly worked in its present form on Broadway, which has surprised me.'

Andrew's religious indifference very nearly matched Tim's. He also believed that the story from Genesis of Joseph and his coat of many colours stood on its literary merits. 'Alan Doggett's invitation was the reason we did it,' he explains, 'but it wasn't altogether his inspiration. That's too strong a word.' It is also no coincidence that their next work, *Jesus Christ Superstar*, was drawn from the same source, the Bible.

Yet Ian Hunter's recollection of the first performance of

Joseph is that it was anything but an immediate success. 'It wasn't particularly memorable, only a ten-minute show,' he says. (Tim remembers it as having 'twenty minutes' worth of music. That's all we were asked for, and that's all we did.' Gary Bond, who starred as Joseph in the version of the show put on at the Edinburgh Festival four years later, says 'when it began it was fifteen minutes long'.)

Hunter continues: 'I enjoyed it, but it didn't amount to much. Just a piece for the choir to sing, nice and lively.'

He recalls the day, 1 March 1968, as being 'a nasty wet Friday'. The parents dutifully assembled in the afternoon. 'They did their best not to seem bored by it all, that is those who didn't appreciate the lively tunes and lyrics,' Hunter says. 'Personally, as I say, I enjoyed playing, and Alan was obviously having a great time conducting. It was fairly singable, you know. But I didn't think much more of it than that at the time.'

And indeed this might have been its one and only airing, had Dr Lloyd Webber not put in a very useful oar. Andrew's father, in addition to his other duties, occupied an organ post at the Methodist Central Hall, Westminster, as musical director. His enthusiasm for *Joseph* led to an invitation to Tim and Andrew to expand it to a full twenty minutes for performance by the school choir and a pop group called The Mixed Bag in the hall itself.

It was there, on a Sunday in May 1968, that a most remarkable blend of fortuitous circumstances occurred. A boy at the school persuaded his music-critic father to attend the performance. The critic's name was Derek Jewell, not only occupying a noteworthy position as jazz and popular music reviewer for the illustrious *Sunday Times* but also a communications director of the Thomson Organization, its then proprietors. His son Nicholas was ten at the time. Jewell says: 'He came home one night and said, "Dad, you've got to come to this concert, it's really great." And I said "Oh Lord, have I?" Because I hear a lot of music and I love most of it, but school concerts are not particularly my thing. Especially when I knew perfectly well that my son was not musical and could scarcely sing in tune, though he was in the choir. So I said finally: "Oh, well, I suppose I will," and I went to it with my wife.'

What Derek Jewell found at Central Hall that night was to grow into an extraordinary work. Yet at the moment when young Nick Jewell was bending his father's reluctant ear one of the pair responsible for it was wondering whether he had been right in writing a Biblical cantata for a prep school at all, when he and Tim might have been using the time to write more pop songs. Andrew was asking this, and other, fundamental questions. For instance, wouldn't one of their songs, one day, take off and get into the charts?

At the same time his indulgent father was almost kicking himself. As Dr Lloyd Webber told the *Daily Mail* ballet critic David Gillard subsequently: 'A lot of friends thought I'd been mad to let him [Andrew] come down [from Oxford], but I wasn't prepared to force him. I thought he ought to have a shot at what he wanted to do because if he didn't he'd be fed up all his life.' Not many fathers would have said, or even thought, as much.

This was a changed Andrew. The years with Tim had been sadly unsuccessful, yet formative. His natural eccentricity was giving way to style. The hair was now worn long, curling over his shoulders. A *penchant* for velvet jackets had superseded Westminster gunmetal-grey or black, and the Carnaby Street cut was considerably accentuated on his thin frame. The predominant note was Mozartian, with the high collar of an eighteenth-century frock-coat running down to a waisted and full-buttoned, deep-skirted garment – suggesting that its wearer might have an unpublished manuscript, or music-score, tucked away in its tail. Two features stood out: his shirts, which were as bounteously floral as a tropical garden and his leonine eyes.

Tim, too, was beginning to cut something of a dash. More inclined towards flannels and sports jackets, and indeed far more Anglo-Saxon than Andrew in appearance, he seldom went over the top except in hairstyle. In this his flowing blond locks, curling poetically to his shoulders, became the most noticeable characteristic of the pair.

And in all their new finery they were both there at Central Hall, of course, on the night. Nobody, least of all the composer and lyricist, could possibly have anticipated what was to come of it.

9

Miraculous Joseph

THE trouble, as Dr Lloyd Webber pointed out, was that you couldn't put on a twenty-minute show at Central Hall and expect people to pay to come to see it. *Joseph* had to be expanded, and when that proved impossible beyond certain limits it had to be added to. Dr Lloyd Webber helped. He gave an interlude performance on the organ, playing Bach's Toccata and Fugue in D Minor. Also roped in were John Lill, on piano, and a solo by Andrew's 17-year-old brother, Julian, on cello.

The joy for Tim and Andrew was that they at last had an assured audience of real people, not just parents. Only a handful (David Ballantyne counted 46) in fact turned up, but they were genuine paying customers. And among them, though the composers had no way of knowing it, was the reluctant critic, Derek Jewell.

'How very nearly I missed it,' he says now, almost in wonder. 'It really made me sit up. I thought it was absolutely great – quite splendid!'

Even before the moving and thrilling last number, 'Any Dream Will Do', Jewell had realized that this was far, far more than a school piece jazzed up to amuse grown-ups. His notice – one he had not intended to write, but which he was unable to skip once he'd heard the show – appeared in the *Sunday Times* of 19 May 1968 entitled 'A Springboard called "Joseph"'. A springboard it was, with plenty of bounce in it.

He opened the piece with four of Tim's lines sung by the choir in a mid-show number 'Help Us, Help Us':

> 'Give us food,' the brothers said,
> 'Dieting is for the birds,'
> Joseph gave them all they wanted,
> Second helpings, even thirds . . .

'Even on paper,' Jewell wrote, 'the happy bounce of lyrics like these comes through . . . the effect is irresistible.' He called it a 'pop oratorio'. 'On this evidence,' he predicted, 'the pop idiom – beat rhythms and Bacharachian melodies – is most enjoyably capable of being used in extended form.' One of the very first to realize what Andrew had long nursed and defended (the conviction that rock, pop and every other strain of contemporary sound were legitimate members of the musical family), Derek Jewell was plainly delighted. But not wholly satisfied.

'Musically, *Joseph* is not all gold,' he wrote. 'It needs more light and shade. A very beautiful melody, "Close Every Door To Me", is one of the few points when the hectic pace slows down. The snap and crackle of the rest of the work tends to be too insistent, masking the impact of the words which, unlike many in pop, are important.'

But, as the critic continued, 'Such reservations seem pedantic when matched against *Joseph*'s infectious overall character. Throughout its twenty-minute duration it bristles with wonderfully singable tunes. It entertains. It communicates instantly, as all good pop should communicate. And it is a considerable piece of barrier-breaking by its creators, two men in their early twenties – Tim Rice, the lyricist, and Andrew Lloyd Webber, who wrote the music.' (Andrew's twentieth birthday had followed the Colet Court performance.)

As Andrew and Tim joyously agreed, nobody could have asked for more than this unbelievably fortunate stroke.

When Tim showed the review to his colleagues even the great Norrie Paramor was impressed. 'I was still with EMI,' Tim explains. 'We hadn't made any money by then. Anyway, it was all remarkably good experience, recording groups like Cliff Richard and the Shadows, and The Scaffold.'

Ian Hunter, too, was re-appraising the work. 'I could see that in the expanded form it had much more to it than I'd originally imagined,' he admits. 'I played the harpsichord at the Central Hall version, which was a very different performance from the one we'd been able to put on at the school. I realized then that both Andrew and Tim were far more gifted than I'd thought at first.'

Andrew had struck a slightly bizarre note at the prep school. Hunter remembers him at rehearsals, 'wearing the most extraordinary long coat with a high collar, like Beau Brummel; the collar *always* turned up.' Hunter found him 'Very temperamental, or perhaps sensitive is a better word.' He adds, 'I did notice that he took offence easily, while Tim on the other hand was always very, very nice and never went out of his way to hurt anybody's feelings.' Whereas Andrew, it seemed, often trampled over them to get the effect he wanted, however unintentionally. Hunter says: 'I quickly realized that, young as he was, he did not suffer fools at all gladly!'

The music teacher had also witnessed Andrew under more relaxed circumstances, when the young composer invited him to dinner in the Harrington Road flat. Hunter remembers how Andrew was 'very different at home, much more boyish and good humoured. His parents were out and I think he cooked for us. Lasagne, I believe, and jolly good, too.'

Andrew's interest in exotic food was growing, leading him to obscure restaurants in all parts of London. He was constantly searching for excellent, unusual cooking and, equally important, value for money. He and Tim spent most of their spare cash on meals out, regarding them quite properly as 'business expenses', since their whole conversation and concentration was on whatever musical project they were currently involved with.

Having to pay his way on these occasions was, however, becoming embarrassing. Tim, at least, was in a job. But Andrew, according to friends who knew him at the time, was kept very short of cash because he earned so little. Barrow remembers his grandmother, Molly, 'subbing' him occasionally. And John Lill thinks the old lady might well have been helping the family in more ways than one. 'They weren't poor in the slightest,' he says. 'With two boys at public schools, how could they be? No, I've certainly never known them to be without.' The trouble was that Andrew was finding that his taste in clothes and restaurants outran his finances, and nothing or almost nothing was coming in.

In something like desperation he had sent a clip of Derek Jewell's review to a wealthy property man called Sefton Myers, suggested by his friend David Ballantyne. Myers happened to be a patient of Ballantyne's father, a doctor in Walton-on-Thames, and he had some arrangement with Ballantyne's manager, Marcus Harrison, which served as an introduction. 'I'd heard that Myers was youngish and very interested in the theatre,' Andrew says. 'I wrote and told him that I just had to get some sort of a job if I couldn't sell my music anywhere. Things were that tough.'

Almost a year had gone by since the Colet Court presentation of *Joseph*. Though Paramor had recorded the show, the album had not yet been released. Any royalties from that first disc seemed a long way off in a highly doubtful future.

'I mean, we needed money in the broadest terms,' Andrew says. 'Tim and I were broke. All we'd got was *Joseph*, which was no more than a calling card at that stage.

We couldn't get anybody to stage it, other than St Paul's Cathedral, which was putting it on in November.'

Fortunately, Sefton Myers was an unusual man with a flair for finding talent – particularly in beautiful young women – and backing it with considerable courage. He and Andrew took to each other straight away. But success required a magician more than a benefactor in this case.

Myers' major connection with the world of show business was through a managing agent, David Land, who at that time had offices in Charles Street, Mayfair. He handled the Dagenham Girl Pipers. Land's recollection of Andrew's introduction was that, perhaps coincidentally, a photograph of the agent with Myers and their two motorcars, both Rolls Royces, had appeared in newspapers to promote a girl singer called Andy Silver. Andrew, he says, 'had seen it and written to me. He told me he and Tim wanted to start a theatrical museum and we arranged a meeting.'

The meeting took place with results which were impossible to forecast, and which owed nothing to the world of museums.

'They came to the office,' Land says, 'full of this idea, but I could see that it would cost too much. I liked them, and their enthusiasm was infectious. Before they left I asked casually, not really meaning anything, "Are you working full time?"'

'I knew they had some sort of publishing arrangement with Southern Music. I really only just threw this out as a sort of throwaway line. But Tim – and these are his exact words – said "No, we're not. What can we do for bread?"'

'As I say, I liked them. I said, "Whatever you're earning, we'll give you, in that case." They'd played us their single of *Joseph* and I thought there was something there. I said I'd pay them £30 a week each, and two or three days later they rang up and accepted. We became their managers.'

Land and Myers were both popular and hard-working members of the Variety Club, showbusiness's indefatigable charity. 'Sefton had been Chief Barker and I organized the cabarets for them,' Land remembers. 'That was how we'd come together originally.' A shrewd businessman under his cordial bonhomie, David Land was quick to realize the potential of his new clients.

'They were writing pop songs for Southern, for which I believe they'd been paid something like £100 between them for a year's publishing agreement, giving them the use of the recording studio in Denman Street and offering whatever they could produce in the way of demo tapes or discs to singers. Also, by the time they came to us they'd done a musical on the life of Dr Barnardo, *The Likes of Us*, which was never produced. But I urged them, on the strength of their *Joseph* (which I went to see at Central Hall, Westminster) to concentrate on a Biblical subject. "Anything but Jesus Christ," I told them.

'To me, not a religious man (but I'm a Jew and respectful), that was too sacred for entertainment. Anyway, they went away and wrote *Jesus Christ Superstar*, and you'll see that on the sleeve of their *Joseph* record, done in 1978 by MCA, they acknowledged me.'

The acknowledgement reads: 'Andrew Lloyd Webber and Tim Rice dedicate this album to David Land, without whom, not only would *Joseph* have remained in obscurity, but also *Jesus Christ Superstar* would never have been written.'

Behind this tribute was a smart piece of business which Land pulled off. As he explains, 'They'd been stuck for an extra tune during the album recording of *Superstar*, and I managed to help them out.' He also helped himself to a profitable bargain. 'Andrew never wastes a tune,' he says. 'I knew that. I'd heard some of the stuff they'd written for Southern, and remembered one song called "Sunset Morn".

Would it do, I asked Andrew? It would, but Southern owned the copyright.'

Land offered the music company £50 for the song, without elaborating on the fact that it was desperately needed for a major album. He may not even have mentioned the fact. Anyway, the deal was struck. He can hardly suppress a wide grin of the successful showman when he says, now: 'Imagine! Andrew and Tim re-wrote that and it went into the show as "I Don't Know How To Love Him" – one of the great hits. By now it's made quarter of a million!'

Nobody could seriously accuse Southern of being sleepy over this deal, since to them Tim and Andrew were an unknown pair of amateur public-schoolboys dabbling in the overpopulated world of pop music. And with only one small school cantata to their credit. To everyone but Land and Myers, they were fledglings in a jungle.

Andrew and Tim (who actually produced the album for EMI) had been paid 'about £100 each' for the original *Joseph* recording. The money soon went. If Land and Myers had not sent word that they would see them, if they had not taken them on, persuading Andrew to abandon his museum notion and stick to composing, it is a tantalizing thought that Andrew Lloyd Webber might today be a solid businessman or banker. There were, he says, 'a number of things I wouldn't have been too bad at, and I really did mean to give the whole music and theatre thing up if I couldn't make a living at it.' The fates, plainly, were not going to permit any such thing.

Andrew's idea for a 'pop museum' was only one of several suggestion for making money. 'My idea was that I'd get hold of items of real interest to the fans, like Elvis's guitar and P.J. Proby's pants – which were always splitting. When we went along to the meeting with Land and Myers I thought that that was what we were getting into.'

Fortunately, Land's gentle rejection of the idea didn't dash his spirits too much, and the man himself impressed Andrew. 'I thought "what an imposing man",' he later recalled. 'He seemed to have the music world buttoned up. And, fortunately, he and Myers had heard our record of *Joseph*. They wanted to back us, but to write musicals not to run a museum.'

Andrew still thinks of Sefton Myers as one of the most helpful props to his career. The confidence he and David Land showed in Tim and Andrew when they had so little to show was indeed extraordinarily far-sighted.

'They undertook to pay us three grand a year, going to five grand after three years with options to extend it on and on, so that basically it was for ten years if they picked them all up,' Andrew recalls. 'Quite respectable, really.'

But tragically Myers would not live to enjoy the fruits of it. To David Land, on returning from a doctor's visit, he confided that he was suffering from 'the dreaded lurgy'. A terminal cancer had been diagnosed, and in little more than a year from then, in 1970, Myers died, at the age of forty-three. He had formed a public company with David Land, in order to offer shares in their business – now including Tim and Andrew – to the public at large.

His death was especially distressing to Andrew. 'I believe Sefton would have become a vital part in everything we did,' he says. 'He had that kind of mind. The sadness is that he never took part in what rightly belonged to him, our success.'

Myers and Land had taken a professional gamble of the sort that marks out showmen from the herd. By banking on the futures of two unknown and fairly desperate youths, they had shown both courage and flair. But they were not entirely alone in valuing the pair's talents.

At the St Paul's rendering of *Joseph* which took place on Saturday, 9 November 1968, the reporter who had thought

so little of their first record in the *Evening Standard* offices
was in the audience. Ray Connolly left the cathedral that
night with a very much enhanced opinion of the pair. 'I
don't know how long it will be,' he wrote, 'before someone
composes a good pop symphony, but I do know that
Saturday night's performance of *Joseph and the Amazing
Technicolor Dreamcoat* brought the likelihood of such a
production considerably closer.'

He had, he said, been 'elevated' by the show's 'strong
sense of humour and its awareness of pop history'. As he
said in the notice which appeared in his paper the following
Monday, 'Despite what many prefer to believe, pop is
already a serious and experimental art form with its own
history (however brief) and its own standards, with truly
exciting prospects for its immediate future. Too often,
however, in its attempt to be taken seriously it can be
pretentious and gimmicky. No one could accuse Andrew
Lloyd Webber and Tim Rice of any such conceit.'

How much Alan Doggett's enthusiasm had been responsible is a moot point. The original handwritten score, with
the words added in schoolboyish, longhand capitals under
musical notation of extreme simplicity, offers a wry
glimpse of those early rehearsals in the old Colet Court
music-room and the tiny attic above. Ragging of Doggett
by the composers seems to have been part of the process of
gestation. Such instructions as 'With un-Doggett-like
expression!' appear in place of the usual forms. Somebody,
presumably Andrew, had written for posterity under the
final chords, 'Doggett Mobbed!' Had he lived to see the
many hundreds of school and professional performances
which followed the little work he had commissioned with
such zest, perhaps Alan Doggett would have felt that such
acclaim was a fitting reward. He died in 1973.

Colet Court and ex-headmaster Collis also merit a share,
though as Ian Hunter says without bitterness: 'It does

seem rather wonderful. It was the first time the school had been involved in anything like it. A triumph really. But ironically, whenever we present the show now (as we did before Christmas 1982, and have done at other times since the first performance) we have to pay the Performing Rights Society £20 to put it on!'

In musical circles, as Hunter knows, money rarely flows in the direction of the most deserving. And Andrew, too, was learning this. 'Sefton's original contract provided certain guarantees,' he explains. 'If he took up the options, we stood to make a great deal more money. I mean, *Joseph* did take quite considerable sums of money, eventually; but it's all been more or less signed away. So many contracts down the line. And although they can't absolutely ride roughshod over Tim and me – because, clearly, we could make a noise about the style of a production and so forth – financially any production of *Joseph* that gets put on we get literally nothing out of. I mean, it's like we get twenty per cent of five per cent of five per cent of ten per cent!'

Andrew accepts that this is another harsh fact of theatrical life. 'Anything that happened with *Joseph*,' he says, 'I regard slightly as a bonus. I do feel in a way that everything has come out of it and this has to be reckoned.'

Yet he was, after all, an absolute beginner, still at the Royal College (where he helped out in the library) and richer in ideas and inspiration than accomplishment. The Land–Myers' contract gave him and Tim freedom to write as they wished, and they had plenty of – perhaps too many – musical ideas. At this point Tim proved invaluable as a sheet anchor to Andrew's drifting thoughts. 'It was his idea as much as mine to write a show round Judas Iscariot, treating Jesus as a minor character,' Andrew acknowledges. 'I needed a lot of prompting to get down to doing it.'

As well that he did, because *Jesus Christ Superstar* was to become their second outstanding triumph. And in the meantime Andrew had stumbled on another notion which he had long wanted to put into modern musical form, the heroic tale of Richard Lion Heart. '*JC* [*Jesus Christ*] was only one of the projects we talked about at first,' Tim says. 'We wanted something with a strong central character. And when we wrote *Come Back, Richard: Your Country Needs You* – we did one performance of it in London, and it was recorded in 1969 on the RCA-Victor label – we thought we'd got it; but it was an enormous flop. We had to begin thinking again.'

Tim's enthusiasm for the Bible story was deeply, strongly rooted. Andrew's developed in stages. 'I can remember having a very entertaining discussion with the vicar of – what's that church in Queen's Gate? – St Augustine's – when I was at the Royal College of Music. He said what a fantastic idea to do a musical on Christ. And I said it would be a terrible idea because it would never sell!'

Tim recalls: 'The more people, especially clergymen, told us it was OK the more we went off it, ironic as that might sound.'

Andrew's discussion is well remembered by the Reverend Kenneth Hewitt at St Augustine's, though he is unaware that it influenced the hit show. 'We did have quite an excited conversation,' the priest recalls. 'At the time, I was chaplain to the Royal College of Music and one of my aims was to try to get the church used more by music students. With Andrew, I think I took the line that there was a mass of excellent material in the Bible, and I quoted the current interest in medieval mystery plays, like Eliot's *Murder in the Cathedral*. What I was really trying to show was that the concept of a relationship between the arts and religion is perfect justifiable, and we had a fairly spirited chat about that.'

Not a wholly convincing one, obviously. The actual urge to write *Superstar* is none too reliably remembered by either of the collaborators. It was very largely need which gave it birth, plus Tim's boyhood fascination with Bible stories. As he explained to Michael Braun, compiler of a book on the production (*Jesus Christ Superstar*, Pan Books, 1972): 'I suppose I was fascinated particularly by Judas Iscariot and, corny though it may sound, the Dylan song "With God On Our Side" which has that all-time great lyric "I can't think for you, you'll have to decide; did Judas Iscariot have God on his side?" That really made me think, well, there's a fantastic story here: and I've always had, since I was about ten, an ambition to one day write a play about either Pilate or Judas, and bring Christ in as an incidental character; although in *Superstar* Christ is much more . . .'

Tim went on to explain how little faith they had in the original idea. 'We were thinking more on the lines of theatre,' he told Braun. 'We only did it on record in the first place purely because we wanted a demonstration disc to impress some theatrical man to put it on. Nothing more really.'

Tim recalls writing the lyrics 'just before Sunday lunch at my parents' home in Hatfield'. The main theme tune was already in his head and had been plaguing him for several weeks. It had come to Andrew almost out of the blue. He tried to explain how it did so to Ray Connolly:

'Well, I'd been told that there was a certain shop in the Fulham Road that had an original copy of an old Ricky Nelson album, and I went down to buy it. And so excited was I to get hold of it that I came out with this music running through my head - rushed into the nearest restaurant, demanded paper to write it down, and then telephone Tim to say I'd thought of the most fantastic tune.'

As he explains, the music was his own – not derivative of the Nelson disc in his excited hands. And the restaurant was Carlo's Place, still a popular eating-place on the Chelsea outskirts. There may well be a blue plaque on its walls, one day, commemorating the occasion.

The tune, of course, became the unforgettable theme melody of the show, its opening chorus stamping itself on many million minds: 'Jesus Christ, Superstar, who are you, what have you sacrificed?' At the time, as Andrew says, it could have fitted into any of their current schemes and dreams. The fluid workshop of their two minds discarded nothing good, adapted whatever suited and kept a store-house of tunes, lyrics and ideas from which to draw. Tim once tried to convey their collaborative process.

'There was no moment when we went "pow" – like when Lennon found his McCartney, or Rogers his Hammer-stein,' he said. 'It seemed to come more slowly. Basically, we think of an idea for a theme, then Andrew goes off and thinks up some music for it, and then brings it back to me and I try to put lyrics to it. Then we both get together and go over what we've got.'

Not a very precise explanation, but it demonstrates one thing about their working relationship as it then was: the fact that neither had any idea how popular they would become. They had then no more thought of today's multi-millionaire success than David Land had when he listened, with well-concealed lack of interest, to the idea of backing a museum for the memorabilia of pop stars.

10

Super Jesus

IT had taken Andrew until May 1969 to realize that *Superstar* was their best bet. Then, as he says, 'we decided there just had to be a musical possibility in the story of Christ somewhere.' As he'd got to know Martin Sullivan, the Dean of St Paul's, during the performance of *Joseph* six months earlier, it was a reasonable assumption that this wise and worldly man (unfortunately no longer alive to see the continuing success of his progeny) would have thoughts on such a project. He had indeed.

'He was the only man, the only person, who warned us that we might be accused of anti-semitism,' Andrew recalls. 'And although we didn't think that was on for a moment, it did make us aware that the subject was going to be controversial.'

Significantly the idea of *Superstar* preceded the first meeting with the Myers-Land office on the day in November when the Rice-Webber team professionally came of age. But it was still only a possibility, lying around with other half-developed plans. Nevertheless the contract they'd signed, cheerfully agreeing to everything in it, bound them to deliver a workable script for a musical within a reasonable time . . . or else.

'We really didn't have any alternative,' Andrew says. 'There was an idea of doing the Kennedy Cuban crisis, but it never really got off the ground. No, we came to the conclusion that there was no other story we wanted to write at that time . . . It was Jesus or nothing.'

Tim's words and Andrew's inspired chorus written on a restaurant table added just enough weight to ensure concentration on the Biblical notion. They'd already decided on one fundamental: it should be built round Judas and the Crucifixion. And a title came to Tim rather as the theme tune had come to Andrew. 'We just wanted a really good moving rhythm track,' he explained to Michael Braun. 'Originally I'd written "Jesus Christ, Jesus Christ" four times over. I thought, "that's rather boring, you know. Can't I call him something else?" Superstar scanned, so I put it in.'

As he admits, up to that time he'd never heard of Andy Warhol, who might have laid claim to the title himself. 'It was just a word I'd heard once or twice in *Melody Maker* or something, to describe a really stupendous artist.'

The next step was to find somebody to sing it, which Tim, still being a hireling of EMI, was in the best position to do. It so happened that one of the people he was recording at EMI was a singer called Murray Head. 'Nobody would talk to him,' Tim says, 'because he had a contract for three songs and the two he'd recorded so far had both flopped. I got him and the Grease Band together.'

By now Land had recovered from his shock at discovering that the two young artists he and Sefton Myers had taken on (gambling largely on Myers' hunch that they would come up with something worthwhile) were actively at work on a Biblical musical featuring Judas, Jesus and Mary Magdalene. He offered the *Superstar* single to the British Decca recording company, who turned it down as 'too controversial'. He then tried it on other British labels with the same negative result. And without too much hope he also approached RCA, who took no time at all to snap a 'not interested' reply. For a while the likelihood of *Superstar* ever being more than a shelved idea seemed remote.

Then Land remembered his friendship with Cyril Simons,

the publisher of MCA-UK, one of the country's largest record companies and the British subsidiary of the giant conglomerate Music Corporation of America, owners of Universal Studios, four recording labels and a mass of other companies and enterprises. Rice, too, had a friend at MCA-UK, Alan Crowder, who had worked with him at Paramor. It was Crowder who introduced the trio – Rice, Webber and Land – to a man called Brian Brolly who was head of the British MCA office. And it was Brolly, a mild-mannered, discreetly retiring Irishman (now the chief executive of Andrew's production company) who put them in orbit.

In October the single was recorded on eight-track tape at Olympic Studios in Barnes, London, with Murray Head, who had played in the London production of *Hair*, singing the part of Judas. Originally MCA-UK had tried to hold the composers down to a strict budget of under £10,000, but Andrew's need for musical perfection would not be so restricted. 'They thought we were off our heads,' he says, 'but Brian Brolly backed us all the way. He was the one man at MCA-UK who did.'

At the last minute Tim changed the title to include 'Superstar' because, as he explained, 'I believed that if we called it "Jesus Christ" we'd have had it, despite the fact that Cliff Richard had recorded "Jesus" and got away with it.' Sensibly he realized that what an evangelical Cliff Richard might do successfully could spell disaster for them.

In England, in fact, reaction to the possible heresy and sacrilege of putting the Bible story into a pop-music record was slight, but elsewhere in the world the single created varying degrees of controversy. Brolly refused to be put off. 'He'd fully understood the basic thinking behind the project,' Andrew says in admiration, 'and he was aiming for a complete concept album – that is, one filled out to the length and shape of a stage musical – in spite of the fact that nobody as yet wanted to risk putting *Superstar* on the stage.'

Traditionally, record albums follow closely in the wake of successful stage shows. Brolly was putting the musical cart before the commercial horse. Even Land and Myers were doubtful about the likelihood of success, and unwilling to commit Tim and Andrew to the task of writing a full score, if it meant tying up their artists for weeks on a project which nobody seemed to want to risk money on. Andrew is speaking euphemistically when he says, 'There were discussions.' In fact, not everyone in Charles Street agreed. In the end, Brolly's quiet and discreet manner won the day, but it was greatly helped by the interest coming from his parent company in the States.

Elsewhere, too, the single was doing reasonably well. In Australia, Belgium, Holland and Canada *Superstar* was an underground smash hit with the 'bubblegums', or pre-teens. Records of it were being played on all-night radio stations across America, where sales reached 100,000. According to Ellis Nassour, whose account *Rock Opera* was published by Hawthorn in 1973, a copy of the disc was in the hands of Richard Broderick, the International Vice-President of MCA, when he attended the company's executive meeting in New York on 4 November 1969. 'This is something quite unusual, gentlemen,' he told the assembled brass. 'I feel it can be something monstrous.'

He'd picked an interesting word. The reaction of some of his more puritanical colleagues to putting out a pop record with Jesus in the title was predictably horrified. Some believed they would face Federal censorship. In England, the BBC had initially refused to allow the record airtime. However, at a time when MCA's Decca label stood in dire need of a hot-selling album, it looked just good enough. The American company decided to gamble. They put the single out, later commissioning the complete album.

Tim and Andrew knew nothing of this until much later. The news of British sales of the single was depressingly disappointing. A total of 36,941 copies were finally sold, sending the composers' spirits into their well-worn boots. What they had psychedelically imagined would be a soar-away hit – and which had got them on the David Frost show in London – proved to be just another middle-of-the-road number. In the States the single never escalated above the high eighties in the charts.

Doubly galling was the splendid, lavish reception by the critics of Britain's music papers. If nothing else, they taught Andrew never to take too seriously the view of the insider, the committed. At the time, he and Tim were in something like shock for quite a while.

'Tim told me one day,' Andrew remembers, "Look, it hasn't made it. Let's face it, it's back to the old drawing board. We'd better do one on Robin Hood!" Then word reached us that it was, thankfully, doing somewhat better abroad.'

So, when Land called to say that MCA were ready to commission the album, Brolly's keenness had already inspired them to roll up their sleeves and get down to work. The problem was how to build what was only a slender theme, mostly still in their heads, into a full-scale musical opera long enough to cover four sides of a double long-playing stereo album.

'That was quite a task,' Andrew recalls. 'We had to write the rest of the opera which we'd talked about as if it existed but which really was only an outline in Tim's subconscious. I had a few snatches of tunes which I thought might fit, but that was all.'

Not surprisingly, a certain amount of panic hit them.

'We took off,' Andrew says. 'There was no way we could see ourselves churning it all out unless we got completely away. There was a hotel in a quiet little place in Herefordshire, the Stoke Edith Hotel in Stoke Edith village. We booked in there on the understanding that we would have use of a piano and be left entirely alone.'

It was the week before Christmas 1969 and bitterly cold. Andrew was due to spend the holiday with his aunt Vi and uncle George Crosby in warm and still fleetingly sunny Ventimiglia. He was working against the clock.

Villagers heard strange sounds – chords and choruses sung, played and vamped – coming from the hotel. The place was as good as its word, the composers left severely alone. In five and a half days the whole score was done.

'The most unusual thing for me was that practically everything was expressly written for *Superstar*,' Andrew says. He sounds genuinely surprised. 'Instead of using things that we had already done for something else, it was more or less all new stuff. At the end, about half of what we had musically was rock, the other half classical, or show music.'

Doggett, still sympathetically in touch, had heard the theme tune and suggested it should be used for a musical based on the *Daily Mail* Air Race, then attracting a lot of attention. The composers toyed with the idea, understanding his motivation. The song had just that sort of uplift. But so it had for a more celestial subject, they decided. It had to be the theme for Jesus Christ on the cross.

'That expensive single we'd made had clinched it in my mind,' Andrew says. 'I must say I'm still very proud of the orchestral sound which, for a single, was pretty incredible. When we got to work on the album for Brian Brolly I knew we'd got to hang everything on it, which was how it turned out.'

At first, Tim had problems with some of the lyrics. He

has joked since about them, but they were real at the time. 'I had most difficulty with the song "I Don't Know How To Love Him", funnily enough,' he told Braun. 'Patter songs like "King Herod" are relatively easy. It's the spare and simple lyrics that are always the most difficult to write.'

Andrew found that Tim's talents exceeded anything he might have expected. 'May I say, the lyrics are unusually literate for pop music,' he says, with the kind of understatement Westminster would approve of.

Tim's identification with pop was affecting Andrew in an increasingly formative way. 'I'd always been fascinated by pop, and really wanted to work in the medium,' he told Ray Connolly a few months later, with obvious sincerity. Yet now he sees this as a discarded part of his early development. 'Tim's very interested in pop,' Andrew says. 'Which I am only interested in if I happen to like it. I mean, if I hear something on *Top of the Pops* that I like, then I'll buy it. But I'm not interested in pop from the point of view of the pursuit of pop itself.'

Superstar, he admits, needed the youthful innocence and excitement of pop. Without it the show would have had to be Wagnerian in size and scope. As it was they could pour all they had into a musical tale which, though haunting and moving, never tried to be a grand opera. Arguably it is all the grander for that.

Brian Brolly was one of the very few who realized what he had set in motion. He had handled the original, single recording with flair and total commitment. It was largely his persuasion that had swung the cautious management into putting £14,500 of their money – a lot for any recording by unknowns – behind the production of the album. All he could offer was the outside chance that, in the wake of the album, the single would take off eventually in Britain as it had overseas – what, in the trade, is known as a 'sleeper' – and that the show would be staged and a hit, adding measurably to sales of both records.

In October 1970, when the album was released in Britain, Brolly's head was on the block. If the album failed, or if Andrew and Tim found they couldn't make the plot work, his future was 'in the salad', as the French say. He also had had to put his professional judgement behind the argument that the record-buying world was ready for a wholly religious theme, however spirited the music. Would it be distasteful, his bosses wanted to know? Could it be banned?

When they emerged from their Herefordshire hideaway the composers were in no mood to settle such fears about their use of touchy material. They'd written the passion of Jesus into the script with the zest of first-hand observers. Unhampered by any overbearing religious views, they had treated one of the Christian world's most sacred and poignant events as theatrical chemistry: the cross and the crucifixion as prop and dramatic scene. To Connolly, who sought out their feelings about the real story, they admitted that they had barely given it a thought. Did they believe in God, he asked? 'The short answer is yes,' Tim told him. 'But I don't believe that Christ was God, which I think makes his story all the more amazing.'

And the timing was right. Miraculous, you might say, since they'd had no more idea than the anxious MCA directors that a religious revival was under way. 'It was just incredible luck,' Tim told Connolly. Andrew adds: 'You see, the whole idea of doing anything on record *first*, instead of as a stage musical, was a total accident. It was forced on us by the fact that nobody would touch the piece.'

According to Andrew every management (including the prestigious Robert Stigwood office) had listened to the idea for staging *Superstar* and declined with varying degrees of shocked horror. As Andrew recalls now with bitter humour, 'We were turned down by literally everybody. *Every*body I mean. Stigwood wouldn't even let us have Jack Bruce, a famous recording bass guitarist under contract to him, because he didn't rate the idea. And there wasn't one single producer you've ever heard of we didn't contact along the line, half of them really big and famous names like the Grades and so forth. Nobody wanted it, but nobody.'

Casting the album was the next problem, and it was not an easy one to solve. Until the recording was almost finished they had failed utterly to get it right. Then, only by chance, it came together. 'We still hadn't found the right Mary Magdalene, or a Pilate,' Andrew recalls. 'At this point the whole album was almost finished, so it was very, very tight. But one night I went down to a place in the King's Road where they had cabaret turns, to see Jon Hendricks who might have been good for Pilate. And there was this soft-voiced, angelic girl singing "Blowing in the Wind" and playing a guitar. The moment I saw her I knew we had found our Mary.'

The singer was Yvonne Elliman, from Hawaii. She is not likely to forget how Andrew approached her after her performance that night. 'He just walked up to me and said, "You're my Mary Magdalene," I said, "Okay." Actually, I didn't know who she was! Except that I had a vague idea she was Jesus's mother. And I thought, "Oh, he must be some Jesus-freak who wants to do an album." You know, a religious hot-gospel kind of thing. It didn't exactly turn me on. But then he began explaining what it was they were really doing.'

What they were doing, if slowly, was putting together a hand-picked cast of principals for the record, backed by some of their old and faithful players.

Barry Dennen, playing in *Hair*, was a musical comedy singer. They found him only just in time to sing the Pilate

role. He did it magnificently, despite the fact that he'd
never played in opera or sung rock music in his life. Others
were harder. Murray Head was filming, and could only be
used in odd spare moments. Ian Gillen of Deep Purple was
another fitful participant, coming to the studios when his
own group's frenzied schedule allowed. In the background
was the steady nucleus who'd worked with them before and
would have broken their necks to do so again.

'We had the same great mob who did the single, like Pete
Robinson, Chris Mercer and the Grease Band lads,' Tim
recalled later, 'and our irreplaceable engineer, Alan Duffy.'

It was an exciting, strenuously testing time for both Tim
and Andrew. On David Frost's nationally syndicated
American TV-show in November 1971, Andrew went into
details. 'We had two or three [songs] that secretly we were
getting very unhappy with. There was one thing which was
using the same tune as "Heaven On Their Mind" – where
Jesus cursed the fig tree in the Bible – but we just didn't
think it worked very well.' As he told Michael Braun: 'I did
re-write a lot, for instance the middle part of "Gethsemane"
was practically the last thing I did because I felt the thing I
had originally just wasn't right.'

Tim went on that Frost interview with him, in a
nationwide American peak-time hour. By then *Superstar*
was making headlines all over the world, both for its
record-breaking success as a recording and as the stage
show it had become. Frost wanted to know if the King
Herod song which had caused much of the shocked outrage
had been specially written.

Tim told him: 'Yes,' then corrected himself. 'It's had a
strange history,' he said. 'Andrew wrote the tune a long
long time ago and initially it was called "Saladin Days",
which was an atrocious pun based on Saladin who was a
rather violent cove who hung around in the Middle East
when Richard Lion-Heart was on his crusades.'

As with other melodies brought out of his past, it was an example of how Andrew finds ways to adapt old tunes to fresh words – in this case Tim's – which fit the piece. 'It's the same tune exactly,' Tim explained. 'It just goes "Oh, so he was a Christ" where before it had been "Those were the days, good old Saladin days".'

He confided to Frost: 'We entered that one for the Eurovision Song Contest under the title "Try It And See" as a sort of knees-up, boom-bang-a-bang type of record. It was rejected.' Like so much of their early work, it had then been put on the shelf to be re-vamped at some future date. 'We still thought it was a good ghastly tune,' Tim said, 'so we gave it to King Herod, because he was just the sort of horrible guy who'd say "Show me a miracle!" Which is what it says in the Bible, really.'

As they both agree, the hardest part of *Superstar*'s ultimate creation was finding the right blend of mood and tone for the role of Jesus Christ. And Andrew admits that his use of a sudden switch in the musical style from rock to a Richard Strauss-style sentimentality failed to get across.

'The idea was to try and fuse all the elements and everything together in that last part, the Crucifixion of Christ,' he says, 'but the point was missed by virtually everybody. The overture, the first act and the opera all end in the same way, leaving you with this sort of heavily over-romantic music suddenly coming in. People wondered what on earth was *that* doing at the end of this rock musical, but they missed the whole point.'

As he explains, 'I didn't mean it as a sort of satire, exactly. That's the wrong word. But I did want to point up the irony in the horror of this Crucifixion in which a man is being killed in a ghastly way, but which is remembered and taught as a sort of sacchariny kind of "two-lambs-and-the-good-shepherd" image.'

Andrew adds, with feeling, 'That, I think, is how it has

been lumbered on young people, it certainly was on me when I was at school.' Thus, in an inverted sense, the teachings of his English public school contributed to *Superstar*'s remarkable success. Religious instruction, or scripture, as traditionally expounded in Westminster and similar schools (and especially in preparatory schools where those running them can give unbridled expression to their own religious beliefs, however archaic) has changed little since the days of John Knox, as he had been perceptive enough to see.

But there were those at MCA in America who still doubted whether such a deliberately provocative album could succeed. When it became known, through a delighted Brian Brolly, that Yvonne Elliman's beautiful British recording was 'superb', they hid their feelings. In the States prejudice against the use of the Bible story and the Crucifixion of Jesus Christ as the basis of a rock musical was rising.

By the time Andrew and Tim were invited on to the American Frost show this had blown up into a gale of puritanical protest. Pickets were blocking the entrance to theatres where *Superstar* was being played. Wild and abusive letters and phone calls were sent to the cast, including Yvonne Elliman and Barry Dennen. On the night when an invited audience watched Frost put the composers on live television the front row contained some of the most outspoken and vehement of these protesters. For showman Frost, they were sparky material.

Turning the cameras on them, Frost said. 'I know we've got three or four people here who have strong objections . . . do any of you think this is something that shouldn't have been attempted at all?'

A man answered. 'The very concept of staging something about Jesus whose name is sacred to millions is abhorrent. I think the album is blasphemy, a distortion, and here we have this tinsel idiocy, giving those who think like it something to chat and joke and jest about.'

This was greeted with derisory whistles from the studio audience, but it represented a strong body of thinking in America. Tim answered, to applause: 'I would just like to say that if Christ cannot be taken into the streets, into the fields and houses, then He has no meaning at all. If He is only gettable at in an obscure church down the end of the street, with lots and lots of ceremony, then that is why He has become meaningless.'

Andrew added: 'I remember the Dean of St Paul's in London saying "Please try and take Jesus down off a stained-glass window." I don't know whether we've succeeded in doing that, but I certainly agree with Tim wholeheartedly. If Jesus can't be discussed on the David Frost show in a serious manner, what relevance has he?'

He added, with feeling: 'I'm sure if he'd been alive He would have been very happy to have come and talked on the programme himself!' Whether He would have enjoyed or approved of the show was left unasked.

11
—
The Big Dollar

WHEN he took his first look at the Statue of Liberty from the deck of the Queen Elizabeth II in June 1970 Andrew may have wondered if the great arm holding aloft its torch would light his way home in triumph, or bitter failure. He had little reason for optimism. The trip, made with Tim (and, because of his suspected high blood pressure, taken by sea rather than air) was only to attend the premiere of their cantata *Joseph and the Amazing Technicolor Dreamcoat* which two go-ahead priests were staging on Long Island.

But the album of *Superstar* was finished. And America, having overcome its worst scruples, was about to release it. So Ellis Nassour, a publicity man for the New York record company, MCA, was there to meet them. For Ellis it was 'kind of my job to take them around, take care of them, make sure they were happy, without spending any money. That was the company's philosophy in those days – keep the artists happy so long as it didn't cost us anything.'

Andrew and Tim had enjoyed the voyage. 'We'd been lucky. Beatle George Harrison, a very friendly cove, was travelling with us,' Andrew recalls. 'That made it very much more interesting, though the days did drag a bit.' It was also not the best time for them to be paying their first visit to one of the world's most expensive cities. 'At that time they had no money,' Nassour says. 'I think they were kind of living off the stipends David Land was paying them.'

Tim made no bones about it. He told his host, 'Look, I've no money. Can I stay at your flat for a couple of nights?' Nassour has a small, comfortable working apartment on Horatio Street in Greenwich Village and willingly agreed. He and Tim had immediately hit it off, while Andrew was finding it harder to adjust to American ways.

'The trouble with him was that he gave an impression of being very stuck up,' Nassour remembers. 'The first time I saw him, dressed in a way that New Yorkers would have thought was poofy and flamboyant (though nobody could be straighter, in fact. Tim liked the skirts, and so did Andrew), I said "what a stuffed-shirt!"'

Tim on the other hand had got off to a royal start with the MCA representative. 'He had a great sense of humour,' Nassour recalls. 'Knew a lot about American music and was fascinated by it. Also, he was a big fan of the cartoon characters, Tom and Jerry, and so was I. We had lots to talk about.'

'In fact at one point I thought Tim was talking so much about Tom and Jerry I believed he was going to write a book about them!'

Tim's height (well over six foot) was a shade more than Ellis Nassour's spare couch would take. 'He had to sleep on cushions on the floor, I believe,' he says. 'But he didn't seem to mind.'

The record company were throwing a party to launch the album of *Superstar* in an old church, St Peter's, on Lexington Avenue. By now the composers were being housed at the company's expense in modest rooms at the Drake Hotel. But when Andrew ordered wine with his meals, the tight-fisted company jibbed.

'I thought they were being so petty,' Ellis Nassour says. 'If Andrew wanted a bottle of wine, why shouldn't he have it? But those problems were still causing trouble because nobody really knew if the record would sell or not.'

And he was quite right about their finances. *Joseph* was a growing success in England, where several schools were seeking licence to put it on, and they had the small weekly payments from Land and Myers, but neither Andrew nor Tim could afford to pay for very much on their own. Murray Head's single had still not taken off in Britain. And those critics who felt that the composers were walking a dangerously heretical path in using and 'distorting' stories from the Bible were increasingly hostile.

Worse, the search for a producer who would actually stage the show continued but with little hope of success. 'What made us mad,' Andrew remembers, 'was that we were being accused of everything from money-grabbing to anti-semitism, but largely by people who had never listened to anything we'd written.'

Fortunately miracles do happen, and not only on the stage.

'I got a call at the office one day from a gentleman called Robert Stigwood,' Nassour remembers. 'I'd never heard of him, but I later learned that he was an Australian who had part-managed the Beatles. He'd been in recent financial difficulties, but was now a public company owning *Hair, Oh, Calcutta* and *The Dirtiest Show in Town*. I also gathered he was building up an international theatrical business, despite the issue of his shares in September 1970 being described in an English financial paper as "one of the most dramatic new issue flops of all time".'

Nassour listened politely while Stigwood asked if it would be possible for him to meet Tim and Andrew. He'd heard of their record of *Superstar*, knew that MCA were putting it out in the States and sensed that he might have a lot to offer the young, obviously talented, but equally inexperienced, pair.

'That evening at dinner,' Nassour recalls, 'I told Tim and Andrew that a man by the name of Robert Stigwood had called and wanted to meet them. I asked how they felt about it. They said they'd be delighted. So a couple of days later a limousine arrived at the Drake to pick the three of us up.'

Andrew adds, admiringly: 'By then we were into the first week of the record's release. It was doing fantastic business. In Britain it hadn't made the charts even in its first two weeks – which is when it has to succeed or die. But there it was soaring up, and we could hardly believe it. Managements were calling us from all over, but Stigwood was the only one sensible enough to send a car.' During the next decade record sales would exceed six million, with another two million from the recording of the film's sound-track, and numerous others from stage productions.

Over dinner that night, foundations were laid for a future with the Stigwood Organization which was even more unbelievable. Myers had retired following his terminal diagnosis and was on the point of death. David Land remained the composers' personal manager, but Stigwood bought out their contract, plus all its available options. This meant that they would be bound to his Organization for the next nine years.

The deal Stigwood made was one which neither he nor the composers would have agreed to later, but at the time both needed each other in almost equal parts. In exchange for 150,000 shares in his still unweaned company and £20,000 cash advance against future royalties Stigwood bought a 51 per cent interest in their present employers (a company, New Talent Ventures, operated now solely by David Land). Land stayed in, with a 49 per cent share, but Stigwood also took over the rights to 25 per cent of Andrew and Tim's earnings for the next five years, as well as all rights to stage and film production of their works in the English-speaking world.

Since MCA in England had already acquired the rights to

the record of *Superstar*, and also the publishing and performing rights, there was no way Stigwood could take these over. But as the record's success in the States became assured and its moneymaking potential a certainty, he hammered the record company to renegotiate his new clients' contract, and shamed them into doubling their royalties – neatly including, of course, his own 25 per cent of these – in return for a portion of future Rice–Webber compositions.

He didn't stop there. For a further cash-down sum of £80,000, plus 100,000 more of his shares, the Australian bought out the last 49 per cent of the Land–Myers contract and set up his own publishing company, Superstar Ventures, to publish all future works of the authors. He now owned them lock, stock and barrel.

As packages go, it ranks among the world's more impressive. Two years later, when *Superstar* was a successful stage show, the financial journalist David Palmer called it 'a deal Midas himself would have been proud of'. Nevertheless, like many others in those early days who saw the suspiciously sudden rise of Andrew and Tim's theatrical star, Palmer was asking 'But how long can it last?' It is easy now to look back on that question with amused tolerance, but at the time it was realistic. In spite of the success achieved by the *Superstar* record in the States, the future was still in doubt.

When Tim and Andrew paid another visit to New York in the second week of November 1970, they were astonished to find themselves famous, and at the centre of a nationwide furore which their work had created. Religious fanatics were damning it. Music critics adored it. Whereas in England it had raised little interest, here it was provoking tremendous controversy. To Ellis Nassour Tim privately joked: 'Somebody had better tell England the record's out!'

MCA released the album under their Decca label in November. It first attained the Number One spot on the American charts in February 1971 (and, historically, climbed back into top position in all three of the major US trade papers twice more). A jubilant Decca cabled this news to Andrew and Tim in England: 'Breaking open a bottle of champagne to celebrate'. Well aware of the company's tight-fistedness, the composers replied somewhat acidly: 'Be bloody careful you don't cut yourself!'

For Andrew it was as much a spur as anything. He was composing furiously, producing a volume of work which was to show up in several of his future shows. More important, in January that year he had fallen in love with a girl he met at a party in Oxford, which he only attended because, unexpectedly, a friend gave him a lift to the town and he was at a loose end.

Sarah Tudor Hugill was sixteen and still at school, swotting for A-levels. Andrew was twenty-two. Though nobody would have described him as immature, there was an engaging boyishness and innocence about him. With Sarah he could enjoy all the pleasures of puppy-love while at the same time relying on her commonsense outlook and intelligence to balance his natural exuberance.

Ten days after their first meeting he invited her to dinner and she accepted, though with some trepidation. Andrew's youthful appearance made her suspect that the evening might be something of an ordeal. As she later told Vivien Lind of Thames Television: 'He took me to this restaurant, and I sat through the whole meal wondering if he expected me to pay my half when the bill came!'

Fortunately, she was able to disguise her anxiety and, as she says, 'not actually descend to rummaging in my bag'.

Sarah's father, Anthony Hugill, was then a director of the sugar firm, Tate & Lyle. He and his wife hardly expected the news that their schoolgirl daughter was planning marriage rather than university or a career, but Andrew's obvious sincerity – and persistence – overcame any scruples they may have had. In any case, there was no doubting his affection and regard for Sarah, and hers for him. They seemed perfectly matched: ideally, radiantly happy.

That Christmas Andrew went to stay with his aunt and uncle in Ventimiglia, and this time he took Sarah with him. Another couple were staying, the Fleet Street journalist Peter Hawkins and his wife Diana. Diana remembers Andrew's pride in his schoolgirl fiancée, and the obvious fuss which their romance had created, certainly in her family if not his.

'Her mother kept ringing up and asking Vi if all was well, and would she keep an eye on them and so on,' she recalls. 'Vi was *very* parental. Nothing improper was going to take place under her roof!'

She remembers too how taken up Andrew was with plans for *Superstar*. The record had caught on all over Europe. 'It was actually being played from the loudspeakers in the streets of Bordighera,' Diana remembers. 'I'm very un-musical but Peter was tremendously impressed. He could see that Andrew's music was going to be a sensational success, and he tried on his behalf to get film people – through my father, Maurice Carter, a production designer – interested.'

Later during that holiday, Peter Hawkins and Andrew talked over new ideas. 'Andrew was anxiously searching for a new subject,' says Diana. 'Peter wanted to propose one, and suggested doing a musical on Aleister Crowley, the man who professed to be the world's most evil man, practising black arts and so on. For a while, I think Andrew was really quite keen on the idea but nothing came of it.'

Meanwhile she and young Sarah, who seemed 'just a schoolgirl' at the time – as indeed she was – were enjoying

Aunt Vi's always welcoming hospitality. 'Sarah was
obviously in love,' Diana remembers, 'but she and Andrew
didn't give any impression of being rapturously taken up
with each other. They got along splendidly, but I don't
remember them showing any signs of uncontrollable calf-
love.'

In fact, as Sarah later confessed to Vivien Lind, she 'had
eyes for nobody else' once she and Andrew fell in love. As
she explained, 'It had a terrible effect on me sometimes.
Soon after we were married I drove into the back of a lorry
because he was in another car and I wanted to wave to him!'
Sarah laughed. 'I was always doing things like that, which
would infuriate Andrew. But then the funny side would
strike him and we'd have a good laugh together.'

Less funny were the many technical problems of *Superstar* which were involving the young composer more and
more. A version of the Lord's Prayer which he had
composed music for, intending to use it in the show, was
played at his and Sarah's wedding in the little church of
Holy Cross, Ashton Keynes, on Saturday, 24 July 1971.
Sarah's A-level papers, completed the previous month,
were still waiting to be marked.

For Andrew, the marriage began twelve years of happiness and achievement. Their first country home was a six-
acre farm, Summerleas, at East Knoyle, near Shaftesbury in
Dorset. Andrew and Sarah both worked hard at renovating
and improving the place and, according to neighbours, a
great deal of money was spent on it. For a while it seemed
ideal, both as a working haven for Andrew and a social
playground which they could enjoy with their friends. A
swimming pool was installed. But after two years they sold
it and moved nearer London where Andrew could be more
in touch with an increasingly demanding public.

By this time it was already becoming noticeable that
certain areas of Andrew and Tim's lives were moving in

sharply different directions. This barely affected their work together, except when Andrew's compulsive concentration failed to find its echo in his partner. But Tim's attitude was that work was fine only while the mood was on him. Given a tune by Andrew (or anyone else) he had no great difficulty in fitting words to it. If the theme was already clearly defined, his extraordinary talent was in being fluently able to convey any aspect of it, and with a brevity and feeling that was (and is) his particular style.

Andrew was the toiler. A perfectionist, he worked long, exhausting hours shaping and selecting melodic frameworks and orchestrations for his compositions. The excitement for him lay in using fresh, original sounds – indulging the fascination for these which John Lill had shared with him at Harrington Court. Too often now Tim was reluctant to be fully or wholeheartedly involved in these sessions, preferring the company of girlfriends and pleasures which Andrew found unrewarding.

Apart from restaurant meals, which he continued to indulge with selective care (and, of course, in the company of Sarah) his idea of a good time was largely to spend long hours at the piano, or playing with such innovations as the moog synthesizer, which he had incorporated in his score for *Superstar*. Had it not been for the exhilaration of their shared success in the States, and the demands laid on them by the new contract with Stigwood, these differences might well have deepened, the scratches becoming lasting cuts. As it was, they passed almost unnoticed.

There was good reason for putting them aside. Stigwood had decided to stage the show first on Broadway, where interest in *Superstar* was fanned by publicity and excitement lacking in England. His prime need was to get it out fast, since pirate companies were springing up all over the States, singing the opera as recorded but presenting it as a live piece of original theatre.

With a bevy of lawyers the producer fought to prevent these invasions on his property, but with limited success. One of the chief malefactors, New York impresario Betty Sperber, even went so far as to bill her show 'the original' production. Outside America, too, the album was proving an irresistible temptation to a number of theatrical opportunists. In Europe a touring group was passing itself off as 'the official American company'. Stigwood, in rehearsal with the genuine article, went for them, producing his own 'authorized' touring company in self-defence in Pittsburgh's Civic Arena on 12 July.

But some of his zeal misfired. In Australia his legal agents descended on an unlicensed concert, obtained a court banning order, and herded it off the stage – only to discover that the show was being run by nuns entirely for charity. The embargo raised scandalized public reaction.

Seeing Stigwood's embarrassment over this gaffe, Andrew and Tim organized a leg-pull for their producer, persuading one of the New York cast to dress up as a nun with an Australian accent. At a time during rehearsal when Stigwood was relaxing in his usual position in the orchestra pit, enjoying a picnic meal with a glass of wine, the 'nun' came up to him and accused him of heartlessness. Stigwood's astonished reaction gave the cast a few moments of memorable light relief. As one of them said: 'The pressure of putting on the show was getting to us, and seeing Robert's face just about doubled us up.'

It was one of the few moments of mirth in what was increasingly becoming a tough and tense production. For the stage version Tim and Andrew had to work a lot of the recorded material into entirely fresh shape, and the trauma of setting the various numbers in a fast-moving, highly sophisticated series of dance and action routines, with design problems on top of the usual lighting and other complexities, would have extended far more experienced writers. Housed in two adjoining suites at the Waldorf Astoria Hotel on Park Avenue, they found themselves battling through a seemingly endless stream of re-writes and adaptations, with new numbers to fill out awkward corners. It was work requiring total, 24-hour commitment.

For instance, in one afternoon Tim not only finished off the crucial lyrics for the number 'Could We Start Again, Please', but also managed to write the words for a much-needed additional insert for Pontius Pilate. In Andrew's judgement, 'all of it was superb, but then Tim is the best there is'. His respect for Tim had never varied, but in the mounting pressure it was becoming ominously clear to both of them that their ways of working differed radically.

Put simply, Andrew works like a terrier while Tim, to use the same analogy, darts in and out of his creative role like a retriever. So while Andrew applied himself to composition with the minimum distraction, working single-mindedly towards his goal, Tim's flair was sporadic. It came as a shock to Andrew, for instance, when Tim announced that after they'd finished work on the show he was planning a brief holiday in Japan. A friend of theirs saw how this led to their first disagreement, though the friction had been building between them for some time.

'Webber got really quite upset,' this observer noticed. 'He told his partner that they should be going back to England to help on all sorts of other tasks they had going. Rice was unmoved by that. He'd worked hard and reckoned he deserved the break – probably needed one, too. Anyway, the two had a heated argument in the taxi on the way to the theatre that day and it's probably significant that Webber went to London alone and Rice to Tokyo.'

In the opinion of this man, Andrew was altogether too inflexible to avoid conflict over such matters. 'I think he resented Tim's being able to relax as he did,' he says. 'Where Tim Rice went out on the town and had a good time now and again, Webber was always holed up in that hotel room. They just saw life differently.'

In American eyes, the supreme difference was in their utterly separate way of treating the people who worked with or near them. As Ellis Nassour remarked later: 'Tim was an easy-going, happy-go-lucky chap who smiled his way through crisis after crisis, coming up with the goods when needed, maybe at the ultimate last moment but always delivering. Andrew seemed to be suffering from tunnel-vision.'

Tim, he says, 'wrote the lyrics for *Superstar* originally on a restaurant napkin in London, over a meal in The Great American Disaster on Piccadilly.' That this is not supported by what either Tim or Andrew has said, and seems physically and mentally impossible, has not altered Nassour's opinion that Andrew was the cause of much of the trouble between them, undervaluing Tim's ability to 'write from the hip', as it were.

Unfortunately, it was not just the writers who were sometimes at loggerheads over the show. As the weeks passed, leading up to the concert tour in July and the Broadway staging in late September, stress was reflected in a number of ways. Stigwood was trying desperately to root out the trouble, sensing Andrew's depression and the growing friction. Finally, using the excuse of a motorcar accident, he replaced the director, Frank Corsaro. It was regrettable but understandable in the circumstances when he was at full stretch, that the producer – generally renowned for generosity and kindness – did so without any message of sympathy to the injured man. Corsaro was given a weekly percentage of the show's future (and unknown) takings in settlement for all his strenuous efforts, and released.

Well, you might say, that's show business. And when a show like *Superstar* is exhibiting signs of failing on

Broadway, any measure is pardonable. It is just unfortunate, perhaps, that Andrew has been connected with a number of such painful incidents in his brief and highly successful career, however little he has personally been responsible.

The new director, Tom O'Horgan, who had directed the very successful *Hair* in America, took over in early August. It would be nice to say that his arrival made all the difference. It did not. Andrew found him to have an entirely different view of the piece from his own. He was never happy with O'Horgan's conception, and nursed deep gloom over the outcome, which he confided to Sarah.

She had come to America with him, and was suffering much of the tension and depression of these weeks in rehearsal. Their lowest point came when, after the tours which tended to confirm the worst of Andrew's fears, they actually got the show into the Mark Hellinger Theater on Broadway. Then, all too obviously, the sound proved hopelessly inadequate.

Jesus Christ Superstar was to open with the first of several previews – regarded by the cast, gratefully, as 'just paid rehearsals' – on 27 September 1971. There was absolutely no hope of meeting the date. 'Technical difficulties' enforced cancellation and an exhausting and confusing refunding of money for tickets. The same thing had to take place the following night. If it had not been for a life-saving operation by one of the most distinguished sound experts in America, Abe Jacob, it might never have opened at all.

As it was, Jacob, veteran of ten international tours and sound director of *Hair* among many other hit shows, ordered radical changes in equipment, swapping police microphones for more conventional ones and generally playing Old Harry with everything that had been causing trouble. It worked. The show finally made its delayed debut on Wednesday the 29th without a hitch.

But it wasn't, it still wasn't, the show Andrew craved.

The cast were finding the changes almost impossible to adjust to in the time, their intricate and dynamic routines confused by the sudden switches. Andrew never allows himself to interfere with a director, once his work has been given into such hands, but the sense of foreboding still nagged him unmercifully. It is still with him today, reminding him of how the show *might* have been. As he says, with feeling: 'If it [the show] had been presented properly I'm sure we wouldn't have suffered as we did with the critics.' And he blames that bad press (actually divided fifty-fifty, and with some highly redeeming plaudits among the reviews) for the sometimes cool reception given to future works of his and Tim's.

Andrew goes on to explain his feelings in some detail. For him, *Superstar* was, if not a disaster, at best a besmirched presentation in the one area – the highly critical arena in which so very few foreign showmen have triumphed – Broadway, where he would have given everything to achieve perfection. It was not to be. 'There wasn't any alternative,' he explains. 'Well, there was this other producer, Frank Corsaro. And if he'd done it, who knows? It *might* have been a complete disaster. I think it would have been an interesting one, though.'

His inability to control the medium, which he knows to be so intensely dependent on collaborative effort, was at the root of his disappointment. He was twenty-three. And already he was looking ahead, weighing this unsatisfactory (to him) production against the future he was confident would be his. After the New York opening he told Sarah, 'It will take us six or seven years to pay back the dues of this thing in America.' It was an accurate forecast. Eight years later, critical acclaim for *Evita* was muted, despite its ultimate success.

Most galling of all, Andrew cannot understand why the staged *Superstar* should have failed. 'It had been a terrific hit as a record,' he says. 'Yet it was never a success to any major extent in the American theatre. The only productions which were successful were in London, Australia and other places abroad.'

One valuable result of his frustrating months in America with *Superstar* was, however, that he and Sarah were able to travel around the vast country almost at will, taking in quick visits to both concert showings and the tour of the Broadway production before it came to New York. In that time they got to know a fair amount about trains, using them as much as possible for their journeys. Twelve years later, some of the experience of those travels took shape in the music he then had no idea he was going to write, the great score of his musical *Starlight Express*.

And he now credits the show's weaknesses with one other advantage. 'Nobody else cloned it,' he says. 'Every production thereafter was different, because the Broadway one was such a long way from being definitive. It left enormous scope for individual interpretation and improvement.' Since there have been, he reckons, 'some twenty productions' of *Superstar*, this has allowed him to see it done in a number of ways, and the variety convinces him that the show itself is far sounder than was realized on Broadway.

By late 1983, *Superstar* had actually been staged in no less than 37 countries, including Iceland, Yugoslavia and Zambia. In South Africa and Zimbabwe it was a smash hit, and wherever it appeared the advance publicity aroused by the controversy almost always guaranteed sell-out shows for the duration of the run. In the English-speaking world especially it broke several records for box-office takings and bookings, being heralded as 'one of Britains's greatest musicals' in Canada, New Zealand, Malta, Kenya, Trinidad and Singapore. In Japan, they somehow managed to make its message understood to an audience who may have had less acquaintance with the Bible story than with the works of Charles Dickens.

The one glaring exception, in Andrew's unhappy recollection, was O'Horgan's interpretation on Broadway. Which is not to say that the cast, headed by Yvonne Elliman and Barry Dennen, were any less great than they had been on the record. They were rewarded when Universal Pictures, the giant motion picture company owners of MCA, promptly took up rights to film the show, appointing the Oscar-winning Canadian director Norman Jewison to make it.

Jewison watched the company play it live on the stage then signed them for the same parts in his film. He shot *Superstar* in Israel, persuading the government there to contribute a million of the four-million-dollar budget.

Nominally Andrew and Tim 'were to supervise every frame' but in fact Andrew seldom visited the locations in Israel and lost interest in the film when it became clear that he could have no control.

Jewison never intended to make the film in any but his own way. He was later quoted as saying 'those kids [Tim and Andrew] were trying to take Jesus down off the stained-glass window. They had this very modern concept of the music. But when it came to the visuals they lapsed right back to sheer Hollywood 'thirties.' He re-wrote the script with Melvyn Bragg.

Today, Andrew understands Jewison's motives and approves the result (the film won an Oscar for musical adaptation, naming Andrew with André Previn and Herbert Spenser), but at the time it was something of a put-down. Andrew resented the mere thought of another artist, however accomplished, altering the work. He confesses: 'I got that completely wrong. At the time I didn't particularly like it, although the film did quite well outside America and wherever the stage show did not go. But I saw it again four or five years ago. I'd been most concerned because I thought it would date, or rather a lot of the things in it would date. Actually, I think Jewison was hugely ahead of his day. There are lots of images in *Superstar* which are quite remarkable.'

At the time, as he freely admits, he had 'had it, right up to here'. The way *Superstar* was being done in the theatre was so different from how he would have liked it to be done, and so many people were coming between him and his goal.

In one sense, nevertheless, the milestone of Broadway production passed with what, to lesser perfectionists, might have seemed triumph. The cast overcame the most extraordinary technical difficulties to put the show over. Yvonne, the star, declared afterwards that she had 'sung one number for the first time' at a preview. Few more demanding challenges could be put to an artist, but this girl who had caught Andrew's eye in a Chelsea nightspot singing for her supper as a 'warm-up act' at £5 a night proved herself capable of carrying a star role on Broadway. Whatever the critics said – and unfortunately they based their notices on an early preview which was improved beyond recognition by Abe Jacob and the enormous efforts of the entire cast and company – *Jesus Christ Superstar* was destined to be a hit.

12

Et Tu, Clive Barnes?

CHIEF and most feared among the reviewers was Clive Barnes of the *New York Times*. An Englishman. Andrew and Tim called his home one evening, late. Could they drop round for a chat? They'd like his experienced views on a few things they, in their innocence, were not yet sure about. Barnes says: 'I found them charming, delightful and above all, sincere. They told me they were not primarily interested in making money, and I believed them.'

He and his wife Trish kept the composers talking for two or three hours, listening to their experiences with the show, the highly controversial attacks being made on it by religious groups, and their own reactions to America, its theatre and the highly-charged emotionalism on subjects close to its still young and bleeding heart. There were amusing tales to tell.

Yvonne Elliman's role, as the woman in love with Jesus, had been widely criticized. Andrew was astonished. 'She's become a sort of cult figure,' he said. 'People come to the stage door asking her to touch them! They actually believe she has healing powers!'

There were many more serious manifestations of the shock to puritanical America's nervous system. Arch evangelist Billy Graham was leading a campaign of vilification. 'It [*Superstar*] borders on blasphemy and sacrilege,' Dr Graham had stormed. 'I do *not* endorse the production. Nor do I urge young people to see it.'

How did the composers feel about it themselves, Barnes wanted to know? Were they aware that the torch they had lit was burning at the roots of many people's most sacred beliefs?

Tim told him: 'I'm not particularly religious, but people who say my lyrics are sacrilegious just can't have read them properly.'

Andrew hinted that he did not go all the way with everything in the story. There had, he said, been 'long arguments' about what should and should not be included. One of the points stressed by objectors was the absence of the Resurrection. 'I would myself have liked to include it,' he said, 'but it wouldn't have been worthwhile, because there's too much about it that Tim and I can't agree on.'

As he had revealed to an American interviewer who dug into the question of how his religious beliefs differed from Tim's: 'I don't go along with some of the things Tim has written in the opera. His lyrics are extremely good, but I don't necessarily agree with all of them.'

Barnes was interested in their working methods. Tim explained: 'I always prefer writing lyrics to a tune that already exists. But in the case of a theatrical production like *Superstar* you've got to have the plot first. So with us it goes plot, basic structure, then the tune. And then the words. That's the way round we do it.'

He has since qualified this, adding: 'You know, I have occasionally written lyrics – though only very rarely – as it were, on their own. But I don't like doing that. And, I think, obviously with one or two exceptions (such as Elton John or Gilbert and Sullivan) on the whole you'll find the best songs are those in which the words follow the tunes.'

As he says, in the case of a show like *Superstar*: 'We didn't have to make up the story. It was already there, as it had been with *Joseph*. It was just a question of choosing the stories and, having chosen them, making sure they worked dramatically, both in the music and the lyrics. Very much a fifty-fifty thing with us, I mean I only write the words and Andrew only writes the music. We hardly ever cross over at all. We do give advice, or comments, to each other's department, but it's up to the guy who does the words to get the thing going. He's the one who has to make sure the thing has a good structure.'

Nursing what may still be a private grievance between them, Tim says firmly: 'And I don't think you can really measure contribution in terms of time spent.'

That night with Clive and Trish Barnes the contribution was out of all proportion to the time spent – several late hours after an exhausting day. What they both hoped for, and believed could hardly be harmed by the visit, was a fair, even a friendly notice in the *Times* from their fellow-countryman. What Barnes wrote came as a nasty jolt.

The music struck Barnes's ear as 'pleasant though unmemorable . . . cheap, like the Christmas decorations of a chic Fifth Avenue store.' His metaphor overlooked the fact that for ordinary mortals the sight of Saks and other Fifth Avenue department emporia decked out in their majestic finery at Christmas-time is more inclined to conjure visions of glamorous wealth than cut-price banality.

Allowing that Andrew's score 'does have the bustling merit of vitality . . . extraordinarily eclectic', the critic diluted this in the next sentence. 'It runs so many gamuts it almost becomes a musical cartel,' he quipped. 'Mr Lloyd Webber is an accomplished musician – he is one of those rare birds, a Broadway composer who produces his own orchestrations – and he has emerged with some engaging numbers.'

With that faintly praising damnation Andrew had to be satisfied. But Tim got it really in the neck – and from one of the most amiable and fair-minded journalists alive and working in a commanding position in an alien field. 'For me,' Barnes wrote (and Trish now says 'That was *his* opinion, not mine. I was sorry Clive was so disparaging'), 'the real disappointment came not in the music, which is better than run-of-the-mill Broadway and the best score for an English musical in years – but in the conception. There is a coyness in its contemporaneity, a sneaky pleasure in the boldness of its anachronisms, a special undefined air of smugness in its daring.'

Concentrating this low-level attack, Barnes accused: 'Mr Rice's intention was clearly to place Christ's betrayal and death into a vernacular more immediate perhaps to our times. His record sales would presumably indicate his success in this aim, but he does not have a very happy ear for the English language. There is a certain air of dogged doggerel about his phrases that too often sound as limp as a deflated priest.'

Tim's reaction, on a morning when other (unfortunately, less influential) reviews included at least one rave, was understandable fury. To every caller that day – and the phones in the joint Waldorf apartments kept up an incessant invasion – Tim would announce on picking the receiver up: 'This is the Clive Barnes fan club. Yes?' The acid joke was lost on all but a few, and those mostly British, who understood the measure of his hurt.

Yet Douglas Watt in the *Daily News* had made it sound better than good. 'So stunningly effective a theatrical experience that I am still finding it difficult to compose my thoughts,' his notice read. 'It is, in short, a triumph . . . Andrew Lloyd Webber's score is vibrant, richly varied and always dramatically right and much the same can be said for Tim Rice's lyrics.'

Did the critics, then, not know their own minds? Clive Barnes, for all his experience of theatre and his eminence as the *Times* reviewer with a make-or-break reputation, was concerned solely with drama. Watt on the other hand had previously covered both jazz and opera for his paper. In London, Derek Jewell condemns all critics of musical theatre who have not worked in music.

'The trouble is,' Jewell says indignantly, 'that very few London theatre critics know the first thing about music. They are stone tone-deaf. Yet newspapers will insist on sending these theatrical critics – who don't even enjoy popular music and who would turn up their noses at rock and pop, and who never listen to Radio One and Two in their lives, and know nothing about it at all – on sending as I say these dreary, dry creeps who are totally out of touch with the public taste to review musicals! It's laughable!'

Only Jewell isn't laughing. In his position as a director of one of Britain's major newspaper groups and jazz critic for the *Sunday Times*, he feels and expresses righteous fury. As he well knows, neither Fleet Street nor its New York equivalent can afford to retain specialist musical-theatre reviewers on their staffs. It is a misfortune from Andrew's viewpoint which currently has to be accepted. He himself is philosophically tolerant of reviews, provided they are reasonably accurate.

But Derek Jewell continues to campaign. 'I've always insisted that a drama critic who wouldn't know a bloody good tune from a bag of apples shouldn't even go near – and certainly never review – musicals, because he doesn't know what he's talking about!'

The most damning critic of Andrew's music is Bernard Levin. Reviewing *Evita*, Levin castigated the show's 'trivial score'. Jewell exclaims: 'Who the hell cares what Bernard Levin thinks, with respect, about a popular musical? Bernard is one of an infinitesimally small minority who like classical opera, who will go to classical opera. So what the hell would he know about popular music? It's ridiculous!'

He continues, even more forcibly: 'To my mind Andrew and Tim are great *modern* opera composers. And there *are* critics in this town determined that Andrew will *not* be put down by these people! Jack Tinker of the *Daily Mail* is one. He knows what he's talking about. And I'm one. But quite a few of the others are out to crucify Andrew – because they don't know the first thing about music. They go to judge the play not the music!'

Jewell shakes his head at what he sees as the unfairness of it all. 'Andrew has been too successful for his own good. That creates envy in this town. And on Broadway. He's just too bloody good. He makes the rest look like amateurs. Yet, after Ellington, I'd say he's the most significant popular composer of our century.'

Does this explain Barnes's lukewarm reactions, not only to *Superstar* but to everything Andrew has written since? In Jewell's view it does. 'There are a lot of knives out for him, everywhere,' he says. 'People love to review something of his badly, because he's a perfectionist, and perfectionists make a lot of enemies.' He shrugs. 'I am a compromiser. A lot of the time I'll say "Oh well, that will do". Most of us do that. Andrew Lloyd Webber *never will do it*! That's what's remarkable!'

'He's five foot nothing . . . what does he remind me of? An Oscar Wilde kind of person, in a way. But the steel in his soul is quite extraordinary. He will *never, ever* let anything go unless it is absolutely right.'

To Jewell, this explains why Andrew and Tim were finding it harder and harder to work together during the frenzied pre-premiere days of *Superstar*'s stage debut. 'One reason has to be that Andrew's a workaholic. Tim just doesn't want to do quite as much as Andrew wants to do. Tim wants to have a bit of fun, and do the effortless thing. They're just two different people.'

So different that Jewell, who values them both as friends, candidly and sorrowfully accepts that their attitudes to work, success and commitment have immeasurably widened a gap between them.

'Tim is a talented dilettante,' he explains. 'That's exactly what he is. He'll go on things which do him no good at all. And which Andrew, I would imagine, must shudder at. That's the difference.

'The second is that I suspect – and I'm not saying Tim Rice is idle, that would be nonsense – but Andrew Lloyd Webber is a single-minded workaholic, whereas Tim Rice is probably again a dilettante workaholic. He loves to play cricket, and he loves to go on tele shows. He'll do a book here, he'll do something there, and so forth. Andrew is almost Messianic.'

Has he seen the friction between them building? 'No, I've never observed rows between them, but it's obvious that these differences separate them. I don't mean this in a nasty way, but of course there has to be conflict between them. They are just different people.'

As Clive Barnes shrewdly observes: 'I've noticed that Lloyd Webber has produced his best work since they split up. What has Rice done in these past six years? Maybe they did need each other when they were both young, but that's something else.'

The night they came to his apartment on 72nd Street, overlooking the Hudson River, Barnes had difficulty in deciding who was the leading light of the two. 'Which one wielded the more power at that time I really couldn't make out,' he says. 'Indeed I couldn't manage to sort out which was Tweedledum and Tweedledee! I may even have mixed them up a couple of times, calling Lloyd Webber Rice and vice-versa. It just seemed to me that the taller, bigger man was more likely to be the composer. They were very together then.'

But since that time Barnes admits that he has thought more carefully about their work and how much it depends on their collaboration. 'It's notable to me that the three musicals Lloyd Webber did with Rice all had strong storyline, while *Cats* has none, and yet is probably his greatest work to date. I tend to think so.' The veteran critic, now reviewing for Rupert Murdoch's tabloid, the *New York Post*, adds: 'To an extent I have had to recant on some of the things I said against their early shows. But their success still surprises me.'

It surprised many others, particularly those American executives of the MCA record corporation who had been against the thing from the beginning, doubtful of its appeal and openly concerned that the religious controversy would harm the company image. In the month after the Broadway opening Robert Stigwood flew back to England, in the words of the *Observer*'s Mammon column, 'a happy and a busy man', and with ample reason to be both.

The record had gone into *Variety*'s best-selling-album charts three weeks after its release and stayed near the top for forty consecutive weeks, earning close on £13 million. Stigwood's quarter share of Andrew and Tim's royalties and the success of his touring and Broadway companies in the stage version of *Superstar* was bringing him £16,500 a week, apart from the $7\frac{1}{2}$ per cent management fee his organization collected for handling the production. His publicly quoted shares had recovered all they had lost at the time of his undersubscribed launch the previous year. He was well on the way to becoming a multi-millionaire.

Andrew and Tim had never known such opulence. Every day's post brought news of more and more money pouring into their coffers. A lack of interest in mere wealth, as described to Clive Barnes, may have been true when they voiced it (as it is of most people who seek artistic rewards with little or no hope of financial gain). But now they were tasting an altogether new sensation: the seemingly inexhaustible flow of hard cash. Though they clung self-consciously to old ways and standards, these could not last.

'Perhaps we spend a bit more on nice restaurants and wine,' Tim admitted to Ray Connolly, one of their better acquainted Fleet Street contacts, 'but I still drive my Triumph and Andrew still has his Mini.'

He added that, yes, he had just bought a house in West London: 'But only because it was such a bargain, and had been a case of snap it up or lose it.' Andrew was still living in his small basement flat in South Ken, with Sarah, when not in New York or paying visits to the various production companies which were putting on *Superstar* in several overseas countries. He had also acquired the old farmhouse in Shaftesbury, Dorset, to accommodate his still-unquenched love of old buildings in remote corners of England. As to any suggestion that the money rolling in had changed his life at all, he was firmly negative. 'Marriage has actually lowered my expenditure, if anything,' he told Connolly.

But he was beginning to open his eyes to the fact that control over the product was what really counted in the theatre. The success of *Superstar* was so terrific and in a way so unexpected that it had taken him, as it had Tim, entirely by surprise, while Stigwood's shrewd business sense had assured a share of the pie which would increase rather than diminish with success. The lesson was clear:

'We'll never know the extent to which we probably lost some of our control over *Superstar*,' Andrew reflects. 'But we do know that an awful lot of people made just as much if not a great deal more money from it than we did.'

Tim's view was more cynically detached. 'After *Superstar*, even if Robert says, "I've got something that can make you two million quid," and even if he really thinks it could, and even if it did, I'd think, "Well, so what?"' But with both of them the impact of sudden wealth was forcing a new scale of values in both professional and private life, whether or not they acknowledged it themselves.

On holiday in Ventimiglia, Andrew took Sarah to meet an old acquaintance, his Aunt Vi's friend, British film writer-director Ronald Neame. Neame remembered Andrew as a precocious 14-year-old who had 'visited my home, borrowed the piano, and made tape recordings'. Now, nearly ten years later, he was interested to learn that the young upstart whose 'exceptional talent' his aunt had constantly enthused about ('There are a lot of aunts in the world with talented nephews,' Neame comments drily) was a published, apparently highly successful, Broadway composer.

'Once before, I'd suggested to Andrew he might like to write a song on "spec" for a musical I was preparing,' Neame recalls. 'He did, but I never got the film off the ground and he told me he'd used his melody in *Jesus Christ Superstar*, where I believe it became one of the hits.'

It was also one of the themes Andrew incorporated in the entirely fresh score he was writing for the film of *Superstar* which the Canadian director Norman Jewison was to make in Israel. Film music interested Andrew. It was a new and different medium which he plunged into with great enthusiasm. Already, under Stephen Frear's direction, he had completed work on music for the film *Gumshoe*, produced in 1971 by Michael Medwin and starring Albert Finney and Billie Whitelaw. When Ronald Neame suggested he might get together with producer John Woolf in England on the film he was at present making for Columbia Pictures, *The Odessa File*, Andrew accepted at once.

The film did not do well, but the music which Andrew wrote in association with his brother, Julian, has a pleasant, lively quality. There were three themes, the main one sung by Perry Como. And Neame, in a sleeve note to the recording, wrote: 'Composers have always made an important contribution to motion pictures. In this respect Andrew is no exception. The second [theme] is musically the most important: a fugue for cello – played by Andrew's brother, Julian – with a rock group and full orchestra. It is probably Andrew's most provocative and original composition to date. It cannot fail to cause a great deal of attention in the world of music.' Auntie Vi had been right!

Tim wrote lyrics for the film, but few of the words made impact. For all Derek Jewell's belief in his dilettanteism, it did not seem that Tim was especially enamoured of film work. Andrew, who regards the cinema as an area he still hopes to expand into musically, enjoyed it. 'I was really very interested in getting to know how film scores worked,' he says. 'Though I don't consider myself a cinema animal, it is something I always thought I'd at least be able to hold my own in. So the important thing was to find out how it's done technically.'

In *Odessa*, according to the conductor of the London recordings (and the man who was to become Andrew's musical director in many future productions) Anthony Bowles, 'much of Andrew's music for the film was cut, but I'm sure he's used it in other shows since. He's always doing that.' Julian laments its loss. 'It has some of his best stuff,' he says.

Whether or not Andrew's film work would develop to the point where it might take over from other commitments was never really considered. He was simply trying it for size. And, like many other aspects of creative work – especially the cinema – it was frustratingly slow in delivering its verdict. Meanwhile, he was struggling to keep his feet and head in the right ratio to one another.

For Tim the problem was not so acute. He basked in the astonishing tributes which success with *Superstar* was showering on them both. 'He was always the front runner, then,' Andrew reflects. 'Somewhere, dragging along at the back, was Andrew Lloyd Webber. It's changed now, but that's how it was then.'

So Tim could afford to be glib about the lack of direction which suddenly seemed to have developed in their working collaboration. There were still ideas to discuss, magnificent dream-canvases which an evening together over a meal and a bottle or two of wine would conjure up and elaborate. 'The temptation was to follow up with something immediately,' Tim explains. 'We had great plans for several things, like launching The Scaffold [a British pop group] in the States, using techniques we'd learned over there, for one. Andrew was busy with his film scores, but I just hung around. It would have been fatal, I felt, to come in with something like *Adolf Hitler Superstar*. So my feeling was that we should just sit tight until people started wondering when we'd come up with something else, if ever.'

It was an attitude, and a pace, which suited him far better than Andrew. As Andrew sees him, and others agree, 'Tim is one of those people with an awful lot of skills. He's a very good broadcaster. A very able public personality – which, I mean, I am not, really. He edits these intelligently put-together pop books. And he enjoys doing all of them. He therefore has succeeded in an awful lot of different ways in his own right.'

But when their work on the film of *Jesus Christ Superstar* was done (according to Ellis Nassour: 'it amounted to very little. They just had to write and adapt the music a little. I don't think they visited the location in Israel more than once, and they probably didn't approve of how Jewison was handling the production, anyway') there was nothing of any consequence to take its place. Which suited Andrew not at all.

'There was a hiatus, you see,' he explains. 'From that time in 1971 until the early summer of 1974, nearly three years later, we didn't work together on anything terrific. Only the Mark Two *Joseph*, which had to be considerably re-written for its first professional performance at the September 1972 Edinburgh Festival, and two months later at the Round House in London.'

And he breaks off to say, in explanation of the way things in theatre seldom go as planned, 'and *that* is the version running on Broadway now, and has been running for the past two and a half years! Absolutely against anything I would have predicted. In fact, if you'd told me when we wrote it that *Joseph* was going to be a hit Broadway musical, I'd have told you "Listen, mate! I mean, re-examine things!" Let me tell you that when they first wanted it, I was really quite anti letting them have a go. I just didn't believe it could work at that level.'

The big problem with the hiatus was that it never·lacked attractions, and these could so easily divert their energies from more important projects. For example there was the highly successful London opening of *Superstar* at the Palace Theatre on 9 August 1972. That involved them, and was immensely flattering. Then the two *Joseph* professional try-outs were followed by a seven-month West End run at the recently renamed Albery Theatre (previously the New). That was on Saturday, 17 February 1973, the year in which Andrew formed himself into 'The Really Useful' company, taking over Brian Brolly, who'd backed *Superstar* against MCA opposition, to direct his whole operation from a house in Eaton Place, London, SW1.

In the same year, 1973, he found, bought, and began the renovation of a large country house near Newbury. Young as she was, Sarah ran Sydmonton Court with a firm and sure hand. The advantage of the place, apart from its appeal to Andrew's restorative zeal (being a mass of architectural contradictions, added over the years), was its tiny chapel. This, electronically equipped and given stage and theatrical provisions, could become the working, grown-up counter-part of his boyhood model theatre. Three years later he opened it with the first of his annual Sydmonton Festivals.

In one sense these annual events are casual 'happenings' in which carefully selected guests are invited to witness Andrew's latest musical and theatrical compositions while still in the 'ideas' stage of development. The performers are quite often famous artists who enjoy the experimental nature of the Festivals, safe in the knowledge that Andrew swears all who attend to absolute secrecy. 'The whole point is that anyone can get up and make a complete idiot of himself,' he explains. 'It's really like a country houseparty in that sense, with everybody taking part in discussions and activities. Their opinions are very valuable to me.'

While the programmes feature much of his own work, this is not always so. 'They change spontaneously,' he says. 'Somebody may leap out of the woodwork and do a complete ad/lib.' In July 1982, as well as being privileged to hear the music he had written for *Starlight Express* guests were treated to a musical appreciation of jazz-pianist and bandleader Duke Ellington, written and produced by Derek Jewell.

The following year Andrew equipped his tiny church with highly sophisticated electronic sound equipment and technical aids. His private collection of 'high-tech' material is housed at Sydmonton and is said to maintain very professional standards.

Andrew likes each of his annual Festivals to follow a theme. In 1983 for instance the underlying thread was 'nuclear disarmament', involving a unilateral debate, a hypnotist and lecturer on mind and brain-power as well as the customary Festival Evensong, held in the chapel on the final Saturday night as a conclusion to the four- or five-day event.

During the previous days and nights the guests, who included at least one senior cabinet minister (an indication of the loyalty Andrew expects, and gets, from his audience is that no news of the identity leaked out to the media), were treated to recitals by Andrew's then future wife Sarah Brightman and violinist Nigel Kennedy. There was also a video recording of the workshop production of *Starlight Express*. Andrew's own contribution was what he termed 'a cabaret' with songs from his show *Aspects of Love*, for which Trevor Nunn had been pressed into writing special lyrics. As usual, the Festival should have ended – apart from the Evensong – with a cricket match in which those taking part played against a team of local villagers, whose interest in the Festival has decreased since the price of tickets went up almost to West End heights. But this event was rained off.

In the same year that the Festival began, Tim honoured his old school by taking a company down to Lancing to stage *Superstar* in the great chapel. An unsigned interviewer, writing in the school magazine, asked him: 'Did you go into the Chapel with equanimity?' Tim agreed that school memories of the place were 'pretty grim'. But, surprisingly, he asserted: 'I used to enjoy Sunday services. I liked the singing.' His young interviewer wasn't going to resist the challenge of criticizing the work. 'The language . . .' he said, 'reminds me of a 1950s' movie magazine.' Tim laughed. 'You could be right,' he said. 'My years of influence were in the 'fifties. I'm far more influenced by Presley than by the Beatles. I tend to like the oldies but goodies . . .'

This was well before Jim Woodhouse, by curious coincidence Andrew's ex-housemaster at Westminster, came to Lancing as headmaster. He now knows Tim best for his cricketing interest, which Woodhouse obviously does not share to any great extent. 'Tim has remained quite close to Lancing,' he says. 'He plays cricket for the Old Boys. Cricket is really a sort of dignified comedy, don't you think? Perhaps that is how he sees it.'

In October 1973, Tim joined the new London commercial station, Capital Radio, as a disc jockey, tempted to try his hand at a role which had always held a distinct attraction for him. It was one more example, if that were needed, of his widening appetite for a many-coloured life-style – one that Andrew had no need of, and was privately at odds with. But around this time something happened with which Andrew could not disagree.

Tim switched on the radio in his car one day and caught the tail-end of a play. It was written round the controversial first lady of Argentina, Eva Peron. And it started a small vein of interest in his creative mind. She was glamorous, sexy, beautiful, adored and had swayed the fortunes of an entire nation. All right, she was a superbitch, but who had that ever robbed of interest? Her cruelties, hypocrisy, even the use she had made of men and her own body, had never been seen as vile enough to quench the mesmeric ardour of her subjects. *How would a Western world receive a musical version of her life, he wondered?*

As always when an idea held possibilities, Tim put the suggestion to Andrew, who agreed that it was potentially exciting, involving as it did the fiery Latin music of Argentina which such composers as de Falla and Ravel had captured. The passion and glamour of the project were undeniable. But first, he insisted, they ought to complete another work which he and to a lesser degree Tim had been toying with haphazardly for some time: a musical to be based on the Bertie Wooster novels of P. G. Wodehouse, one of his favourite authors.

Private reservations about Tim's notion of a musical Eva Peron story also influenced him. To Bob Swash, Stigwood's co-producer in London, Andrew confided: 'I really don't want to do another piece about an unknown who rises to fame at thirty-three and then dies . . . we've just done that with Jesus Christ!'

So it was now up to Tim, and his turn to be reluctant. Seized as he was by the Peron story, he nevertheless valued Andrew's judgement. Above all, he recognized that the composer could never work well unless his full and total enthusiasm were engaged. After much lengthy and sometimes acrimonious discussion and debate, he grudgingly agreed to try his hand at the Wodehouse idea first . . . provided that Andrew would also agree to put in some spare time on his *Evita* notion, composing whatever he could for the words Tim had already written.

Tim was acutely aware that Wodehouse, much as he revered him, was not really suited to the musical stage, or at least not to the type of lyrics which he could fluently write for richer and more romantic material. To try to transpose the world's greatest living humorous writer to the rhythms and disciplines of the musical stage was asking, he believed, far too much. However, no other course was open if he wanted Andrew to work with him on *Evita*, so he took it on.

P. G. Wodehouse was by now a very old man living in America and Andrew had won his approval to the general idea of doing the work, but with the cautionary postscript from Wodehouse that, 'It's been tried before and failed.' To secure his full approval and advice Andrew went over to the author's Long Island home. Wodehouse again advised him to be careful since the pitfalls were great. Andrew was under no illusion, but on meeting the frail old Master of the Bertie Wooster stories he more than ever decided to press on with the project. He very much wanted to achieve success in Wodehouse's lifetime. And he equally strongly felt the music for the subject beginning to form in his mind. *Jeeves* it had to be.

13

Win Some, Lose Some

IN one way money was no longer a problem, at least not the problem it had been when Andrew's mealtime wine consumption was queried by American recording company executives. Andrew had moved to a £140,000 house in Knightsbridge. His hand-made, gorgeously flowered shirts came from a smart boutique in Beauchamp Place, Deborah and Clare. Tim was advised by his accountant that his earnings, like Andrew's, had passed the £200,000 mark in each of the two previous years. After a long search, he had found the house in the country he was looking for (and where he now lives with his boxer dog, an adequate wine cellar, and his cricket gear) in Oxfordshire. On 19 August 1974 he married Jane McIntosh in London.

Tim had met Jane at Capital Radio, during his occasional stints as a DJ for the broadcasting company. She was a secretary, and colleagues still talk about the day they found her desk empty, a note pinned to her typewriter, and the terse message 'Gone abroad with Tim Rice.' Announcement of the marriage came soon afterwards.

When Tim and Jane's first child was born, a daughter, they christened her Eva-Jane, after the Argentine dictator's wife who, by then, was not only fascinating Tim but was also the means of showering him with money. The *Evita* publicist Genista Streeten maintains that Tim had become wholly devoted to the legend of Eva Peron, to the point where he saw her in an exalted light. In Genista's view,

'Tim has always been impressed by demi-gods,' which, if true, would explain his choice of several of the subjects which he and Andrew chose to develop (from Saladin, Richard Lion-Heart and the great philanthropist Dr Barnardo to the Biblical stars of *Joseph* and *Superstar*).

The drawback to these new responsibilities and possessions for both Andrew and Tim was that, inexorably, they changed the focus of their individual lives. It became harder to meet, to argue over plans and projects until all hours, and during restaurant meals. Socially, the gulf between them was widening, each developing associations and friendships of his own. 'When you don't have money,' Tim tried to explain to Peter Dacre of the *Sunday Express*, 'you don't worry about it. Now, one has to be careful.' Andrew echoed this, with feeling. 'We were unprepared,' he cried. 'The first time we met to discuss our financial situation was during Lionel Bart's bankruptcy! A salutary lesson!'

As Tim summed up the dilemma, 'A lot of our old friends don't like to ring us up now, because they think we're so grand. That's really sad.' He diplomatically avoided any suggestion that the divisive nature of their new wealth was having an equally corrosive effect on their partnership. Geographically if in no other way, they were now apart more often than they were together. The old days of adjoining flats and impromptu meetings at any hour were giving place to 'fitted in' appointments and interviews.

The adjustment was from having barely had enough cash, to enjoying an apparently inexhaustible bank balance. At Oxford, Andrew's closest friend, David Marks, had been struck by the ease of Andrew's pocket, despite an obvious lack of means. With money, some of this wore away. His lyric-writing schoolfriend Robin Barrow remembers an embarrassing occasion, prompted no doubt unintentionally by this.

'We'd gone along in a party of old friends to one of Andrew's favourite Kensington restaurant haunts,' Barrow says. 'It was quite a modest place, which suited the rest of us because it was only Andrew who'd struck it rich at that time. And he was believed to be rolling! So when after the meal he joyfully ordered expensive brandies for everyone I thought he was giving us a treat. Not a bit of it. When the bill came we all had to stump up our share, so that in effect we were subsidising his entertainment – because we would never have lashed out on brandy unless we'd thought it was on him.'

As Barrow says, not unkindly, 'I find it irritating to think, let alone talk, about money like that, but I must say I do remember that occasion. I suppose Andrew had not the remotest idea how we felt.' And later, when the party pressed on back to Andrew's flat, there was another enlightening experience for Barrow. 'Andrew produced a tray of drinks, then pretended he'd forgotten how to pour whisky,' he recalls. 'I thought it was complete affectation, as if he wanted to show us that he hadn't got into expensive ways.'

But what was sadder was the pressure that sudden wealth, marriage, property and fame was heaping on his and Tim's working relationship. In the year he married, Tim backed out of the *Jeeves* project because, he said, he 'had come to feel that I am not going to be able to do justice to the source'. Artistically, Andrew had to accept this, knowing that Tim's respect for Wodehouse amounted almost to reverence and was certainly as great as his own. If the Master's words were too sacred for Tim to touch, his magnificently benign satire on English life too delicate, then so be it. But privately, as he admitted later, that was not the only trouble.

'We had this intense period of working together and then it all happened and we allowed people to come between us. It's ridiculous. Tim and I are very close, really,' he told Sydney Edwards of the *Evening Standard*.

The 'people' were never named. But Andrew had sensed a sea-change in his partner which was disturbing. If Tim was to tie himself and his many talents to other creative areas, once again he might find himself without a lyricist. The frustration of Robin Barrow's departure and those empty years until he and Tim met recurred with worrying intensity.

There were, of course, other writers, other lyricists. And he was no longer an unknown tyro. Bob Swash suggested Alan Ayckbourn, who had long appealed to Andrew's boyish sense of humour, his comedies rich in all that could be desired by a writer who might blend his genius with that of the Master. Intrigued by the novelty (he had never written a musical), Ayckbourn agreed to try and shape the thing so that Andrew would have an original storyline. Andrew's hope was that, with this, he could encourage Tim to come back and write lyrics for the show.

But in this, as in so much else to do with *Jeeves*, he was disappointed. For Ayckbourn's acceptance was reportedly qualified by reservations which would have put any 'Plum' Wodehouse fan's nose out of joint. Though never admitting as much, Tim was not taken with the idea of working with a writer who thought musicals 'pretty damn boring' and who asked aloud 'who the hell is Jeeves? I mean he's just a figure who says lines!' So Tim finally and absolutely backed away from any connection with the piece, while waiting for Andrew to deliver the score for his own cherished notion of the legendary Evita.

'I don't know quite why he wouldn't do it,' Andrew says. 'I don't think he really rated it, you know. And probably with hindsight, it was the right thing to do. Because as everybody knows I went ahead with Alan Ayckbourn and it was a disaster.'

If Tim had written the lyrics, could that have achieved a

better result? Andrew tactfully declines to condemn
Ayckbourn's words altogether. 'No, but the lyrics would
have had an easier turn of phrase,' he says. 'Alan's lyrics
were simple, direct and tremendously effective. And the
real truth is that *Jeeves* was nothing like as bad as it was said
to be. But, at the same time, it was not as good as one or
two people have subsequently said that it might have been,
if . . . well, I mean I'm always being asked about a revival of
it.'

There may have been other reasons, also. Anthony
Bowles, the experienced musical director of Andrew and
Julian's *Odessa File* film score, points to them with some
force.

'Andrew had never written anything directly for the
theatre before,' Bowles says. 'Both *Superstar*, which I'd
directed musically for him at the Palace, and *Joseph*, which
I'd also directed at the Albery, were only turned into
theatre pieces after they'd been written for recordings. I
don't think in those days he really had the knowledge to
read the theatre.'

It was well known that both these earlier shows had
needed a lot of re-writing to fit them for the live stage.
'*Joseph* had had to be entirely re-orchestrated, re-cast and
expanded for the West End,' Bowles recalls. His experience
of how *Superstar's* London version came into being was one
he says he will never forget.

'I'd been asked to do a musical arrangement of *Superstar*
for what was to be its European premiere, in Paris,' he says.
'I'd never met Andrew, and I didn't know anything about
him or his music then, so I had to get LPs and listen to
them. Then I rang him and said I thought it needed quite a
few things done to make it viable for the stage, did he
mind? He told me: "Well, if it's going to be done in Paris,
go ahead and do what you like with it."'

'He didn't seem particularly interested, perhaps because

he was into other things. *Superstar*, I gathered, had been a sort of youthful folly which he'd written when he was only nineteen or so.

'Anyway, I went to Paris and messed about with the score. I didn't know anything about the rock world. It was new to me. But I speak French. We rehearsed in the vast Palais de Chaillot, and when we opened it caused quite a stir, with pickets outside. Quite lively. Andrew had come over with Tim, and Robert Stigwood was there for the opening. He told me afterwards "Your version is the one we'd like to use in London." There was no date fixed, but they wanted to do it there. So I said, "Please ask me at the time."'

Bowles makes it quite clear that Andrew had raised no objection to any of the changes he had made. 'Not in the slightest,' he says. 'I'd tried to take off the hysteria from the early stages, so that it was a much slower build-up to the climax. Originally, it tended to have constant orgasms – virtually from the word go. So I tried to give it a more gradual dramatic line, without interfering with the composition as such. The changes weren't really major, but they were quite far-reaching in little ways.'

Within 24 hours of Bowles's return to London he got a phone call from the Stigwood office asking him to attend a meeting with the director, Australian Jim Sharmers. At this, he says he agreed to take on the show, but with one important alteration to the plan. The orchestra had to be in the pit, with Anthony Bowles conducting it from the usual place, facing the stage. 'They'd schemed it at the back, with me invisible to the company and watching them through closed-circuit television,' Bowles explains. 'I told them I was a musical director, not an accompanist.'

After that, everything went smoothly. The show when it opened was immediately successful. It ran for eight years, breaking all musical records for London. Bowles says: 'I venture to suggest the reasons were that it wasn't as lavish a production as in the States where, as a stage show, it wasn't so successful. I mean, it wasn't a paean of bad taste as I heard the American one was, though I didn't see it. Also, despite the cast changes during that long run, it was a very, very happy company with the most wonderful feeling about the show. You see, Andrew trusted the people he was working with. He knew they were all doing their best, and all for him.'

And having worked on *Superstar* (and later, *Joseph*) Bowles struck up quite a friendship with Andrew and Tim. 'We were all on the friendliest possible terms,' he recalls. 'I don't think Andrew even remotely resented any changes I made. We used to have meals together and seemed to get along fine. I used to hear tales about Andrew being potty about one-armed bandits, and having them installed in his house at Sydmonton, but that side of his life escaped me completely. We talked almost entirely about music and the theatre.'

The plans for *Jeeves* were under constant discussion, Bowles remembers, even before he was invited to direct it musically. 'Actually, I'd spent a year in Stuttgart as musical director of a ballet company, only flying back to do two performances of *Superstar* every month and to keep my eye on it,' he explains. 'It was right after that that I took on *Jeeves*.'

His first surprise was the absence of Tim Rice. 'Nobody said very much to me about that,' he says, 'and to begin with I kept expecting Tim to turn up with some of the lyrics. But then I realized that he wasn't going to have anything to do with the show, though I gathered Andrew would have liked him to do so. It just wasn't his cup of tea.'

On the surface, Bowles accepted that this should have made no difference to the merits of the production. Ayckbourn had brought in Eric Thompson, who had directed all his great successes. As Bowles saw it, '*In theory* it couldn't fail. To put the most successful young British composer with the most successful comedy writer on a piece by one of the world's most gifted and celebrated humorous authors, and then to have it directed by the man who had the most West End shows running at that particular moment – five Ayckbourn plays were running at the time, if you count *Norman Conquest* as three – and on top of that the show was being choreographed by the new young choreographer of the Ballet Rambert, Christopher Brice, so I mean . . . But in practice it failed miserably!'

Anthony Bowles is too experienced to suggest that this cannot and does not happen in the theatre. All the most popular playwrights and composers produce flops from time to time. But in this case he puts the failure down to Ayckbourn's unfamiliarity with the medium.

'Alan hadn't the remotest idea of how to write a musical in those days,' he says. 'I understand he's written them since, but then he was absolutely without experience. He produced the most *involved* plot. Very ingenious – as indeed were all of his plots. A very good Wodehouse pastiche, really. The lyrics weren't stunning, but they were singable. *And* settable – which is more than you can say for some lyric-writers. But it was so enormously long!

'It was also, and I mean I'm speaking now from a purely personal opinion, *totally* escapist. You couldn't justify it on any grounds of social or political importance whatever. It was an utterly escapist thing, which only the most ardent and knowledgeable fan of the Wodehouse books could have appreciated. Added to which, it was something like thirty-five minutes before a female came on to the stage.'

Bowles, who had worked on flops before, was made doubly miserable by what he saw as the lack of grasp which Ayckbourn and his director were showing. 'Andrew wasn't to blame,' he believes. 'He'd written some charming music for it – quite a bit of which has turned up since, I've noticed, in *Cats* and so on – but the production fell into every mistake it's possible to make. For instance, the first four numbers all went to Bertie Wooster!

'Then, when it actually got going, the director, Eric Thompson, showed that he too hadn't the remotest idea about directing a musical. He'd never, ever done one before, in spite of having directed all of Alan Ayckbourn's successful plays. He'd got a good company to work with and there was nothing wrong with the music, there are some smashing tunes in it (indeed, it's the only flop I've ever done which had an LP released after the show had come off!). But there was nothing anybody could do with the script. Nothing at all.'

The first read-through of Ayckbourn's script took, Bowles remembers, unhappily, five and a half hours with music. 'When we eventually opened in Bristol,' he declares, 'even after all the cuts which had been made, it was still something like four and a quarter hours long! And, of course, the plot was so complicated and involved that when you cut pieces out people began to do things which didn't make any sense.'

He recalls one scene 'where everyone was drunk, but you hadn't seen them *get* drunk, or been given the faintest idea *why* they were drunk. It was preposterous!'

The cast were beginning to think so too. 'We all knew it was totally unsaleable,' Bowles says. 'Which made the whole thing deeply miserable. And it wasn't helped by the bad blood which, as always when a show isn't going well, was beginning to flow.'

Andrew and Alan Ayckbourn had become firm friends. They remained so. 'He was fantastic to work with, and I hope we can do something together again,' Andrew announced later to confirm this fact. But Bowles watched even these two come close to friction. 'They were showing signs of strained relations at times,' he says, 'though they were the best of friends. But Eric was the main victim. Poor chap, he didn't know what to do. He'd been used to dealing with intimate Ayckbourn plays and moving no more than three or four people at a time about the stage. Then, suddenly, he had a company of thirty – or whatever it was – and he hadn't the remotest idea what to do with anybody.'

As Bowles points out, the pressures were terrific. *Jeeves* was to be the premiere of the year. 'Quite apart from the money,' he says, 'and I saw later they lost £110,000 on it, everyone was expecting it to be a smash, while we all knew it wasn't – not that kind, anyway.'

And at the first night the audience got the message. 'I was astonished how cold the house was,' Bowles remembers. 'There was no dissenting voice, nothing said. Just a well-behaved resistance. We knew it wasn't going over.'

And by then the last vestige of belief in the show as it stood was hard even for Andrew and Alan to maintain. 'Eric had been sacked,' Bowles recalls miserably. 'But it was too late. We opened on the Tuesday and he was sacked on the Friday before. Alan came in to direct it himself. With no experience at all of directing a musical, for him to try and lead the show was even worse!'

And the bad blood boiled over. 'We were all on our knees by that time. Ever since we'd left Bristol we'd done nothing but rehearse, all day every day. Every night there were changes, never for the better. Just different. And of course everybody got to the state where they didn't know what was going where. They didn't even know which scene was in and which was out. By the time Alan took over we were all numb.'

Eric Thompson was the only one spared, but he too felt nothing but despair. In a theatrical director's life there are always thistles among the roses. Thompson died in November 1982. His widow, the West End actress Philida Law, watched his distress at the time. 'Eric had always felt there was a lot wrong with it,' she recalls. 'Of course he did. After five weeks of rehearsals and the previews it would have been obvious to anybody. It just didn't work.'

Philida Law thought the production 'fell between fifteen stools, all different'. In her professional view, it had a tremendous lot wrong with it. 'But I don't think you can say who or what was specifically to blame,' she says. 'Eric of course felt absolute despair when it failed, but I think he realized that they were all a bit out of their depth. None of the three – he, Andrew or Alan had ever done a musical before. Well, Andrew had some musical experience, but that was pretty slight. One just can't apportion blame. You must get a script and see for yourself.'

The script does indeed reveal a curious blend of long-winded comedy – Wooster, played by David Hemmings, sharing choruses with members of the Drones Club, while the inimitable Jeeves played by Michael Aldridge stood by – and contrived cues for Andrew's music. But it's impossible to tell from the record (now a collector's item) how poorly the show was received. It lasted at the Her Majesty's Theatre in the Haymarket for less than five weeks, the final curtain ringing down on 24 May 1975 on what critic Sheridan Morley has since called its 'all too short-lived' run.

To Andrew, it was never anything but a failure of theatrical chemistry. 'I learned a lot from it,' he says. 'And I still believe that it only needed one different piece in the chemical mix to have made it a success.'

Is he perhaps thinking, when he says that, of the good

that can come out of even the most costly theatrical disaster? In the chorus of *Jeeves*, noticeably attractive and fresh, was a young musical actress by the name of Elaine Paige. The future Evita was enjoying her first taste – a bitter one – of working for and with Andrew Lloyd Webber.

14

Don't Cry for Andrew

IT was fortunate that his old partner's infectious enthusiasm for Eva Peron had kept the idea fresh in both their minds, because Andrew turned to it now if not with relish, at least with none of his earlier reluctance. On the last night of *Jeeves* he'd received a cable from the American director Hal Prince urging him to 'bank the score' of the *Jeeves* show, which he proceeded to do. Frustrating though the failure had been, it had left him with a fount of tunes which, if kept more or less intact, might one day lead to its resurrection, or at least provide inspiration for another vehicle. *Evita* needed an altogether different approach, and the contrast was welcome.

But first there was an imperative need for a holiday. He and Sarah had been invited to a Greek island by their friend Gary Bond, who had starred in the version of *Joseph* performed at the Edinburgh Festival. On impulse, Andrew sent Bond a cable accepting. They set off with only the haziest notion of where they were going, but after the disappointment of the closure the prospect of leaving civilization was irresistible. It's doubtful that they even realized that the island retreat was in fact almost exclusively used by nudists.

'I'd been there for three or four days and was sunbathing when the ferry dropped them off-shore,' Bond says. 'They had to wade the rest of the way. One of the funniest sights of my life was Andrew, in long velvet jacket and trousers rolled up to his knees, splashing towards the beach. Even funnier was when I had to introduce him to nudist friends. He simply didn't know where to look!'

That the holiday could have caused Andrew to relax was most unlikely in any circumstances. Like the American comedian Woody Allen, Andrew does not care for holidays as a part of life. 'Frankly, they bore me,' he admits. The need to be within reach of his numerous pianos, his personal group of devoted musician friends – who notably include jazz-rock keyboard player Rod Argent, drummer John Hiseman and his saxophonist wife Barbara Thompson – and who will rush to help him whenever he wants to try out a tune, is far too insistent. In his relations with Tim Rice this had played an increasingly divisive part. It is not simply that he does not enjoy leisure but that, unlike Tim, he really finds it destructive.

Much of the irritation he had felt during their work on *Superstar* in New York was still in his mind at this time. 'When I look back now,' he says, 'I suppose one must say that different people have different work rhythms, and going off to Japan or whatever when I felt we should have been working was probably a good thing for Tim to do. He needed the experience of different people and new places. But from my point of view I was keen to get on and write. I just needed lyrics. I still need lyrics. I eat lyricists up.'

Lacking the strength which success with *Jeeves* would have brought him, Andrew was in no position to dictate terms. *Evita*, as the show was to be called, was Tim's idea. It belonged to him, needing only music such as Andrew could readily furnish to support his lyrics. In essence the story was already there, as the stories of *Joseph* and *Superstar* had been. But by introducing Che Guevara as a symbol of Eva Peron's victims Tim rounded out history. *Evita*, therefore, was to be by 'Tim Rice and Andrew Lloyd Webber', in that order.

Epicurean tastes in food and wine rarely include a liking for humble pie, but in this case Andrew could be grateful for the role of composer to a story and a theatrical design which came to him, as he freely admits, ready made. 'I didn't need a lot of persuading because I thought that anything that had got Tim that fired up had to be a good idea,' he reflects; 'my only slight concern was how one would handle a piece like that politically.'

Against this was the obvious attraction of Eva Peron as a romantic figure. Andrew was enthralled by the legend. 'I find it hard to put this simply,' he says, 'but I was feeling a great desire to write something which would allow me to show, on a really large screen, a full-blooded romantic story.

'I suppose many composers wouldn't have worried about the politics in the slightest.' he goes on. 'I mean, the violence and so on. But *Evita* from this point of view did worry me. On the other hand it also intrigued me, partly I suppose because of what was going on in Britain at that time.'

Andrew points to the concern he felt for the tide of violence which, in 1975, was revealing itself in the rise of private armies, vandalism, football stadium hooliganism and the plummeting decline of wealth as shown by the record drop in the value of shares quoted on the London stock exchange. 'It was very worrying to see it all,' he explains, 'and particularly so for those like me who passionately believe in the democratic way of life.'

He saw *Evita* as a 'possibility of doing a sort of bitter-sweet political commentary opera. I was beginning to play around musically with the really extreme emotions affecting life – mortality and so on. It was therefore a marvellous subject.'

He saw it, too, as a cautionary tale reflecting some of his own deeply-held fears. 'People forget,' he says, 'but it was a very terrifying time. Financially I, like a lot of others, honestly thought that I was going down the pan.'

His first child, a daughter, Imogen, was born a year later, in 1976. He had bought Sydmonton at what was not so much a worryingly high price as a portent of what his future load in life would become if the pressures continued. As he says, 'I really could see no way of continuing to make ends meet. *Jeeves* had been a costly loss and top income-tax was 83 to 90 per cent.'

Costs everywhere were soaring, and Andrew's taste of theatrical disaster made him flinch from any production in which he did not have total faith. He was still far from convinced that *Evita* would work as a stage show, though the music he was composing for it was as exciting as anything he had written. Long discussions with Tim and with David Land, their agent, had so far failed altogether to relieve this pessimistic frame of mind. The shock of failure with *Jeeves* had been too searing to be banished lightly.

Bob Swash remembers his worries coming to a head. 'We were well ahead by then,' Swash says. 'The record had been made as a 'concept recording', which is done to promote a forthcoming stage show as much as to sell the disc, and it was a success. Julie Covington's single of 'Don't Cry for Me Argentina' was consistently topping the charts. But Andrew still felt nervous, he said, about putting the show on the stage, and I took him to lunch with Tim at L'Escargot in Soho to thrash it out.'

Over lunch, Swash says he put it to Andrew that the show *must* go on. 'What are we going to do?' he asked. 'We've got this hit song, and a wonderful book and lyrics. What's to stop it being a hit on the stage?'

Andrew looked glum. 'I can't see it,' he said. 'Anyway, not unless we have at least fifty musicians.' Swash says he couldn't believe his ears. Neither could Tim.

'With that number in the orchestra, we'd need Covent

Garden [the Royal Opera House] to fit them all in the orchestra pit – apart from having about an extra £3,000 a week to pay for their sessions. It was an absolute killer, and Tim told him so.'

According to Swash, the partners then had a stormy row lasting half through the lunch. 'I'm not going to say who won,' Swash says now, 'but I can tell you this, Andrew did *not* get his fifty musicians.' An assistant in another room offers him verification of the current orchestra in use in the London show. 'How many are there? Ah, twenty-five! I thought so.'

Settling that one point seems to have acted on Andrew like a cleansing downpour of summer rain. If he and Tim had further stormy scenes, they are not on record. His enthusiasm for the show rose with every rehearsal, and his work on it had never been excelled in anything they had done previously. Yet his nervousness never altogether left him.

He has a frightening recollection of sitting through an early private staging of the show at the Prince Edward Theatre in London. 'I thought the management were mad! A lot of well-meaning people – connected with the record and so on, but seeing it on stage for the first time – were in the audience. And they were *terribly* depressed. I could feel it, and I was sure it wasn't going to work.'

Such agonizing doubts about a musical show are common at the stage when, as Andrew well knows, technical defects have to be laboriously ironed out in rehearsals and previews during which, quite often, there is little lighting and poor sound. As he says of that first ordeal: 'It looked to me as if it was staggering slowly, blindly towards completion. Half the time the audience couldn't see what was going on. How could they appreciate it?'

Yet, when it opened on 21 June 1978, all London

welcomed *Evita*. Some of the critics almost ran out of superlatives. *Classical Music* magazine gave it the accolade of 'serious art'. In the reviewer's words, Elaine Paige starring as Eva Peron had 'scored a great triumph, singing with power and feeling, dancing prettily, acting superbly.' As Che Guevara David Essex's whole performance was 'excellent, the irony nicely calculated, the singing pointed but never self-conscious'.

Derek Jewell was even more fulsome. 'Magnificent, original, compelling,' he extolled in the *Sunday Times* on 25 June; 'Lloyd Webber is perhaps the most remarkable musical child of his generation . . .'

Jewell, as one of the critics who *did* understand music, had perceived what some had missed. 'The score . . .' he wrote, 'is an unparalleled fusion of twentieth-century musical experience. Echoes of the past, Tchaikovsky, Puccini, and church choral music, shimmer hauntingly through. But it is the interweaving of pop, rock, jazz, Broadway, Latin and other elements which make the brew so astonishingly potent.'

The whole production, Jewell felt, was 'breathtaking'.

Three months later, *Evita* was playing to capacity business. Scalpers outside the Prince Edward were getting two and three times the price of tickets for seats which could only be booked three months ahead. On 3 October Andrew and Tim enjoyed one other astonishing first – *Jesus Christ Superstar* had broken all records as Britain's longest-running musical. With *Joseph and the Amazing Technicolor Dreamcoat* returning to the Westminster Theatre for a further run, they now had three hits in the West End at one time.

Andrew could look back on his early tremors of apprehension with relief. But his anxieties about the political nature of the show lingered. They are still with him in some degree, as a story he tells illustrates:

'While boarding at Westminster I went along one evening to hear Sir Oswald Mosley, the one-time Fascist leader, speak. Not from any interest in his politics, but because I was studying the art of speaking.

'That night Mosley used a ringing sentence which, when I told it to Tim later, became a strong line in the *Evita* show. Mosley said "What a shame! And what a disgrace!" We used it in the business with Evita where she says "Our dignity! Our pride!" And it fitted perfectly.'

Mosley's speech had made little impact on him otherwise, but there was an interesting distraction at the meeting. 'The front row was full of pretty girls taking notes,' he recalls. 'I thought it very weird until I learnt that they were first-year students from the Royal Academy of Dramatic Art, brought there to study speech-making. After that, I wasn't so much fascinated by what Mosley had to say as by the fact that there were twenty-four gorgeous girls, all very interested in the schoolboys sitting at the back!'

The problem with *Evita* was that there was no such light relief. He was being forced to take a position about a woman regarded by many as a poisonous, indeed murderous, dictator in her own right. 'I had to accept the fact that there would be people who would charge us with glorifying Fascism,' he says. 'Of course I worried about it. I do worry a lot about everything I do, more or less, and especially about the moral position. If that charge proved to be true, I reckoned, then there were good reasons why the piece should not be allowed out, however good it was in itself.'

What evidence was there? Tim had no qualms. 'People tended to have extreme views about Eva Peron,' he has since explained. 'They either loved or hated her. I was somewhere in the middle.'

Also, he had probed far deeper into her background. 'I'd

read a few books about her, the only ones available in England,' he says. 'But there was no one, definite work which you could call reliable. So I went over to Argentina to get the feel of the place.'

He thereby experienced the extraordinary, semi-mystical legend which, combined with the poignancy of her death, had made Eva Peron a cult idol. It was this charismatic allure from the grave which excited him, and which he passed on to Andrew. In the end Andrew had to admit: 'She was easily the most unpleasant character I've written about, yet I found her story fascinating. Dying when she did – which must have infuriated her! – there had to be something about her which made people admire her. I'm sure Puccini would have adored her.'

And the inspiration for his music was all there. The hostility of the military and the aristocracy to this jumped-up actress from the sticks, combining effectively with her illness to create a feeling of inevitable doom, was very exciting to compose for. 'In *Evita*,' he explains, 'I tried not to self-consciously ape Latin American styles which are obviously not part of my background. But you couldn't escape the richness and colour of the setting – I may even have bent over too far in responding to this.'

As with their previous shows there was no crippling adherence to any one particular style, either in the music or the action. In *Joseph*, French and Western American musical themes had been used. In *Superstar* the variations ranged from grand opera to a satirical take-off of Elvis Presley's rock motif. Andrew composed some of the *Evita* music – including part of the song which was to become the world-famous 'Don't Cry For Me, Argentina' – while in Bristol for the first performance on tour of *Jeeves*. 'I'd basically written it before then,' he says. 'But I remember developing it, playing around with it, and getting a lot of it right while we were there.'

Everything Andrew composed was now in keeping with the spirit of glamour overlaid with terror which Eva Peron evoked. 'We had to make a great many changes,' he admits. 'For instance, it wasn't until almost the very end of the recording of the *Evita* album in November 1976 that Tim came up with the line "Don't cry for me, Argentina" for the song. Until then it had been in the dialogue, but not in the lyrics anywhere.'

In fact the switch to the key line was made so late in the day that the singer Julie Covington had to be called back into the studio to re-record it. 'Julie came back in and sang the line over, then we dubbed it on to the track,' Andrew says.

Her recording of what was to become one of the greatest-ever British hit records struggled into birth during a gruellingly long and anxious labour. Andrew, Tim and the cast of singers had by then come close to suffering dizzy spells, but the result was tremendously satisfying. Anthony Bowles, called in by Andrew to direct, was unashamedly buoyed up by it.

'It had the smell of success from the start,' he recalls. 'And the Olympic Studios at Barnes where we'd recorded the first *Joseph* were smashing to work in. Imagine, we had the entire London Philharmonic Orchestra backing the singers. That was probably the first work of its kind they'd done, and they loved it. Then, apart from Julie, we had Colm Wilkinson who'd done the Judas take-over in *Superstar* doing Che. And Paul Jones as Peron.'

Andrew was still trying feverishly to achieve a perfect balance for the theme, knowing that its setting and the timing of its use were crucial. It was at this almost too-late hour that the title line came under scrutiny, because Tim was pressing him to agree on a title which would, as he said, 'sit well on the record'. To Andrew, this was less important than the complex interplay of the music – in effect two joint melodic concepts – in the body of the opera as a whole. 'But there was a deadline panic coming up,' Tim recently recalled. 'We were almost on to the last session, and still it wasn't set between us what we'd call it. Andrew told me: "Oh, look, stick it in as 'Don't Cry For Me, Argentina', it sounds nice and we'll alter it later for the stage show.' Of course we never could alter it – thank heavens!'

But as they both admit, the title line didn't really make any logical sense. The rest of the lyrics were supporting their original title line, so that the song should have read 'It's only your lover returning, the truth is I never left you; in all my wild days . . .' and so on. As it became, it left an enigmatic mystery: 'Don't cry for me, Argentina, the truth is I never left you . . .' But the non-sequitur was never challenged.

Andrew looks back almost with wonder now on the way this turned out. As he says: 'It just shows you, the difference between it being just a song and having the right alchemy to make it a hit was *that* close! How do you explain that? You don't.'

The whole show was a demonstration of the fickle nature of success in theatrical life. For *Jeeves* the 'mix' had been, on the face of it, better than good. A 24-carat writer, composer, director presenting a pre-sold best-seller in musical form, every part of it had seemed to guarantee success. *Evita* on the other hand was a daring and politically explosive piece about a woman many theatre-goers would shun. Yet Jeeves lost Andrew's backers their shirts, while *Evita* has been paying satisfying dividends virtually since it opened at the Prince Edward Theatre on 21 June 1978 – and is still doing so, despite the closure of its first Broadway run in July 1983.

According to Stigwood's independent British associate, Bob Swash, Andrew's multi-millionaire producer was discriminating about his own share of the cost of the shows. Stigwood had subscribed to the British production of *Superstar*, knowing that it had every chance of success after its Broadway run. David Land had put £10,000 into the show, the rest, he says, 'coming largely from backers of *Hair* who'd made money on that and wanted to come in'. The whole production had cost no more than £120,000.

With *Jeeves*, carrying a big cast and orchestra, the cost soared. It topped £200,000, of which Land had put up £3,000 and lost the lot. He and the other unfortunates were slow to push their burnt fingers into their wallets when it came to *Evita*, despite the show's obvious attraction.

Swash says: 'When Stigwood came over and I told him *Evita* was going to cost £400,000 to stage in the UK, he couldn't believe it. "Good God, you can't spend that amount of money on a musical!" he told me (today it would be more like a million). Finally, I convinced him and he asked me "Well, can you raise it here in Britain?" I told him we could manage, and he didn't knowingly put a penny into the show.'

Unknowingly, Robert Stigwood had a small stake in *Evita* in London without having to worry his head about it. 'When I'd finally got the money together, there was still something like £625 outstanding,' Bob Swash says with a chuckle. 'I put it down for Stigwood without telling him.'

Even before the royalties due on that modest investment can have reached him, Stigwood had got the message about the show's tremendous money-making potential. 'For the Broadway production of *Evita*?' Bob Swash asks. 'Oh, that was altogether different, of course. By then he knew it was a hit. Although that was a much more expensive production, Stigwood backed the whole thing himself. Nobody else could get a look in. And since that was after the event he couldn't fail, could he?'

Which, as Andrew agrees, is the hallmark of a good

showman. To be able to pick winners and avoid losers is a fine art in theatrical production. The only technical difference, on the surface, between *Jeeves* and *Evita* was the fact that the music of Jeeves was not made into a record and put on sale until *after* the show. *Evita* had reaped the enormous rewards of Miss Covington's persuasive recording of 'Don't Cry For Me, Argentina', made more than eighteen months before the show opened on stage. In Anthony Bowles's view this more than anything had assured the musical show's success.

'It went into the charts as a single very soon after we recorded her singing it,' he says. 'It was a great surprise to me, let me say, because it was nothing like any of the numbers which were hits at that time. I never doubted that the show was going to work, but the way that record took off did astonish me.'

Once he realized what was happening, Bowles tried to persuade Andrew to let him take a financial interest in the show. 'I did everything I could – offered to conduct sessions virtually for nothing, all that sort of thing. He wouldn't budge.' He was told that it was never the policy of Andrew and Tim (as Ellis Nassour had discovered when he, too, had tried to make a profitable investment out of *Superstar* in New York) to invite people they were working alongside to subscribe. Bowles had to be content with his 'not bad' salary, which, as he laments, 'would have been a minuscule part of what I'd have made if I had only been able to share in a tiny part of the royalties. Then I'd have been in clover, but no way!'

Getting backing for *Evita* had, in fact, been considerably easier than for their early shows, in spite of Andrew's failure with *Jeeves*. It was left to prospective 'angels' to think what they liked about that. Most believed that the fault lay in Tim and Andrew's not having done it together, and now that the two were collaborating again, and jointly sharing enthusiasm for the project, it was an altogether different ball-game. The way the funds rolled in allowed for certain extravagances.

'For instance,' Bowles says. 'We had that expensive orchestra playing at all the recording sessions. And not just a normal line-up, but the *augmented* LPO! There must have been ninety or more musicians in the studio sometimes. I well remember Tim saying, round about the second session when we were still only just starting: 'Well, we've already passed what *Superstar* cost us!'

To Bowles, as the sessions proceeded, the music was far superior to anything of Andrew's that he had previously directed. 'I think it is his masterpiece to date,' he said early in 1983. 'It's a very sophisticated score. And not only the music but the lyrics are so much better than *Superstar*. Yes, it was *very* nice doing the recording. Lovely! But the show was another kettle of fish.'

As soon as the stage show was decided on, Bowles was asked by Robert Stigwood to stay and direct that as well. The stage director was to be Hal Prince, the great American showman. But Prince would not be coming over from the States until the very last possible minute, Bowles was told. Meanwhile he and a small team of specialists were to keep the show together.

Ray Holder was the dance arranger. Working with Andrew for the first time posed awkward problems, he found. 'My first meeting with him was just before Easter,' Holder remembers. 'He told me – which was very unusual – "anything I don't like of yours, I'll throw out." I found him, personally, very difficult to understand, and that's not sour grapes.'

It was the first time Hal Prince had agreed to originate a show in London, which he felt 'clung too tenaciously to rigid demarcation lines between operetta and musical theatre'. He had no time for convention. 'I didn't get on with Hal,' Holder admits. 'He ignored my first "good morning" and outstretched hand, and he went on ignoring it right through the show. I found that intensely insulting.'

To Anthony Bowles, who was abruptly fired while on holiday during the early run of *Evita*, Prince was a director who, 'let's say, I would never in any circumstances hope to work with again'. The reason why this senior, highly experienced musical director was dismissed from the company has never been fully explained, he says, even to him.

In Bowles's view, the *Evita* cast enjoyed his musical direction of the show without exception. He feels baffled and hurt. Andrew, who values Bowles as 'a smashing person to work with', seems also unable to offer a very convincing explanation of the mysterious sacking. 'It wasn't my management, you see,' he says. 'Stigwoods were running the company. There was nothing that could be done from my side once Hal Prince had been appointed.'

As Andrew does say, 'For some reason Anthony, from the word go, didn't seem to get on with Hal. A great pity. I'm very, very fond of Anthony, but Hal is a strong-willed man and Anthony is equally so. Hal is an emotional man too, but in a *great* way. He's so talented that you can't – I mean, it's just one of those things, really.' He makes an expressive gesture.

To Bowles, astonishingly barred from the theatre and the show he had done so much to help create, Andrew's diffidence was anything but 'just one of those things'. He was thoroughly alarmed by what had happened, feeling deserted, and with no hint of a reason for the treatment he was getting.

'Why hadn't Andrew taken some sort of action, I kept asking myself? He'd had a fair bit of mileage out of me. Surely, I thought, he'll want to straighten out whatever it was that had caused this incredible situation?'

Bowles says he still cannot believe that his dismissal 'was anything but a grotesque misunderstanding'. Eventually, after the Musicians' Union had threatened strike action on Bowles's behalf, Hal Prince unbent sufficiently to get on the phone to his baffled ex-musical director and attempt some sort of explanation.

'I hope there's no ill-feeling,' Prince said, after a rambling and to Bowles illogical statement about his need for someone who 'doesn't just come in and throw his weight about while just doing one show a week' (as agreed, Bowles says, in his contract). The reply can hardly have justified the call. 'No ill-feeling?' Bowles asked incredulously. 'There are *oceans* of ill-feeling!'

To Andrew, who had to explain to the wounded man that he could do nothing about it as the matter was out of his hands, Bowles was equally forthright. He told Andrew on the telephone: 'Don't be silly, Andrew. Of course you can do something about it. I've knocked myself out for you now for six years. What do you mean, you can't do anything about it? What have I done? That's all I want to know.'

Andrew, he says, told him, 'Well, you were away (on holiday) when Hal wanted you.' Bowles could hardly believe his ears. 'Yes, I know I was,' he said. 'But that was all agreed with Hal beforehand!'

Unexplained as it was, the incident raised questions. 'I freely admit I'm not a very good employer,' Andrew says today. There are those like Brian Brolly, his dedicated chief executive, who would disagree, but other voices persist. 'Andrew can be quite ruthless, obviously,' Genista Streeten says, having worked on Andrew's publicity for *Evita*. 'After the show was a success on Broadway he tried to hustle everyone like mad, and some people found it too much. Why do you think his secretary Biddy Hayward, who'd been with him for eight or nine years, gave up the job recently? I think it just got too much for her.'

Genista herself quit the *Evita* show in London, but not due to Andrew despite the fact that she found him 'highly temperamental, always losing his temper'. Her feeling about him is dispassionately professional, as one might anticipate from an experienced theatrical press executive. 'Musically, I'm not over-impressed,' she says. 'I've heard it said that he's only ever written one tune – "Don't Cry For Me, Argentina" – the rest are all off-shoots of it, and I'm inclined to agree. But I have been amazed at his powers of production, and I must say I admire the way he gets everything together. Andrew is amazing with people. He certainly knows how to use his friends.'

One of the closest of these, David Crewe-Read, is frankly aware of Andrew's effect on people like Genista Streeten, but insists he has always found that anyone who has come close to him has *wanted* to work with him, and enjoyed doing so. 'He'll get his own way, quite rightly so, and I know that a steamroller effect comes out of it sometimes, but with the amount of hangers-on he has to deal with that's inevitable. I think his attitude is extremely useful – people get hurt, but something good comes through in the end.'

Crewe-Read shares Andrew's interest in history and architecture. His own business is in antique pine furniture and they met in 1969 when both were living in flats in the house in Gledhow Gardens from which Andrew was married to Sarah Hugill. 'He used to make such a din composing music for *Jesus Christ Superstar* that my wife, Lisa, and I had to bang on the floor with a poker,' Crewe-Read remembers. 'One day he called up and invited us down. We became firm friends once we found a mutual interest in nineteenth-century art and architecture, which we both love. It began, actually, when we discovered we both knew what the Pre-Raphaelite Brotherhood was.'

There are plenty of others who share this view of
Andrew's personal character, and who believe as Crewe-
Read does that 'he is probably the most genuine and
generous person you'll ever meet'. The theatrical backs put
up by his sometimes awkward and always direct manner in
his professional life are seldom of those who know him in
the way these friends do. But then, as Andrew himself
confesses, 'there are two sides to me – the side that would
be quite happy letting everything go and just enjoying
myself with no regard for the consequences, and the other
side which makes me keen to take hold of a subject and go
through it analytically and seriously.'

Evita fused the two, bringing maturity in its wake. The
first Sydmonton Festival in July 1976 began a pattern
which was to culminate in his desire to own and operate a
London theatre where he would be able to try out the ideas
and musical bits and pieces teeming in his head. In
November that same year the record of *Evita* was finally
made, and its immediate and unquenchable international
success – Derek Jewell's *Sunday Times* review hailed it 'a
masterpiece' – did two things.

Because of the money it earned, Andrew was now able to
stop worrying about the threat of having to leave England.
According to people close to him at that time, the
uncertain political future, his commitments and the
vulnerability of a show-business career had previously
reduced him to forging escape plans on at least three
occasions. 'The first time he was determined to go and live
in New York – which he claims to hate,' an associate said.
'He only lasted there a week, then he couldn't stand it. The
second time he got as far as the airport before changing his
mind. And the third time he held out in the States for two
whole days.'

Evita's gilded triumph therefore provided a strong
incentive – combined with the relief of a Tory election

victory and the removal of some of the UK's most draconian higher-tax levels – for staying put. But it also gave Tim an equal measure of financial security, with less promising results. The point of all this has often been overlooked, and is still less than clear to both Tim and Andrew. It is that, as with Gilbert and Sullivan and many other famous collaborators, freedom from restraint was to test their union to the limit. Artists, as the cliché spells out, work together best when hungry, and *Evita* had swept away any danger of that.

15

Variations and Valerie

THE phone rang in John Hiseman's home in Sutton, Surrey, and a soft voice asked if the British jazz-rock drummer would like to get his group together and, basically, 'play about with a piece of music I'm going to write'. Who was calling, a surprised Hiseman asked? And why him and his group? 'I'm Andrew Lloyd Webber,' came the reply. 'And I just happened to be walking down a corridor a few moments ago in the MCA recording company offices and heard your music – it's exactly the kind of sound I'm after.' 'Fine,' Hiseman told him. But in his own mind he was asking, *'Who's Andrew Lloyd Webber?'*

'It's true, I'd never heard of him, or of *Superstar* or *Evita* at that time,' John Hiseman admits now. In fact, it wasn't such a blind spot. *Evita* was in rehearsal but in late 1977 it still had to be shown. Also the tight, inward-looking world of jazz-rock to which John's group, Colosseum II (produced by Monty Babson of Morgan Studios), belonged was not well versed in mini-operatic works. The record Andrew had heard, 'Electric Savage', was a representative sample of art-style improvization, involving instrumental solos and, wherever possible, themes. Its novelty lay more in the extensive use of synthesizers and very bravura drumming than in anything even vaguely connected with musical theatre.

From where Andrew stood the need for an individually

talented group who could sit in on sessions, which might begin with little more than a thin melody line and develop them using their own ideas and enthusiasm, was now becoming vital. Problems of working with Tim and others had pointed up the urgent necessity for engaging his own team. He was being called on to produce more and more, and given freedom to do so. The frustrating paradox was that he could do nothing alone. The composer of musicals, as he constantly stresses, is not a one-man band.

His first meeting with John Hiseman settled at least one major aspect of this. 'I went to his flat,' the drummer recalls, 'and he romanced on the piano for about an hour. It seemed he had almost a complete score. By the end I was in a state of semi-shock. I just knew we had to get involved.'

Hiseman called his group together and put it to them. 'Don't laugh,' he warned. 'There's this character, Andrew Lloyd Webber, wanting us to help him play around with his musical ideas, and from what I've seen of his work he's astonishing. How do you feel?'

Nobody felt anything. With the result that since then, whenever Andrew has wanted to work out a piece of music or fit a tune to a particular moment in one of his shows, he has had the whole enthusiastic support of the group. It includes John's wife, the saxophonist Barbara Thompson, Rod Argent on keyboard, and instrumentalists John Mole, Gary Moore and Don Airey.

The piece Andrew played over at the first meeting was not, in fact, intended for theatre. It was his own 'Variations on a Theme of Paganini', written largely for his brother Julian. It is an odd story. Apparently Andrew was so dejected by the poor showing of Leyton Orient in the Football League tables that year that he made a bet with Julian that they would be relegated from their Second Division position. 'If they're not,' he promised, 'I'll write a piece for you, featuring your cello-playing.'

Evita finds its home in London's West End

Andrew and Tim in perfect harmony – but for how long?

Evita goes into rehearsal: Andrew checks finer points with director Hal Prince and Elaine Paige

Andrew and Tim, with their manager David Land, watch *Evita* take shape

Evita stars, Elaine Paige and David Essex, in rehearsal in London

On Broadway, Evita is played by Patti Lupone, with Bob Gunton as Peron

Andrew and Valerie Eliot, with a copy of her late husband's *Old Possum's Book of Practical Cats*

BELOW: *Cats* in rehearsal: Andrew with director Trevor Nunn and choreographer Gillian Lynne

BELOW RIGHT: Cameron Mackintosh, producer of *Cats*

With Elaine Paige at the *Cats* opening in London

The Broadway cast of *Cats* on their way to the Heaviside Layer, the cats' heaven

Bonnie Langford, Elaine Paige and Finola Hughes in the London show

Andrew cuts his 34th-birthday cake, watched by first wife Sarah (left) and singer Marti Webb

Longtime fans of the Everly Brothers, Andrew and his brother Julian enjoy meeting Don (left) and Phil (right) during their London concert in late 1982

At Heathrow airport, en route to New York, Andrew announces surprise marriage plans with singer and dancer Sarah Brightman

Andrew buys the Palace Theatre, London, to launch a new chapter in his career

In his first independent production, *Daisy Pulls It Off*, Andrew enjoys a ragging from the cast

Orient fortunately managed to scrape through (though by one point only). But if Andrew lost his bet, Julian and posterity received a valuable musical settlement. 'Variations' gave John Hiseman and his group, as well as Julian, a rich medley of solo instrumental opportunities. It was recorded early in 1978 after a triumphal workshop performance (alongside an early version of *Cats*) at Andrew's second Sydmonton Festival. By February it was at Number Three in the charts.

Only days before, it had been performed on television in the London Weekend 'South Bank Show', and not only was it awarded a golden disc for this success but also lastingly retained as the show's theme music. Andrew regards it as his favourite work 'for reasons which I can never explain' though they are by no means hard to understand. The piece is like the music of *Superstar* in its straightforward continuity. It moves from one variation to the next in an unbroken line.

John Hiseman's first encounter was followed by a call from David Land, at that time still managing Andrew's interests. 'Can you help?' the drummer was asked. 'Andrew needs a sax player who can double on tenor and alto, play equally well on flute and alto flute, and who must be able to play jazz-rock and sight-read music.' It was a tall order, but John's wife Barbara was classically trained and a brilliant saxophonist. She became a featured soloist with Julian on the record.

It took two weeks of concentrated eight-hour sessions in Babson's Morgan Studios at Willesden – where such famous names as Mick Jagger, Rod Stewart and Beatles John Lennon and Paul McCartney have recorded – to make 'Variations' into the monument it has become. The record ranks among the finest post-war British compositions. Andrew tries to pass this off with his usual modesty –'I think it's got some quite amusing variations within it' – but he has to admit that it is outstanding in a number of ways apart from selling more than any of his other records. And he does allow that 'purely as a piece of plastic, it is probably the best I've ever made'.

As he explains: 'It really was brilliantly performed. There is *nobody* on it one could have replaced, or done any more with.' And in this vein Andrew admits that a record which, as Hiseman proudly recalls, 'got to number two in the charts, and all but knocked Abba out of the number one spot', must possess unique qualities.

'Well, it would certainly be jolly awkward to equal anything as well played as that,' he says. 'And with a bunch of musicians at that particular point whose whole idea was that they should not just be background. This was a piece for six virtuoso performers, and the astonishing thing was how everything came together and succeeded, in spite of it being wholly uncommercial!' He laughs at the recollection, then says gravely: 'I mean, England is the only country at all where you could have a success with it.' Yet in the States, where he and Julian performed 'Variations' in Los Angeles and New York in concerts, it was well received.

So the lost wager became a flower in the British musical crown; or more accurately a bud, since its full flowering only came with the use of 'Variations' in Andrew's later work, his vocal and visual entertainment which he aptly calls *Song and Dance*, and in which Wayne Sleep danced to this music. Its use then had a curious history which linked it closely with Andrew's *Cats*.

At the presentation of awards to *Evita* by the Society of West End Theatre Awards, one of Britain's youngest and most successful producers, Cameron Mackintosh, was handling the production of winning excerpts for BBC television. That night Cameron, for all his considerable experience and talent (with, for example, *My Fair Lady*, *Godspell*, *Side by Side with Sondheim*), was having trouble.

Evita was the cause. 'For some reason they – the *Evita* company management – didn't want to do what I wanted them to do, which was to perform only the hit-song "Don't Cry For Me, Argentina". I wanted that because it was simple to set, needing only one microphone, but they wouldn't have it. They wanted a sort of medley which took at least eight microphones and had very tricky sound problems all round. Added to which, everybody concerned kept changing their minds.'

Mackintosh is a mercurial young man who enjoys his active life to the full. Problems of this sort were not uncommon to him after producing some 150 shows, among them successful revivals of *Oliver!*, *Oklahoma* and *The Pirates of Penzance*. But as he ruefully recalls: 'It wasn't the happiest evening of my life and I did drink a slightly more than sufficient amount of claret to sustain me. Andrew didn't help either. He plainly didn't like the result, and I suffered from quite a few of his jibes.'

One insurmountable difficulty was the place they were working in, a hotel ballroom. 'It had the atmosphere more of a village hall than a theatre,' Mackintosh remembers, 'and I felt that in the circumstances the show was the best anybody could have put together. But Andrew made no allowances at all for this, and one remark he made really stung me. "*Evita*," he said scornfully, "only became a great show because it had one of the world's greatest directors, Hal Prince, directing it. *That's exactly what this cabaret needed tonight!*"'

The producer's recollection is that this upset him so much that later, when the cameras had stopped turning and the show was over, he needed all his self-control not to accost Andrew and demand an apology. He vaguely believes he may even have got as far as threatening physical assault, but as the wine by then had flowed even more and it was well after midnight when Cameron finally got himself out of the place and into a taxi, nobody is quite sure if anything of the sort actually took place.

Something must have reminded Andrew next morning that he had inadvertently distressed a producer who was only trying to carry out a very difficult assignment, because a few days after the event he wrote to Cameron saying that 'he had meant nothing personal' by his remark. This, had the producer realized it, was the most convincing evidence of Andrew's feelings since he claims never to write letters, and certainly does so as little as possible. 'Anyway, it was a very nice letter,' Mackintosh says, 'and much later his secretary rang completely out of the blue and said Andrew would like to meet me and would I lunch with him at his London club, the Savile.'

At that lunch, on a bleak January day in 1980, Cameron and Andrew discovered a mutual collection of interests, from good wine to bad theatre directors. 'We bemoaned the lack of expertise among the British directors we both knew,' Cameron recalls, 'and I suggested Trevor Nunn, whose work I admired enormously, as the exception. Andrew had had a very good association with Hal Prince which had shown him how good the Americans could be, but he agreed with me about Trevor. And we talked about the possibility of getting him interested in Andrew's then only notional production of *Cats*.'

Through the choreographer Gillian Lynne, Cameron had already met Nunn and offered to sound him out. As he says: 'I could see that *Cats* was no ordinary show. It was going to need a team all of whom would have to share Andrew's enthusiasm for it to the limit. It had got to me all right, and I saw that it was the kind of thing that Trevor, and probably Gillian too, would be just right for if they'd do it. So I agreed to try.'

Trevor Nunn had never directed a musical, and as the distinguished and eminent director of the Royal Shakespeare Company (destined to inhabit the new Barbican Centre then in preparation) it was unlikely that any popular musical would have appealed to his talents. This notion, combining as it did the words of a great poet, T. S. Eliot, with the music of Britain's most successful and promising young theatrical composer just might attract him, Cameron believed. But when the idea was put to him Nunn was anything but sure. 'He took a long time making up his mind,' Cameron says. 'And I clearly remember the decision to take it on. We were standing in the street outside Joe Allen's where we'd had lunch. Suddenly Trevor said, "All right, I'll do it." It was a great moment.'

It was also the start of a great reward for a most unlikely theatrical idea and the courage and tenacity Andrew Lloyd Webber had shown in clinging to it and developing it through all its stages. Andrew can look back on it now with a well-merited sense of accomplishment. At the time it was often closer to a sick headache.

'It really started as an academic exercise,' he explains. 'Would you believe, I was very intrigued to know if I could set pure verse rather than lines written for my music, or by a lyricist with music in mind. I have, you see, a very sort of Victorian work ethic, which means that I am constantly looking for things to do which I haven't tried my hand at before. I remembered the *Cats* book from when I was a kid, and I knew it was witty, funny and definitely lyrical, because Eliot shows his Americanism every other minute in the book – I mean quite a lot of the lines aren't exactly written by your actual English poet, they're by an American writing in an English style.'

As early as 1975 Andrew was playing around with these lines, working at odd moments on music to express their magical quality. 'I did most of it in my London flat in the evenings, when people came back late with me and we'd sing round the piano, that sort of thing. Then I'd ask:

"What do you think?" They seemed to like them, which was encouraging.'

And at the Sydmonton Festival Andrew saw the thing grow. 'Eventually, I ended up setting the whole book, but of course that only produced a sort of anthology album, on the lines of "Tell Me On A Sunday", which might have been quite fun for television but would never have gone in a theatre. Then Valerie Eliot arrived.'

She changed everything. Andrew had invited the poet's widow to the Festival without any idea that she would bring with her a scenario by her late husband which widened the whole concept of Grizabella and was not in the book at all. 'I remember her coming in on that Saturday morning, when I was doing all the pieces all the way through just as an anthology, and saying "oh, by the way, there is this". She gave it to me and I was pole-axed!'

Andrew had the rest of the Festival to get through but he could think of nothing but the terrific impact of Valerie Eliot's gift. 'I realized she had given me a piece of gold,' he says. 'I was like a zombie, just thinking what it meant. Because what she had given me was a complete link between the cat world of Old Possum – which everyone thinks is a sort of off-duty Eliot in a way – and the whole central body of everything he'd ever written.'

Trevor Nunn had to be told without delay. 'I just crammed my fingers into the dial and called him to come down and see what I'd got as fast as he possibly could. I remember saying "Listen, I think you really must come and read this because it makes all the difference. This gives us what we need to make a musical for the theatre." And he did come down, and of course saw it right away.'

Even so, Trevor's decision to take time off from the prestigious Royal Shakespeare Company for a still hazardous and eccentric commercial musical was a big step which he spent some time making. As Andrew says now, admiringly: 'In hindsight it was a much bigger step than it looked at the time. But thank heavens he took it, and then followed the famous six months in which I was literally scratching around London for the money.'

At the Savile lunch with Cameron Mackintosh 'Variations' had been very much in Andrew's mind, but in loose association with *Cats*. He had yet to link it with the other half of *Song and Dance*, his wholly different creation of songs about an English girl and her American lovers. To Cameron, he had talked happily about the success of this music which, under the title of one of the tunes, 'Tell Me On A Sunday', had just been performed by singer Marti Webb on BBC television and was about to be given the extraordinary privilege of a repeat showing within weeks of the original broadcast.

'It became fairly obvious, fast, that Andrew wasn't having any success with trying to make a double bill of *Cats* and "Variations" into a show for theatre,' Mackintosh recalls. 'We did try, and everyone we approached in England and America turned it down. Andrew's idea was to blend "Variations" in a first-half dancing show, with maybe a troupe of dancers and a narrator taking over in the second half and performing *Cats*, which he'd already scored and tried out at his Festival in the country. Nobody wanted it.'

The songs sung by Marti Webb were another thing altogether. 'Tell Me On A Sunday' was an instant hit record for her and was soon followed by another from the medley, 'Come Back With The Same Look In Your Eyes'. A major film company was interested in filling out the romantic theme, using Andrew's music. The very moving and touching words were by the Oscar-winning lyricist of 'Born Free' and many hit songs, Don Black, and he too was keen to see the piece expanded. The problem was how to make what was essentially a cabaret repertoire into a musical play, and neither Andrew nor Don Black nor even the fertile mind of Cameron Mackintosh could fathom that.

In one way Andrew had overshot himself. The idea he'd originally had for 'Tell Me On A Sunday' had come out of a desire to write something for a one-woman performer. Tim Rice had tried to interest him in putting together a television special for Elaine Paige, but that idea seemed to Andrew to fall down because, as he says, 'It wouldn't have been a complete piece in its own right.' It was a chance meeting with Don Black while he was in America pre-working the New York production of *Evita* (which opened at the Broadway Theater on 25 September 1979 that settled the matter.

'Don is one of those lyricists who do a lot of their thinking from a title. He said something to me like "Come back with the same look in your eyes", and I thought immediately, "What a great title!" So I wrote the song and he wrote words for it. Then I told him I'd had this idea for a long time, about an English girl who had all these love affairs in New York or California, I wasn't sure where at that stage. Don had lived in the States for years and he picked up the resonances.'

The next question was who would or could do it. 'There was talk about Marti, because she was going into *Evita* but only to do two performances a week, doing the stuff that Elaine couldn't – which meant she would be free for us if we wanted her. I suggested we let her try it out, and we did and it worked *wildly* better than we'd originally thought. We did it at my Festival and the performance there was about 90 per cent the same as the one the BBC did.

'And the funny thing was that when they broadcast it at something like 10.30 on a Tuesday evening, without any publicity, nobody at the BBC really rated it. But the day afterwards they held their Music Planning meeting. My piece had had great reviews, so questions were asked. As a result they re-ran it at a peak hour on a Sunday, and we were given the marvellous opportunity of having it shown twice in such a short space of time. It was so obviously a piece that would work, but what was the most important thing to me was that it showed I could do something – this sympathetic piece about a girl – which was really small scale. That was what I found gratifying.'

He still had no conception of the revolutionary use of the song-cycle in *Song and Dance*. That, as Cameron remembers, arose out of a transatlantic voyage they made together on the liner *Queen Elizabeth II*. 'We were both locked up in the ship,' the producer says, 'and we came out with the idea of putting basically two shows together, Marti in the first half singing the "Tell Me" songs and Wayne in the second half dancing to "Variations". That was when I first saw what a marvellous marriage we made together, in theatrical terms. Andrew is the most talented man I shall ever work with in my life, I know that.'

This solved the old problem of fitting Andrew's *Cats* idea and the 'Variations' music into the same show, which nobody had been able to visualize. 'Between us we'd approached all the major people in the States and a number in Britain about it. The response was always much the same, but not because they didn't go along with "Variations",' Cameron explains. 'Actually, they thought that might be rather exciting. But, as they said, who would want to see a show about pussycats?'

To judge by the solid bookings, the long queues, and the tremendous pile of dollars which poured into the New York advance booking office when *Cats* opened there, not a few. Cameron had never doubted. 'I just felt in my gut that there was something extraordinary there, and in the music (although at this point there was no "Memory" – that came later). Andrew works like an onion, he just builds things up in layers.'

An onion, but no vegetable. While the threads of *Song and Dance* were coming together in his mind he was agonizing over whether *Cats* should be a major work, like *Evita*, or a much smaller show for children. He even toyed with the notion of including puppy-dogs – having heard that Eliot's 'pollicle dogs and jellicle cats' had originated in the inability of a young niece of the poet to say clearly 'poor little dogs and dear little cats'. Only when Valerie Eliot brought him that wonderfully exciting new material did the concept emerge in its final form as a vehicle for some of his most thrilling music.

Yet one obstacle remained, and it was a daunting one. Where to stage *Cats* – which could not possibly be performed in a conventional theatre without altering the entire architectural structure of the place?

16

The Sound of Andrew

WRAPPED in thought about this fundamental problem, Andrew was in no mood to take the call from Thames TV requesting his urgent presence at the New London Theatre for final work on some music of his which was to be screened. He went along on that evening of 4 November 1980 unaware that the rendezvous was a ruse, that he was to be put through the embarrassing if flattering ordeal of featuring in Eamonn Andrews' long-running *This is Your Life*. Had he known, he probably would have ducked it.

Instead, he went through the motions, as invariably he goes through all public appearances – with every faculty tensed to avoid saying anything in haste or folly. Only his eyes showed the surprise he felt, but the show was bland and innocuous enough, revealing little of the man behind the celebrity persona. It is interesting to learn that his own thoughts were barely with it, or its many touching reunions.

He was appraising the hall.

Here he was, in a theatre, the New London, which miraculously seemed to offer exactly the right specifics for *Cats*: a broad open stage which, by conventional proscenium standards, was virtually 'in the round' in that it allowed the audience to become part of the play. Immediately the show ended and he could release himself from the warm exchanges and encounters it encouraged, Andrew telephoned Cameron Mackintosh.

'I've got it!' he cried in great excitement. 'This is the ideal theatre for *Cats*. Look, this could be marvellous, and I want you to come and see it and tell me if you don't agree with me.' Cameron, once he had seen it, did agree. He passed on the good news to Trevor Nunn and his RSC designer, John Napier. 'If you can come up with a design to fit, then I think we're in business,' he said.

The one drawback from Cameron's point of view was the unhappy history of the place. 'The New London had never been particularly lucky,' he explains. 'And this weighed with Andrew and me. Call it superstition or what you like, but in the theatre these are factors one takes into account. I was, shall we say, uneasy about its choice.'

But not so uneasy that when Napier and Nunn produced a scale model of the *Cats* set, the fantastic rubbish dump and ambitiously soaring elevator to 'the heaviside layer' from the centre of the stage – a feat since performed nightly with total indifference – he failed to be convinced that Andrew's aims could be realized.

That was before the upsetting news that the theatre management had decided against letting them use it for the show. 'They didn't want *Cats* or anything else there,' Cameron remembers. 'All they did want was to return the theatre to being a conference centre, because that seemed to them to guarantee much more reliable business than a show about pussycats.'

This bombshell hit them in January, with the show due to open in April. Trevor Nunn was committed to return to work for the RSC in May, as was John Napier. If they couldn't get into production by February, the whole idea seemed doomed.

'There were some extraordinary toings and froings then,' Cameron says. 'For two weeks we went through a succession of crisis meetings and emergency planning sessions. There was just no way we could redesign the show for a proscenium theatre unless we had at least another month or two to do it in. We made a few tries at adapting it for the Prince of Wales, but these too had to be abandoned. In the end we had to face the fact that it was the New London or nothing.'

It was at this point that a powerful ally joined them in the shape of impresario Lord Delfont, and in Andrew's opinion he saved the show from extinction. 'Now of course it all seems so easy,' the composer says, 'but then it was frankly terrifying. The cost of it alone – a production nobody wanted to back because the idea still prevailed that no audience would sit through a childlike musical about a bunch of street cats – was absolutely frightening, and I was no millionaire then. As I've said, it would pretty nearly have ruined me if it hadn't worked.'

How it was made to work offers an insight into Andrew Lloyd Webber's personal style. Production of *Cats* against the odds set the hallmark for all that he has written and staged since his career began (with that first questionably 20-minute prep-school rendition of *Joseph and the Amazing Technicolor Dreamcoat* in March 1968). It had taken almost thirteen years. But by the time rehearsals finally began in earnest, and in an assured theatre, for the world and West End premiere of *Cats* in May 1981, Andrew had achieved more than any British composer of musical theatre in this century. He was just thirty-three.

It is tempting to compare such prodigious success with that of other musically gifted mortals, perhaps even with the young Wolfgang Mozart. Andrew had shown a similar ability to adapt the music of his time, from jazz-orientated rhythms and the strident beat of rock and reggae to serious operatic work. In the cautious opinion of distinguished musical contemporaries, his feeling for melody is exceptionally gifted, his mastery of theatrical effect extraordinary, and the use he makes of every known form of musical expression demonstrates a catholicity and adventurous courage which has become the Lloyd Webber keynote.

What an average audience senses, however, is the thrilling quality of Andrew's sound. He gets this by the most determined and concentrated use of technical aids. Andrew Bruce, who had designed much of the sound and lighting of his shows – doing both for *Evita* and *Cats*, and sound only for *Song and Dance*, following an outside tour of *Joseph* – learned early on that Andrew is a demon when it comes to perfection in all these departments. For example, he can detect the slightest falling off in quality of one body microphone in a stage full of prancing, singing dancers.

'He absorbs himself in the technology, very much so,' Bruce says. 'The drawback is that he never gives the opportunity to sit down with him and discuss the problems in detail, which I would relish doing. The only time I ever meet him is when we're sitting around in a group with the whole production team and obviously you can't go into technical detail then. A couple of times I have talked to him, at parties and so on. He knows quite a bit, but there's a level below which he doesn't understand the technical side at all. He just knows instinctively what he wants and expects people like me to get it for him.'

Bruce was not in New York when the veteran American sound expert, Abe Jacob, walked out of *Cats* a few days before the show opened on Broadway. But he values Jacob as a friend and knows something of what prompted the older man's decision to quit. The story casts an illuminating spotlight on Andrew's singleminded pursuit of excellence, which if not learned at Westminster certainly corresponds to that great school's teaching.

'I don't want to pry into what everybody is calling the "scandal of the century",' Bruce says, 'but we've worked with Abe for a long time, and I think he made a personal decision to get out when Andrew brought in another man, Martin Levan, to mix the sound. Andrew trusted Levan's ears to get him the sound he wanted.'

Levan, a talented young Englishman, was not allowed to touch the controls in New York because of union problems. He stood behind Jacob at his console and directed him. 'Martin is very intelligent and easy to get on with,' Andrew Bruce says. 'We worked together very well. But I think that, being that much older, Abe found it more difficult to accept the situation. You know, to be told when the big show is coming to your home town, "Look, I want to bring in somebody I trust" – implying "more than you" – that's a slap in the face to begin with.'

Bruce explains: 'The actual bust-up came, so I've gathered, when Abe had installed the orchestra in what was, basically, a sound-proof room which had the acoustics of a dead recording studio. Normally, this would have been just a try-out and there would have been several other shots at getting the thing right. But Andrew complained it was "too dead". He asked Abe to "liven it up a bit". And for some reason this upset Abe, and he quit.'

Almost certainly, that wasn't the whole story. There had been severe criticism of Abe Jacob's sound in *Evita* in an article in the influential *New York Times*. Andrew Bruce remembers that it had 'made Hal Prince, the director, very jittery'. As he says: 'That probably began it all, but anyway Abe's no fool and I think he'd planned to leave after *Cats* anyway. There are a fair number of people who don't like Abe's sound, which is very definitely American and not something I particularly care for myself. I've always thought we can do better and make it more natural, not so brassy. Abe's sound is very much Abe's sound and I think Andrew has gone away from that. For instance, in my opinion Abe's sound for *Cats* on Broadway didn't give the voices enough body, and the whole thing was too nasal and reedy in the wrong places.'

In technical terms, as Andrew Bruce explains: 'Ninety per cent of recognizable, intelligible speech and sung sound is in a very narrow band, actually between 500 and 3K [3,000 cycles]. That's where most of the information that you perceive and understand is, all the rest is gilding on the lily. So if you're worried about intelligibility you cut out all the gilding. You progressively cut it down until it is very intelligible, but doesn't sound very nice. And that's what a lot of the critics hate and I agree with them. I don't accept that that's the only way you can do it. We've got much more and better equipment these days, so there's really no excuse for using some of the techniques which were necessary in the past.'

Which may explain why Andrew sometimes prefers to rely on flexible and expert young helpers. It also underscores the difficulty he has occasionally encountered while working with established theatrical figures like Abe Jacob, who have their own way of doing things and are fully established in their own techniques.

'We had a serious problem in New York,' Andrew explains. 'It wasn't just that I wanted to ensure the thing was done my way, but Abe had put everyone into a kind of sound-proof room creating no possibility of any kind of live sound at all. His own assistant disagreed with this very strongly. But he insisted. If we weren't going to do it that way, he said, he actually didn't want to go on working on the production.'

Andrew has the greatest respect for artists of Abe Jacob's calibre and knows that such experts must be left to control things as they think fit. Jacob's reaction however took the decision out of his hands. 'We were a little bit dumbfounded,' he says, 'but in the end it worked out for the best. Because Martin [Levan] did take away all of that stuff, and he did it the way he knew I would like.'

For those who work closely with Andrew, this must be the all-important consideration. And it raises the question of how much support he would receive from the experts he depends on should any of his future productions run into disaster. His brother Julian's remark comes back: 'Andrew works best on his own.' Ray Holder, the dance arranger on *Evita* who fell out with Hal Prince, was more explicit: 'I find him very difficult to understand and work with . . . I had the feeling for the first time in twenty-five years in the profession that Andrew, the composer who had entrusted me with the dance arrangements – which meant taking music he'd written, often just a line of melody, and adapting and adjusting it to suit routines devised by the director – might not like, or use, my arrangements at the end of it all! It was a peculiar sensation, and certainly did not inspire great confidence!'

To sections of the press Andrew's insistence on his own standards has frequently seemed to be forging a dangerous rod for his back which one day – presumably if he should ever stumble – could bring much of the popular music press and large elements of Fleet Street down on his neck. 'The press view, generally, is that he owes them quite a lot,' a specialist writer explains. 'They've given him tremendous help over the years, yet he still holds himself aloof as if he owes nobody anything. It's all we can do to get him to pick up the phone.'

This same malcontent scoffs at what he sees as Andrew's 'naïve undervaluation' of the working press. 'No, he's not our favourite in this office by a long chalk, because he's always so inaccessible. And if you want to know why the music press doesn't like him then look at how he handles the arrangements he makes for them. When he was trying to buy the Old Vic theatre, for instance [Andrew offered £500,000 for it in June 1982, following an earlier bid he made for the Aldwych of £1,350,000 in January 1982], he did the surprising thing of announcing to three newspapers the price he was prepared to pay before the bids closed. So Edwin Mervish (the Canadian millionaire store and theatre owner who finally bought it) only had to better his offer by a hundred thousand and he'd got it!

'Andrew's advisers were furious. What did he do? To "put it right" he called a press conference and invited the music papers. The only trouble was he called it for nine-thirty in the morning, a time when few journalists – let alone music journalists and reporters who have probably been at concerts and so on until all hours the previous night – are not usually about. He then kept them waiting a whole hour before turning up himself at about half past ten, by which time the reception was somewhat cool!'

Andrew finally managed to achieve his aim to run a West End theatre when he bought the Palace in the summer of 1983 for £1,300,000, none of which he put up himself. It was a major step forward, giving him both the additional elbow-room he needed to try out and mount his own works as well as equipping him and his production company for other ventures. As Bob Swash, the independent producer who persuaded Robert Stigwood to back *Evita* (provided the money could be raised in the UK), comments: 'Andrew is no longer a composer, he's a producer.'

The Palace is a much-need arena. It extends rather than takes the place of Sydmonton, where Andrew's annual Festivals are still valued as private experimental occasions and an excellent way of getting reaction from people whose views and opinions he respects. A full-scale West End musical theatre stage and equipment allows him to develop fully. Opera is now within his grasp, as is any novelty, however extravagant, in musical invention.

The Palace may lack the large, all-purpose annexe of the Old Vic, but it is far more suited to his work than the

Aldwych. Andrew has found in the theatre a perfect maturity for the dreams once played out in his model theatre of boyhood.

But in September 1983 it was still housing his successful *Song and Dance* with no immediate prospect of his being able to move in and make the very considerable face-lift improvements and alterations which his ambitious plans call for. At Sydmonton, despite the chilly autumn weather, guests were treated to the musical score he had freshly written for a prospective new show, *Aspects of Love* (when not revelling in the warmed waters of Andrew's jaccuzzi). This simple love story from the novel by David Garnett, one of the latter-day Bloomsbury set, seemed particularly appropriate at a time in Andrew's life when romance of a more personal nature was self-evident. Following his divorce two months before, Sarah Brightman had taken her place beside him for the first time. As with the moving passages of his 'Tell Me On A Sunday' cycle, *Aspects of Love* had inspired some of Andrew's most deeply-felt music. And with Sarah singing the words of love which had been written for the occasion, Andrew was able to enjoy a rare fulfilment.

'Sydmonton is a way of life for me,' he says. 'I just have to keep it as a private place.' For this reason, like the royal family, he requires every member of the staff employed there (including those who work on the estate and grounds outside the house) to sign a document promising not to talk about his home, or whatever they may see there.

This is not because Andrew or his family are veiling doubtful secrets in their private lives. News of the jaccuzzi which he installed in 1981 and in which guests frolic at will, often with nubile dancers from his shows, may have led to gossip. But friends who know his home life vouch for the quiet, middle-class respectability of it all.

In his years with the first Sarah Lloyd Webber, the

houseparties were enjoyable relaxed affairs, and Andrew an excellent host. He would delight in playing over pieces from his shows, or new tunes which had come to him. His great love of wine and the fine cellar which, with the help of a knowledgeable friend and adviser (one of the Avery family of Bristol) he has acquired over the years, were a welcome feature of the dinners which his wife cooked with skill and imagination. The comfort and atmosphere of the place, with the children, Imogen and Nicholas, romping about, and Andrew taking video films or playing highly competitive board games – which he also invents – is remembered by all who have stayed under his roof with great pleasure. As his friend Robert Powell the actor says: 'It's just a very large home. You stagger down at whatever time you like in the morning and make your own tea. You just do your own thing.'

Powell and his dancer wife Barbara Lord share Andrew's passion for games and sometimes act as guinea-pigs for his more imaginative try-outs. 'He had us playing one he'd made up called "Insanity",' the actor remembers. 'We all started off in padded cells, and each lunatic had to try and make it to the gate and escape. Andrew thought that he'd ironed out all the bumps, but after about three hours of playing we were all still stuck in the funny-farm and the game never got off the ground.' However, in characteristic style, Andrew refused to let this failure suppress his inventive zeal.

'I have a fairly low level of boredom with games,' he confesses. 'I mean, I don't sit round playing long board games for ages like Alan Ayckbourn. But I do quite like dreaming up stupid ideas.' His latest to go into successful production is 'Calamity', which, he says, with an air of surprise, 'seems, I must say, to work.' To those who know him, the surprise would be if it didn't. As Robert Powell sums it up, 'He never does anything by halves, and is a terrific player. Knows all the rules, will always adjudicate in any dispute and, yes, he's very good, but absolutely ruthless. *Ab-so-lutely* ruthless at games!' At life, too, where making a success of his own ideas and designs is concerned.

The question now occupying the thoughts of those who know this and care about him is how Andrew's single-minded, often wilful, direction of his life will carry him to the goals he has yet to achieve.

17

At Odds with Tim

IT had not taken long for rumours of a split between Tim and Andrew to circulate, once it became clear that they had no joint work to offer after *Evita*. Like celebrity lovers, they were hounded by gossip-columnists and reporters seeking the roots of the trouble. A few stray hints were all that any of the reporters needed. One *Evening Standard* writer even resorted to the old cliché, beginning his piece: 'Tim Rice and Andrew Lloyd Webber would like to make it clear that they are still the best of friends.' Since nobody outside Fleet Street and the murkier depths of Tin Pan Alley had imagined anything other than that, the writer, Charles Catchpole, was well ahead of his field.

'There has been considerable speculation that the hit musical writers are about to go their separate ways,' he reported, hand on heart. Whence came these speculations he did not of course reveal. But the reasons for them trotted off his typewriter. 'Personality clashes,' he reported, adding for the innocent reader's benefit, 'the gossip columnists' euphemism for punch-ups'.

Catchpole further stated, though on whose authority it is hard now to assess, 'Rice readily admits that he doesn't always see eye to eye with the more intense composer Lloyd Webber,' adding: 'but then neither did Lennon and McCartney, or Gilbert and Sullivan.'

From Rice himself, the reporter had been given little

help in forming his view of a split. 'We have our differences. Who doesn't?' Tim was quoted as saying. 'But there's no rift. We are working closely together on the transfer of *Evita* to the States, and after that we'll be getting our heads together on a new project for next year.'

Two 'togethers' in one sentence, but still the intrepid Catchpole was not put off the scent of torn allegiances. 'The rumours,' he wrote, 'which started over reports of rows during rehearsals for *Evita*, were fuelled when it was learned that both were pursuing solo projects – Rice producing records and compiling a book on hit singles, Lloyd Webber working on a setting of *Old Possum's Book of Practical Cats* by T. S. Eliot.'

Yet the hounds of Fleet Street were not entirely off the scent. Derek Jewell, the critic who had given them their first public boost, was now a close friend. He witnessed friction between Tim and Andrew which he remembers as being at times 'intense'. 'At one stage I thought the break-up would be final, but then they got together again,' Jewell recalls. He puts the blame for it on a growing variance in their individual musical and theatrical tastes rather than any personal foibles.

'Andrew wants the Big Idea,' Jewell explains, 'and out of it he'll make the Big Musical. He also wants to build The British Musical Theatre and he wants to do it single-mindedly. That's what his search for his own theatre was based on, the desire to put on musicals – his and other people's – all year round.'

With Rice, he believes the objective is slighter. 'Tim is into pop,' he says. 'He'll knock off a lyric for somebody to do with a song as soon as get to work on a big score. It's largely *that*, as I see it, which has caused such falling out and friction as there is.' And Jewell, a shrewd and experienced observer, is not sanguine about the chances of Tim and Andrew working together again. 'It's closer to being final now than it was,' he says, 'for obvious reasons. One of them is off writing musicals with someone else [Andrew and Trevor Nunn], the other is doing his own things. And if you stay apart long enough, it gets harder and harder to get together.'

Which may or may not, as he says, keep them away indefinitely from concentration on the joint projects which once filled their whole screens. For instance Andrew's reliance on Tim was thrown into sharp relief during the final stages of preparation for *Cats*, in which Tim had up to then played no part at all.

Tim has since made no secret of his feelings at that particular moment. But the roots of the separation, the events which in retrospect seem to have damaged his relationship with Andrew, have stayed in the shadows. There are, as we will see, good reasons for this. What Trevor Nunn calls the 'hornets' nest' dilemma he found himself in while these events were unfolding would make a dramatic plot in its own right. He himself confesses to remaining mystified by some of its complexities.

'My whole connection with Andrew Lloyd Webber began much earlier,' he explains. 'You see, Cameron Mackintosh, the producer, was a friend of mine, as was Gillian Lynne. It was Cameron who wanted me to meet Andrew. They came to my office in the Barbican and we talked about the possibility of making a musical show out of "Tell Me On A Sunday", which Andrew had recorded and which he and Don Black had written.

'I made several proposals which Andrew later politely turned down. He afterwards told me he'd come to the conclusion that "it would make a better film". Frankly, I thought that was just a nice way of saying "I thought your ideas were dreadful!"

'So I was quite surprised when Cameron came back and asked if I'd like to talk to Andrew about another idea – of setting some of T. S. Eliot's cat poems to music. Cameron left an illustrated copy of the Possum book with me, and later on Andrew played me some of the pieces, which I also saw performed at his Sydmonton Festival.'

Nunn recalls his feeling of disappointment at this early unveiling. 'The pieces seemed to me very slight,' he says. 'And aimed at well brought up, heavily protected five-year-olds. Middle-brow, and very set, I thought – rather as if the main ingredient was Thomas the Tank Engine.'

Above all Nunn felt the lack of narrative. 'I wrote a long document to Andrew stressing this. I knew, you see, that Cameron wanted a great, big, expensive show. And I think Andrew believed that some of his best melodic creations had gone into it. I urged that the work should avoid being anthological, which in the theatre has only limited appeal. We needed, I said, something that would tie the material together and give it momentum, interest and interaction.'

Having written all this down, Nunn was fully aware that he was posing a huge problem. 'Because Eliot had never *intended* that,' he explains. 'Each of his Possum poems describes one cat; and usually in the third person, which is another problem for a musical. We see them, each of them, at one moment of activity, or one stage of perception. Here is one kind of cat, we're told – with maybe a couple of illustrations – and *that* is the purpose of the poem. Finish. Just like those figures on Keats's Grecian Urn which are locked, held there, for ever. They have no movement.'

Movement was what the director of the Royal Shakespeare Company felt was needed above all if the poems were to make a musical show. Neither fragmented nor unconnected, but an uninterrupted thread of linking sequences built around one central theme. Yet it had to be achieved *through* Eliot's poetry, and not superimposed on it. Also, all of the poems had to be included, so that nobody would feel that their favourite had been left out.

The problem was largely solved with the wholly unexpected advent of Valerie Eliot. When she arrived with her husband's subsequently discovered notes, indicating that another poem could have been added, there was suddenly, and magically, a climax to the story: the sad, poignant tale of Grizabella.

By now Trevor Nunn and Andrew had worked out a remarkable device for bringing all the cats in the Eliot poems together in one moonlit celebration, the Jellicle Ball. What this fresh ingredient so potently added was a cat who, at first shunned and rejected, is later brought back into the fold by her resurrection to Eliot's 'heaviside layer'. It instantly gave the piece a clear line and dramatic intensity which had hitherto been lacking.

As Nunn happily recalls: 'The jigsaw had at last come together. The present version of *Cats* had arrived.'

Without Grizabella, he says, 'there would have been no basis, no platform for the thing to stand on. There had to be a mythology which all of the cats, that is to say the actors playing them, could subscribe to – whether or not the audience understood it. There had to be a hieratic design and structure to what was going on between the cats. And Grizabella was the focal point.'

Still, the risk was enormous. 'I remember a number of occasions when I had to go and lock myself away, not have contact with anybody else,' Nunn says. 'So great was my terror about the undertaking that I feared passing it on to others. That has never happened to me before or since.'

As he says, 'When you know that there is a vast investment (and a vast expectation, because of Andrew) and that the ice is very, very thin, and you're trying to get people to commit themselves to notions that are tenuous and could easily be scoffed at, even laughed out of court, that is a time to tremble. That is what I *was* doing.'

He was still without an essential musical expression for

the new material. 'One could quite clearly see why Andrew's earlier works had succeeded,' he explains. 'They each had something that could best be described as the "Puccini ingredient" – one huge, sweeping, emotional song. This was absent from *Cats*.'

At first, Andrew did not think so. 'When I first mentioned it, he said, "Oh, but 'Old Deuteronomy' must be used in that way. That's the key tune, and you must use it." Well, it *is* a beautiful tune, absolutely lovely. But I couldn't see it as the essential ingredient I felt the show still needed.'

At this point Nunn's excitement over 'the Grizabella fragment' which Valerie Eliot had provided was mounting, as was Andrew's. But neither had realized its full potential. Nunn says, 'I remember saying to Andrew, "Look, Grizabella should have an utterance, don't you think? She must be the emotional climax of the show." It had suddenly hit me that we now had a candidate for a big emotional role, having been given the subject matter to support it. All it needed was a supercharged emotional song from Grizabella which would sum it all up.'

To his delight, forty-eight hours later Andrew came to him. 'How about this?' he asked. 'It's a tune I thought of some time ago and was saving for something else. Perhaps it could be right.'

Three or four people – the musical director, the show's arranger, and designer John Napier – were in the bare rehearsal room with them at that moment. Andrew went over and sat at the piano. Softly, he played the simple, moving notes of the song we now know as 'Memory'.

They were, Nunn declares, 'absolutely as they are today. Not a note has been changed.' As Andrew finished playing, Nunn turned to the others. 'I asked, "What is the date? The hour? *Remember* . . . because you have just heard a smash hit by Lloyd Webber."'

In his mind's ear, as in Andrew's, it was the perfect musical climax to the celebration, the deeply moving moment when the outcast Grizabella would utter her heartcry of loneliness and misery to the cats who had turned their backs on her, and with it win back their affection. The problem was that it was still only expressed in music. The words would need to be as close to those of T. S. Eliot as it was possible to make them.

'That really *was* a problem,' Nunn says. 'We tried out two lyric writers in succession, both of whom were capable of producing lyrics of beautiful pathos. It simply didn't work. The ingredient wasn't there, and what I knew to be Eliot's intention – to make the material an expression of cats rather than people – wasn't there either. We had to think again. And by now we were desperately short of time.'

What next happened was born almost entirely of desperation. Two weeks of rehearsals had gone by and Judi Dench, rehearsing the lead part of Grizabella, still had no words for her main song. 'As I understand it,' Nunn says, 'Andrew then phoned Tim and asked if he'd have a go at it. Tim said that it would really be better for him not to be involved. Of course, all kinds of construction can be put on that, but I choose to believe the simplest and cleanest: that Andrew was doing a show entirely based on the works of T. S. Eliot and it would be, to say the least, confusing if somebody of Tim's stature came in with merely "additional lyrics".

'Much better, I imagined, for Tim to leave Andrew to get on with this show on his own and then, perhaps, for the two of them to get back together later on and do another Tim Rice–Andrew Lloyd Webber show. This was how it seemed to me. And it was, I thought, perfectly understandable and straightforward from Tim's viewpoint.'

It did not, however, solve the problem. Andrew turned to Don Black, the lyric writer who had collaborated with him on the moving songs of 'Tell Me On A Sunday'. Nunn says: 'What Don came up with were things that fitted the tune perfectly, hot and strong. You know, very bold and good – *but very obviously*, unfortunately, in a different voice from the rest of the show.'

No good. Andrew then, Nunn believes, played the music over to Tim. He left a tape of it with him, then rang and asked if the lyricist had had second thoughts. And, once again, Tim declined to get involved. According to Nunn, he told Andrew he 'would rather pass on it'.

A vital extra week-and-a-half had slipped away. It was now, in Trevor Nunn's recollection, 'a moment of absolute desperation'. A time so critical that he decided to abandon the attempt to teach others the style and feeling of Eliot's verse until he had completely absorbed it himself.

'Fortunately, I happened to be alone that weekend in my house in Hampstead, London. I cleared all engagements and took the phone off the hook. Then I took down my copy of *The Collected Verse of T. S. Eliot* and read them from cover to cover, twice. It took something like six hours, because I gave it a really close reading.'

By that evening Trevor Nunn was surfeited with Eliot's style and meaning. His head reeled with the poet's images. He then asked himself a fundamental question. How, and where, would the unwritten fragment of Grizabella and her plight have fitted into the scheme of the Possum stories *if Eliot had placed her there?*

'I closed my eyes,' he says. 'The one idea that came straight out of that day's reading was "memory". Eliot had shown that, by it, we are all connected to our past. It *makes* us. I saw that it had inspired him in his writing of the Quartets and of the Prufrock period. Indeed, in his "Rhapsody on a Windy Night" there is just the one word "memory", and a section beneath it. Of course, that has nothing whatever to do with the lyric of "Memory", but that's where it started.'

Nunn had written lyrics many times before. Now he wrote down just what he felt. At least, he thought, it would be a guide for some more competent lyricist to follow. And he gave his lyric the title of the theme he had discovered: 'Memory'.

Apart from the second middle section, he says, the words remain today as they were then. Entirely without realizing it, he had composed the hit song which was to be recorded by some of the world's leading singers.

He says: 'The following morning I took it to Andrew and told him: "This may help us to break the deadlock." He took it to the piano and played it. "My God," he said, "you've done it. You've absolutely done it. That's it!" It was, of course, a very exciting moment for me.'

Indeed, Nunn had every reason to be delighted. 'My lyric served the show,' he says. 'I could make it resonate. Tie it in with the rest of the plot. Also, it was full of Eliot ideas – if not in the actual phrases, at least in the themes.'

Unfortunately, Judi Dench, who was to sing it, had been taken to hospital with a seriously damaged Achilles tendon. There was no one to rehearse the song. Trevor Nunn and Andrew were forced to await her return, with her limb in plaster, before the saga of 'Memory's' birth could be completed.

'We now had just a bare three weeks before opening,' Nunn recalls. 'We'd had a copy of the lyric sent to Judi in the hospital, so she'd learnt the words. When she at last hobbled into the theatre it was a wonderfully moving moment for me.'

But a sadly short-lived one. 'Judi is no great singer,' he says. 'What she *is* is a heart-breaker. And on that occasion – in the absolutely deserted theatre where I heard her sing

"Memory" for the first time – it was *tremendously* moving.'

Could she, however, face an actual performance? In plaster, and with a song she had only just learnt, Judi was at a terrible disadvantage. 'She was going to try and do it,' Nunn says. 'We'd scheduled a band call for her. Then she collapsed.'

The injured star was trying to walk across the moonlit set with the help of a stick when she slipped and fell. 'She pitched off one of the ramps into the stalls, damaging her back and jaw,' Nunn says. 'But what really broke was her spirit. She just couldn't go on.'

Twenty-four hours later at a crisis meeting Elaine Paige was frenziedly proposed as a replacement. Her professionalism was well known. If anybody was capable of stepping into the lead role at such short notice, she was. Trevor Nunn took the *Evita* star to dinner that night.

'She had only one question,' he says. 'She wanted to know: "What about this song?" So I wrote it out for her, because stupidly I'd forgotten to bring a copy with me. I just jotted it down on a napkin. Then I tried to explain what was happening, the situation around it.'

Elaine, he knew, was facing an uphill task. 'Just like those earlier lyricists,' he says. 'She was being asked to go into a show she really knew nothing about. With a lyric which seemed to have no connection with anything, and may not have sounded at all like a hit lyric to her.'

At this point Trevor Nunn picks his words with care. His dilemma is obvious. The clash which, had he been able to do so he would have done almost anything to avoid, was almost upon him.

'Next day,' he says, 'I was astonished to hear from Andrew that Tim had changed his mind. He'd decided he would like to have a go at the song, after all. How did I feel? Well, of course I was disappointed, having got so far. But I like to think I was stoic about it. I did recognize that if there was a possibility of Tim coming up with something very much better, then it had to be embraced.'

Stoic is hardly the word. For Nunn, the dream of writing a lyric for an Andrew Lloyd Webber song, one which was to be the pivot of his latest show, was something he never had fully believed could come to reality. 'I guess it's just human to have felt as I did,' he admits. 'After all, I had been enjoying a kind of extra-special excitement.'

And Nunn had no idea why Tim had changed his mind. Elaine was closer to him than anyone in the company. Had she appealed to him? Had she felt, after that first evening, that the words he had scribbled were lacking some quality which only her friend could give to the song?

'It was, of course, perfectly possible,' Nunn admits. 'Elaine, being friends with Tim, *may* have talked to him about it after our dinner together, I don't know. All I do know is that the next morning after Andrew told me Tim had changed his mind, his lyric turned up. I understand that he'd spent just one evening thinking about it. Or one late night. Only one period of time, anyway.'

Nunn implored Andrew: 'Please, for God's sake, talk to Tim about the place of the song in the show. The way it has *got* to connect up. Do tell him the story, so that we don't get back into the previous territory, with something that is not going to seem to be part of the texture of the show.'

So far as he knows, Andrew had done just that.

But, to the director's disappointment, the lyric Rice had written did not seem to reflect this. In Nunn's judgement it was a fine lyric, but 'a number of phrases in it were completely un-catlike,' he says. 'They could only be sung by a woman, not a cat.'

Nevertheless, he immediately began rehearsals with Elaine. 'There was now only a day and a half before she would have to go before the public,' he explains. 'So absolutely no time was left for arguing, or posturing.'

And there was, in fact, only one thing left for him to do. 'I talked to Tim,' Nunn says. 'I told him "Your first version is *very* hopeful. But can I *beg* you to amend one or two things?" From any director, it would have been a normal request. Nunn says he did his best to communicate his reasons.

'Basically,' he says, 'Tim's lyric had Grizabella saying "I'm going off to commit suicide." Now, I don't think you can do that with Eliot. I don't think you can suggest that Eliot would have climaxed the show with a cat going off to finish it all. Temperamentally, atmospherically, you can suggest it. Sub-textually you can indicate it. But I don't believe you can be explicit.'

As he tried to explain to Tim, the un-feline parts of the lyric were being beautifully sung by Elaine – but *as a woman, not as a cat.* 'It was too un-ambiguous,' he says, 'and the previous lyric didn't have that problem. Dispassionately, I had to accept that it had actually got into precisely the ambiguous area that the song, and the show, needed.'

And Tim did listen. But, as Nunn sadly recalls, 'I don't know for what reason, but the next day the reply came back that Tim had looked at it and didn't think that it was necessary to amend anything. He wasn't prepared to make any changes.'

Nunn now admits: 'I don't think I've ever been in a more complicated moral position. In one sense, you see, I felt passionately responsible towards the show: towards Eliot and what we were doing with his material. Equally, though, I could see quite clearly that there was a kind of morally questionable factor in my taking that stance. As director, I had found a piece of material inadequate and wanted it to go – while reinstating my own work in its place!

'Everybody *knew* I was the alternative lyricist. And *I* knew it as well. How much, I had to ask myself, had it coloured my attitude? Because, of course, there was some degree of . . . well, hurt is too strong a word, but certainly involvement, on my part.

He decided to make a set of literary-critical comparisons of the two lyrics, side by side. He says: 'I forced myself through it, put myself through the mangle. I mean, I knew that there was absolutely no point in changing to something, or in changing back to something, for reasons of personal gratification or self-glorification.

'But if the show was going to be better with one than with the other, then I'd *got* to face it. I tried to think of my lyric, to assess it, as if it had been written by somebody else. The conclusion I reached was that unless changes, and considerable changes, were made to Tim's piece – written in something of a hurry, I thought (though understandably so) – unless *some* revision was done, then the previous lyric served the show better.

'What could I do? I didn't want to involve Andrew. That would have been too invidious. The only possible thing was to talk to the producer, Cameron. I asked him not to protect me in any way. If he thought Tim's stuff was better, both in terms of content and commerciality, then I would accept his decision.'

Nunn says Cameron told him that he, Nunn, had made the right decision. In the producer's judgement, the new version was not as 'interlocked in the show'. However, Cameron wanted to put the matter to Andrew before any final decision was taken.

Nunn says: 'I don't know in what terms he did that. But quite soon afterwards Andrew, I think, told Tim that he was very grateful for the version that he had attempted, but that he wanted to stay with what was previously there.'

With the opening set for 11 May 1981 now only days away, the decision unquestionably had had to be made. At whatever cost. But now the delicacy of the situation was massively increased by the fact that Elaine – Tim's acknowledged lady friend, and reportedly longstanding romantic attachment – was the singer of the song. And all her work thus far had been in rehearsing the words of *Tim's rejected lyric.*

Nunn says: 'It was, of course, terribly difficult for her. She had learnt the one version, Tim's, and wasn't particularly keen to learn another. I suspect, too, that she wasn't altogether alive to the minutiae of whether the thing was Eliot-like, or even whether that mattered. Also, she was naturally loyal to Tim.'

Perhaps this, more than anything else, affected her feelings. A professional artist, for whom the show always comes first, no ordinary setback would have stopped Elaine Paige giving, as she did, a most triumphant opening-night performance. But Trevor Nunn – perhaps alone – noticed how she accidentally switched back to Tim's lyric halfway through, on the night of the change-over. As he says: 'Whatever she felt, the point is that she sang the song and recorded it wonderfully. Absolutely wonderfully. My admiration for her is huge.'

He denies any knowledge of gossip suggesting that Elaine threatened to quit the show after the lyrics were changed. 'If it *was* the case, it was certainly never communicated to me,' he says. 'And it wasn't apparent in any way that I could detect. What I do know is that, whenever we had to work together, she was a hundred per cent behind whatever decision I made. Unspokenly, it must have been immensely difficult for her.'

Yet others who know the star believe that she was deeply torn by Tim's rejection, far more so than by the professional difficulty of having to adjust to a completely fresh set of words. 'Andrew's manager, Brian Brolly, spent hours with her that night, trying to explain matters,' a friend says. 'In the end it was Tim himself who had to persuade her.'

And understandably, in Tim, the blow has left lingering bitterness. Perhaps he never shared Trevor's intimate and scholarly understanding of T. S. Eliot's inner meanings. The lyric he had written (according to a composer friend, 'in one concentrated spasm of creative energy, finishing at four in the morning') is soaringly beautiful. It begins:

> Streetlights, and the darkness between them,
> Like the good and the bad sides, of a life almost done.
> Shake the memory of my passions returning to me:
> None forgotten, no not one.

And a later chorus carries the heart-cry:

> Don't look back, no, don't look back;
> So hard to heed, that warning;
> So much temptation, but the past is past . . .'

If Tim had been grieving, with Grizabella, the lost glories of his past – including the great days with Andrew – he could hardly have put it better.

Tim Rice has since talked with sadness of his lyric's rejection. How long he will retain its hurt depends on his own powers of recovery. But to have received the wound at the hands, so to speak, of a rival writer has left a stinging memory of its own, one likely to last a long time if the anger he has publicly expressed is a measure of its power.

Yet in Andrew's situation, as in that of Trevor Nunn, the Solomon-like decision taken was absolutely necessary. Even though it involved rejecting work by his most valued partner, and the writer he wishes above all to rejoin in future works, Andrew had no way of ducking it. No possible alternative. His explanation is not a defence or an attempt to excuse his way out of a situation which has since been chewed over, and not always to his advantage, wherever his and

Tim's names have cropped up. In his own words, it is simply this:

'The position on *Cats* and "Memory" is that Tim never wanted to have anything to do with it whatsoever. He thought it was a rotten idea, so far as I can understand. We'd asked him first off, when we realized that we had access to those additional pieces of material by Eliot, whether or not he'd be interested in completing the missing links for us. He more or less said he had "no interest in it whatsoever" – you know – "no!".'

Andrew's disappointment was understandable, but it was not the end of the story. As he goes on to say: 'Then at very short notice before the opening, Elaine Paige came into the production and Tim changed his mind. He said, "Yes, I'd be interested in helping out with the lyric of 'Memory'" – to see if he could do anything with it.'

But once again, as in the still unexplained case of Anthony Bowles's sacking, Andrew feels he lacked responsibility for the events leading up to Tim's vain work on the lyric and the rejection of the lyric itself. It was out of his hands.

'Trevor Nunn was the director of the show and therefore the only arbiter of decision,' he explains. 'Whatever I may feel, once a director has been appointed he is in charge. He is the governor. And he *most certainly* is when you've got a girl in the show who's just taken over, when you've lost one of the most important actresses in the English theatre [Judi Dench] and when you've got to get the curtain up somehow by the Monday afterwards.'

None of which Tim, or any other experienced theatrical executive or artist, would disagree with. Andrew does not deny that Tim's lyric had quality. But a choice had to be made between the words Trevor Nunn had written and those Tim had sweated out, a choice which could only be made by Trevor himself as director, however invidiously.

'Trevor thought there was a lot to admire in what Tim wrote,' Andrew says now. 'He just didn't feel that it reflected the content of the show as a whole. And he knew that the story of Grizabella was crucial, it was the one element that *had* to be right – which in hindsight I absolutely agree with.'

The decision was no less painful for that. 'No, what Tim came up with was a very interesting lyric,' Andrew explains sadly, 'the trouble is it says something completely different from Trevor's central thesis. And Trevor was right to reject it as he had to do, because only he could take the decision at that point. Personally, I was probably incapable of making a judgement being wholly wrapped up in my music, but I'm sure he did the correct thing. And there's one thing that must be said – there was never any question of Trevor "muscling in" on the hit song, none at all.

'That song of mine was heard by Trevor, the music I'd written for it, oh, six months before. I remember he said at the time that for him it was the "the kernel of the whole show". But anyone who's ever worked with Trevor will tell you that he has only one interest: the good of the show. I have seen him when he's written a piece of work . . . well, let's say, that wasn't as good as someone else's. It happened once with Richard Stilgoe [the television presenter and entertainer who wrote additional lyrics for the show] during *Cats*. Stilgoe had written a lyric for the same song, and it was quite clear which was working better with the audience. Let me tell you, there wasn't even a moment's hesitation for Trevor. His was out: Stilgoe's was in.

'And the moment we put the Nunn lyric for "Memory" into *Cats* the audience was cheering! You know, standing on chairs. But of course that leads to a dangerous argument, which I'm sure Tim wouldn't want to get into, that "the words don't matter anyway". Because that's precisely the point Trevor is making: the words *do* matter.

It's not, you see, that Tim's words were in any way wrong, were bad, but they weren't right for the show. There was no way that, with three days to go to get the curtain up on the musical (with all our enemies rubbing their hands with glee that we weren't going to make the first preview at all!) that Trevor could possibly do anything other than take the decision he took.'

Andrew shakes his head sadly, since plainly the incident is still painful. 'I do feel quite strongly about it,' he says. 'Because it is a ludicrous thing to say that Tim bears me a grudge over this. He's far too professional for that. And it is a jolly good thing, in my opinion, that he has now done a musical [the Tim Rice-written musical *Blondel*] for the first time which was directly for the theatre. Because – put it the other way round – if he suddenly called me and said "Look, we're actually basing all this music on the works of Borodin, say, but we need you to knock off this tune . . ." And I came up with something that didn't reflect that, and at the very last minute – well, now that he's getting to know how this really works in the theatre, he'd have to turn it down. I mean, you can't expect somebody who's spent two years putting the thing together not to have the final say, can you?'

And in the future Andrew believes that Tim's fresh experience on the live stage may bring them together again. 'Now that he's worked with professional people of great calibre, and *Blondel* is a success, it's going to make it far more likely that there's going to be a proper collaboration – a real collaboration – between us. I don't want to sound pompous, but one *needs* to work on original shows for the theatre, as Tim is doing. This was a show that hadn't appeared on record or in some other form first, and that is an experience that cannot be anything but good in my view. I do feel much more strongly that there is a possibility now of Lloyd Webber and Rice working together again, if the right thing comes up for both of us.'

No doubt he does. But Tim Rice has yet to express anything quite so positive in public. Andrew says he and Tim spent two weekends in 1983 with Trevor Nunn to discuss Andrew's *Starlight Express* and possibly the next Lloyd Webber show, based on David Garnett's novel *Aspects of Love*. Curiously, the distinguished director was friendly at the time with Sharon Lee Hill, co-star of Rice's *Blondel* after her dancing role in Andrew's *Cats*. Even so Rice's comments in public since then suggest that it will take more than a couple of convivial weekends to bring them together again.

'We always have had our separate interests,' he told Charles Catchpole, 'and we need time apart to recharge our batteries.' To Simon Kinnersley of the *Daily Mail*, eighteen months after the London opening of *Evita*, Rice was more explicit. 'I think that, as people, we have grown apart. We've both got married, had families [Andrew's son Nicholas had been born six months before] and live totally independent lives. There's no point in working together in the same room if neither of you wants to.'

But it was unquestionably the rejection of his words for 'Memory' which rankled most deeply with the lyricist, and the *Mail*'s normally well-informed columnist, Nigel Dempster, crystallized the situation in May 1981 when he quoted 'a very disappointed Rice' bemoaning the rejection of his lyric for *Cats*. 'The fragile friendship,' Dempster wrote, '. . . has again been strained to breaking point.' Rice, he said, 'tells me that his work has been rejected and adds "I am upset because I thought what I had written was rather good. Andrew asked me for one lyric and I spent three days [not, as informants claim, only *one* night] hard slog on it. He [Andrew] looked at it and told me it wasn't up to scratch, however, and is now using lyrics done by someone else. It failed the driving test and got the Big

Elbow, but it's Andrew's show . . .""

As Tim had told a *Guardian* writer several weeks before the show's West End opening, Andrew worked on *Cats* with 'a dead lyricist. And I failed to pass the audition with the one number I was asked to write – the show's hit song "Memory".' He added, in the most telling statement either was to make on the incident: 'I was *extremely* annoyed.'

And, as Dempster did not fail to note, Trevor Nunn had supplied 'the replacement lyrics which Tim has yet to hear – he has avoided the previews and will not be at the 11 May first night.' There is no denial of any of this on record from either Tim or Andrew.

In the theatre, it was already well known that friction was having noticeable effects on both Tim and Andrew. Min Jones, working on press relations for the *Evita* company, saw them 'fall out over parties. If one went, the other wouldn't turn up.' Her colleague Genista Streeten believes jealousy lay at the root of the discord. 'Tim could talk so easily, he's such an amusing guy, relaxed and natural. I think Andrew was really longing to be able to talk like him and there *was* jealousy there. But also Andrew had to make it on his own, didn't he? He didn't want to be linked with Tim all the time. In his own right he is a lonely, unique genius.'

Lonely, unique geniuses still need support. And Andrew's contention that musicals are 'the most collaborative form of theatre' underlines his deeply-felt need to reunite with Tim Rice. Everyone who knows them both believes it would benefit them immeasurably. One possible shortcut to this would be the filming of *Evita*, which Paramount Pictures have so far failed to do despite an expensively bought option.

Evita was always an attractive idea, in Hollywood terms. It offered glamour, conflict, passion and an unmatchable role for a woman star. The grapevine gossip is that Tim

Rice's insistence on Elaine Paige's playing the title role
chocked the wheels and brought the whole thing to a halt.
'Unlikely,' says Andrew, though whether out of loyalty to
his erstwhile partner it is hard to say.

'I really don't believe that the movie of *Evita* was, let's
say, hanging on Tim saying Elaine Paige was to be in it or
not – though knowing the way these things happen (and
one has seen it over the years) that would certainly have
been an obstacle.'

Andrew's considered view is that 'They left it too late.
At the end, they [Paramount] were just not convinced. And
it didn't help, of course, that the film of the musical *Annie*
came out and was not a success. In fact, a lot of it had to do
with the nervousness Hollywood feels about musicals in
general. There hasn't been a successful film of one – other
than *Saturday Night Fever* and *Grease* which didn't come
from the theatre – since *Cabaret*. That was the last which
did any good critically, and made its money back – though
not much more. And since then the list of flops is endless.
You've got to remember that something like *Chorus Line*
has never even been made. It's a problem for them.'

Claiming to know very little of how such a difficulty can
be overcome, Andrew nevertheless offers statesmanlike
advice to the film makers. 'One successful movie,' he says
with quiet confidence, 'would probably change the whole
thing, and their perception. But they seem to be bogged
down in their thinking. Every musical they consider has to
have a multi-million dollar budget, which makes it
frighteningly difficult to risk making. For *Evita* it was
never less than twelve and a half million dollars.

'My point, because I don't understand anything about
the cinema, is why in the case of *Evita* they are talking
about a twelve-and-a-half-million dollar movie in the first
place? Why don't they make it for five? I just don't
understand where the cost goes.'

As he says: 'If they'd wanted to make *Evita* a vehicle for a superstar, that would have made it a twenty-five-million-dollar budget! So perhaps having Elaine play it wasn't such a bad idea.' In fact, as the British film director Ken Russell discovered with distaste, the budget was already seen in these extravagant terms – even *with* Elaine. In an interview with Diana Hutchinson, *Daily Mail* woman's editor, in November 1982, Russell described how he spent a year at work on the project before deciding that it was 'madness'. He added: 'I knew Elaine wasn't right for the part, but she was hot favourite. Tim Rice was right behind her. Stigwood was very enthusiastic too. But in the first film test she looked extraordinarily like Princess Margaret.'

Tests on Liza Minnelli (too 'American and vulgar') and a meeting with Barbra Streisand, who wouldn't touch the part ('it wouldn't interest me – she was a Fascist'), did nothing to solve the problem, and Ken Russell backed out. Nobody has seriously offered to take his place, and Andrew, once keen to extend his experience of working for the cinema, tends now to talk of the film in the past tense. 'I really think it is dead now,' he said in July 1983 at his London home. 'I really don't see it. It has lost its moment.'

And 'moments', to Andrew, are important. In his life and career to date he has shown an intuitive capacity for timing, with the sole exception of *Jeeves*, which, as he once confessed to John Higgins of *The Times*, 'was rushed straight on to the stage – a great mistake'.

Nevertheless, he does not disguise his disappointment over what could have been another monumental triumph in the one medium that his work has never excelled in. 'I'm sad about it,' he confesses, 'because I think it would have worked. But that would only have been after a lot of re-thinking for the film medium, which would have meant that Tim and I would have had to work on it together. And maybe, just at this moment, with his desire to get on with new things, and mine likewise, that moment has already passed as well.'

It is plainly this realization of a lost opportunity to get back to work with Tim that Andrew most deeply regrets about the lost, or 'indefinitely postponed' movie. He sums up his feelings with an insistence that can hardly be construed otherwise. 'I mean,' he says, 'somewhere along the line I'm sure we'll get back together. Tim is the best lyricist we have, and there's nobody I've ever worked with, or for, who has more than equalled him. So, I don't care how long it takes, the important thing is for it to happen – and not just for Tim and me.'

Andrew laughs. 'Maybe,' he says, 'we'll be like ancient Verdis when it does happen! And perhaps it won't be for twenty-five years or so. But when one has something that we have you don't just let it go.'

18

The Heart Has Its Reasons

ANDREW'S mother was not entirely surprised when, on 19 April 1983, he made his public declaration of love for one of the leading players in *Cats*, Sarah Brightman, and announced his intention of ending his 12-year-old marriage. 'I had slightly suspected that they [his previous wife, Sarah, and he] were perhaps not as happy as they should be,' Jean Lloyd Webber explains. 'And then, and this is the unfortunate thing, he fell in love. I have never really been able to come to terms with that.'

Sarah Brightman, she feels, is taking on a great deal. 'How Sydmonton and the Festivals will work now, I can't say,' she says. 'She and I have had good chats. She's a very warm person and very fond of cats which is important to me. But it *is* a lot for her to run.'

Jean's home is a sunny flat on the south side of London's Old Brompton Road. Far from being alone there since her husband's unexpectedly early death at the age of sixty eight, she has two adored blue Burmese cats – Bandula and Mandalay ('they cost me £25 each') – as constant and intelligent companions. Also, her son Julian and his wife Celia live in the same block, and are constantly in and out.

In her drawing-room effigies of cats, photographs of cats, and her personable and sensitive pets dominate even the grand piano. It is a feline haven. There is no doubt where Andrew's interest in the creatures stems from. Perhaps, too, their notoriously independent spirit is responsible for the doubts his mother has about him, and his future happiness.

As she wisely says, 'Artistic people are less stable, I think. They're going to be up and down. You can't expect them always to behave in a normal conventional manner.' The question, for her and many others who believe that Andrew has yet to produce his greatest music and work, is what this break-up of a steady and well-run existence will do to his output.

At present, he could be compared to a liner leaving safe harbour for the open sea. Every change of course has to take account of the possible danger he runs of injuring others, of running into the shallows. He has his loyal and tested adviser, Brian Brolly, supportive and comforting as a tug. And on the surface all seems calm and well smoothed over, his divorced wife settled in the London house near Sloane Square. But who knows what can come of all this – certainly he is too intelligent to forecast it with certainty.

What he has done is in keeping with the high principles which he has consistently lived by. The house he has settled on Sarah is the one they were always going to do up, to make something of when they found time. Well, time ran out for them both. But if it is ever possible to soften the pain of a marriage break-up Andrew has done all he can in that direction by settling their London house, and giving all possible support to her and their children.

Close friends of both say he has succeeded. 'Sarah is happier now than she has been for months,' David Crewe-Read said at the time of the divorce. 'She's always wanted to get back to London one day,' another friend said. 'She'll soon make a life for herself there, and she's young enough to make a fresh start.'

Young enough and pretty enough, and in many ways a much more interesting and mature person than the schoolgirl who married while waiting for her A-level results. The press can spare Sarah Lloyd Webber (the first) their crocodile tears. Andrew's divorce may have been a legal 'quickie' – the decree nisi was granted on 26 July 1983, little more than three months after he'd revealed his love for Sarah Brightman – but it was relatively painless. He made it clear then that he was in the grip of a consuming emotion which transcended every other value and commitment but decency. It was that which, he believes, made it necessary for him to make 'a clean breast of it'.

Yet he knows, even in the throes of this passion, that he is shooting the emotional rapids. 'I can see that as an artist and writer I do need a stable home life,' he says, 'and this may prove difficult in marriage to a very talented girl who may very well want to take off and get back into the theatre to further her own career. Because then the house in the country and everything just wouldn't tick over.'

Whereas, with his ex-wife, there was always this solid base for his mental and creative workshop. There at their country home he could play around with ideas, develop themes, and always be sure of Sarah's excellent management, her much admired cooking, and the ease with which she ran this and their other establishments and schedules. He knows what he has given up, but there was no other way. 'It had to be,' he says. 'And I can see that, however much I am in love with Sarah Brightman – and I am – it could be me in the end who draws the short straw.'

A chillingly realistic appraisal of the odds, not only of personal happiness but his whole future creative career, which depends perhaps more than he presently realizes on a settled contentment. The risk is to his *oeuvre*, the body of work which is yet to come from his extraordinary talent. His mother recognizes it. 'I think he did get what he needed, stability, from Sarah [his first wife]. It's a big thing he's done, and there are bound to be problems, of course, with two careers. I just hope it works out.'

The second Sarah in his life also knows what she is taking on, but their shared love and Andrew's obvious devotion makes it all seem possible. She feels secure. 'He's strong, you see,' she says. 'When I first met him – he'd asked me to come and audition for him at his flat, before I went into *Cats* – I was absolutely terrified, but he's not really frightening.' She sees him as 'a commanding sort of person, an obvious leader', and is confident about her future in his hands.

It was during rehearsals and while the show was running that Sarah first noticed Andrew's attention to detail. 'He used to come in and go round to every corner of the theatre listening to the sound,' she remembers. 'I don't blame him, that's the only way you can get what you want. It's no good leaving it to others.'

Their romance developed, she says, much later. 'But I'd always felt close to him. At that first meeting in his flat I sat perched on a settee while he stood in front of me telling me all about *Cats*. I don't think I was listening to much of what he was saying, I was more fascinated by this person.'

She is a lover of bizarre clothes. Andrew, she says, 'Always found me highly amusing, because each time we met I was wearing something different and always outrageous.' She laughs. 'I just love clothes,' she says happily, 'all kinds, from the very simple to the very fancy. My feeling for them is like my feeling for music. I like Rock and Roll and I love opera. I'm very open to things, actually.'

So, of course, is Andrew. He looks back on a variety of seedlings which, fertilized in his creative mind, have taken firm root. What will follow, after his preoccupation with *Starlight Express* and *Aspects of Love*, is an exciting thought, more so as it can increase the stature of the first English theatrical composer of musicals to have taken Broadway by storm. Perhaps a hint of future direction lies in what he now feels about those earlier works. As he described them in 1983:

'*Joseph and the Amazing Technicolor Dreamcoat*, I think, has a wonderful innocence. There's a strong core to it that makes it possible to hang anything on it, like an umbrella stand. The original seriousness it had has been completely lost in the new versions, but I still think it's great. It has enormous charm and fun. I think, too, that it's probably the best example of Tim and the least good score of mine in relation to what he did. But it is full of enormous promise and because it was the first one there'll always be people who'll say "That was the best!" There always are those sort of people.

'*Jesus Christ Superstar* also has that innocence, but it's not a very well-formed work. We'd abandoned *Richard* [*Come Back, Richard*] when we wrote it, and Herod's song came from that. The important thing about it for us was that we attempted a lot of things which we'd never attempted before, and the greatest quality it has for me is that it knows exactly what it is going to do and does it. I still feel that, in an extremely dramatic way, it runs in a straight line from A to B. And that makes it work in some kind of operatic terms, however naïvely.

'*Jeeves*, on the other hands, is the biggest enigma. There was probably a lot wrong there, but I still think there are some very good tunes lurking in it. What it did too was let me try to do something completely conventional in the mainstream of musicals, which came out of my love of musical theatre. It just went wrong. And, of course, the major mistake was that we didn't have a team that understood musicals, or in which anyone had sufficient authority to take the lead – paradoxically, since we had so much talent. But there it was.

'*Evita?* Well, my feeling for it is very much love-hate. I love it and hate it in very much the way I want and intend the audience to. Some bits I'm very proud of – I don't think I've ever equalled the waltz yet, and that waltz is my best orchestration. And I dare say it is the best of the works that Tim and I did together. It's also my undying belief that Hal Prince, directing it, pulled off one of the great proscenium productions of all time. But I've always felt very ambivalent about the score. It's not easy to be a full-blooded romantic writer when your political antennae tell you that this is the most loathsome lady in the history of time. I mean, some of the ideas came out of incidents which were anything but romantic – like the chant, which I took from hearing the fans at Stamford Bridge going "da-de-da-de-da *Chelsea*!" with real menace. But to sum up, which isn't easy about this one, I do think there is a case for saying that this is the only one of my things to date which you would find thrilling to hear in an opera-house. And the last twenty-five minutes of *Evita*, and certainly the scene in the bedroom, are still the most daring pieces of harmonic and musical writing that I've done.

'"Variations", as I've said, is my best-selling album in Britain ever and absolutely my favourite piece of composition. It surprised me because it was much more of the rock world, certainly closer to rock than anything I'd done for some time. I suppose what really cheered me up about that was that I hadn't written an instrumental piece before, and I was really intrigued to see if I could do it. And I did, and it became a Number One album!

'Then *Song and Dance* . . . well, the astonishing thing there was that it has the most instant crowd reaction of any of my works. It's an extraordinary sight. I mean, a lot of people who have never seen a fifty-minute dance piece in their lives before! And they suddenly see a company of dancers doing things . . . Up till then, you see, they've always thought anything to do with *corps de ballet* was a bit effete. Then they're faced with this show! What's this? One part *opera*! And a *ballet*! That couldn't possible be for me! But when they get inside they find they actually like it.

'It means a lot to me that I may be pushing the area of their experience this little bit. Because an awful lot of people, after they've seen the show, say, "Well, now, what I'd like to do very much is go to the ballet." Which they'd never before thought could be that entertaining.

'And *Cats* . . . I think *Cats* is far and away the most entertaining of the musicals I've done. If you look at it as an *experience* (which incidentally is how theatre is going to be increasingly looked at in my opinion, because seats are so expensive) then surely it is *hugely* for the medium? It's no good putting on something nowadays which people can see just as well on their video. That's why *Cats* is so popular. They can't get to see anything like it, not at all. It doesn't exist.

'So, to sum up, I'm most pleased of all the work I've so far done with the dance part of *Song and Dance*. Because I think "Variations" is far and away my best piece of actual music. It's funny, but that little segment of just about forty-five minutes or so is probably my best work. There's not a thing in it I'd alter, not a note. Whereas with *Cats*, I mean in New York there are completely different settings of the Rumpleteazer and Mungojerrie, and Growltiger numbers – completely re-written. Of course, the shows get changed all the time. But not "Variations". I'm proud of that.'

Andrew works like a stonemason. In the pit of his creative mind lies the blueprint of what he seeks, forced by the structure of the show to adapt itself to a final shape and theme. He begins with a solid block of musical material. This he chips and hones down to the dimensions imposed by whatever gap the piece has to fill. If it doesn't finally work, then he may have to re-shape it. Again and again. As the Broadway playwright and author Garson Kanin put it in the words of his composer character, Hy Balaban, in the novel of a Broadway musical *Smash* (Viking, 1980), 'I wrote one number into five different scenes sung by four different characters until we found the right person and the right spot.' Andrew will do the same many times.

He begins with a line of melody, a few notes in clearly defined rhythmic sequence which seem to him to suit the mood and theme of the action. A 'score' is just that, it underlines and points up the feeling of action in musical terms. It is not a symphony or song on its own.

Then, on a piano or using tape recordings and such convenient instruments as a synthesizer, the composer will extemporize on this basic line in a hundred, perhaps a thousand, different ways, slowly expanding it and refining its chords and cadences. As the stone-carver knows, so Andrew will know if and when he has achieved what he wants. Or if he has failed. The question of how and why a juvenile prodigy Mozart, a blind Beethoven, or an infantile Lloyd Webber in his nursery days should have this gift while others cannot put two notes together in harmony is for philosophers to ponder.

In his middle thirties, Andrew's record of achievement is extraordinary by any standards. Not only has his music been accepted at the popular level, his shows filling theatres at a time when the world economic climate was emptying many others, but he is respected in the highest musical circles. 'He tinges the simplicity of popular music with something that is tolerable to the majority yet well calculated to be acceptable to a more refined ear,' says John Lill, his concert pianist friend who has every right to speak for the world of classical music. 'And his choice of subject is phenomenal. Altogether, what he has accomplished is amazing. I don't see why he shouldn't go on to write a full-scale opera. Given the experience he has had, I'm sure he could do it. He may well turn to more serious music. And of course he may fail, or he may not. It would be quite extraordinary if he manages to keep up the success of the past few years, and I do think he has got to be careful he doesn't disappear as quickly as he appeared. But everything he tackles seems to turn to gold.'

In Lill's view, shared by many eminent figures in the musical Establishment, 'There are marvellous moments in his writing, but I think some of it borders on the predictable. There's quite a lot of four-square rhythm, and though it's a characteristic style it is slightly limited on occasions. But that applies to many composers.

'I think what he *has* got is the ability to produce a theme with just a shade – almost at a tangent – of what is the predictable pop piece of music. Andrew's music is not pop, of course, which I can't stand. It is far, far better. You can't compare it. There are tremendous qualities in it, and in him. His talent is massive. And it's no coincidence that he's had the success he has.

'It is true that sometimes I do find him slightly banal, slightly empty. But at other times the theme really grips you. It's his themes which to me are so extraordinarily good. They are the best.'

Given that John Lill's praise comes from a musician of the highest calibre, a man who regards pop music as 'a cancer', it is a weighty plaudit. And richly earned. It points the way to a glittering future for Andrew in his new married life, once he and Sarah settle down. The pain of breaking from his first wife is already lessened. 'In these situations,' as he says, 'the person left always feels not only rejection but some degree of humiliation. It's just never possible to get that absolutely right – and I most certainly would feel very upset if it had happened to me the other way round. But there really isn't anything else one can say.'

Financially, of course, it has still to be reckoned. 'By the time this book comes out,' he said in July 1983, 'I will have my theatre in London and that is going to involve a long and costly uphill struggle. Because of my personal circumstances [the terms of the divorce settlement] I've had to borrow to do it, and it'll be a bit touch and go.'

For this reason too, his apparently uninterrupted chain of success and wealth is, he insists, a far less guaranteed haven than it looks. 'People don't realize what a very labour-intensive business the theatre is,' he says with some exasperation. 'They think, gosh, with six shows running round the world – well, five now that *Evita* has closed in New York – he *must* be rolling. But you have to nurse them, because there isn't that amount of money *in* theatre. It isn't there.'

Very often, as he points out, the backers have to risk their investment at odds which few experienced professional gamblers would accept. 'It can be a huge gamble,' he says. 'For instance, Cameron and I did something really inspired, as it turned out, long before *Cats* opened in New York. We took a half page in the *New York Times* and reprinted a smashing review of the show in London from *Time* magazine. We just put on it the New London Theatre phone number and how to dial it from America.

'That was one really smart thing we did, though at the time we didn't realize it. Because although it cost a lot – twenty thousand dollars or something – it was just the sort of grand, defiant gesture Americans go for. And it really was a gesture of defiance! We'd hit a point in London, about six weeks after it opened, when bookings didn't look as solid as we'd have liked. We just said, "Let's really bust it over the edge!" So we put up another £100,000 on publicity, including the New York shot, and we've never had to advertize since, apart from the performance times and so on.'

His experience of the financial ups and downs seems if anything to have made him less cautious, but this could be an illusion. 'I never had anything to do with raising money for the shows while Stigwood handled them,' he says. 'I still don't. Brian Brolly does that for me, that's what he does.'

As a result, Andrew says, he sees a far less exciting return from his successful shows than is popularly supposed, or as a lampoon of him in *Private Eye* in September 1983 (under the heading 'Lloyd Webber Buys Bank of England') might indicate. The tongue-in-cheek story quoted him as saying 'Ever since a kid I've wanted to own it. It is the only bank large enough to contain all my money.'

Andrew comments: 'It's not like the good old days of records when, if you were a pop star, you could be making enormous royalties out of a record company. Nowadays people who are making royalties out of theatre have to accept that if the show is not doing well there has to be a sliding scale in what they are paid. You have to make provision for bad times ahead, also. So it can happen that when a show is just about breaking even royalty payments have to be waived for a time in order to keep it going. The backers will gain later when business picks up, which they certainly won't do if it folds.'

As a producer Andrew does not invest in his own shows except where there is no outside backing available. As Bob Swash says, 'With *Cats* he had to, but that is exceptional. The custom is for shows to be backed by people who want to make money out of success. It's not always easy to find them.'

Andrew fully understands this. He says: 'When you get to a position such as I'm in, with several productions running at the same time, all of them hot, then you do all right out of them, of course you do. But I'll give you a very good example of why there's so much misunderstanding.

'*Daisy Pulls It Off* [his first independent production under the banner of his company] is one of the most successful plays running in London at the moment [1983], and it's making a goodish profit every week. But it's not making enough to guarantee its survival for any length of time. If, when winter comes, it hasn't paid back the whole of its investment and can therefore ride any bad winter weeks, then nobody can be sure it will last. It's just one of those things.'

Depending on one's newspaper, Andrew's own fortune has reportedly varied from a million dollars a week (*Daily Mail*, October 1982) to a 'cautiously estimated just over the million pound [a year] mark' (*Sunday Times*, 23 January 1983). Since his contract with the Stigwood Organization expired in 1979 he has managed himself, through his company run by Brian Brolly, and is a free agent. As Derek Jewell says, 'Both Andrew and Tim felt Stigwood had made a lot of money out of them and was trying to make more. Tim is still with David Land. I presume he thinks life is too short to have to organize everything himself, while Andrew is totally different. Single-minded. He, I suspect, thinks he can perfectly well do it himself. And probably he doesn't much like the Stigwood Organization anyway. It was all very well when it started, but now he probably thinks "I've outgrown this. It *is* worth my taking time to get this thing right."'

And the road to this independent success appears to have been paved with solid gold. In June 1972 Andrew and Tim could count their share of the proceeds (though, as they bitterly realize, they received only $2\frac{1}{2}$ per cent after meeting costs and profits for all the artists) on more than four million copies of the *Superstar* record in the States; and money was cascading in to the show's Broadway box office. Andrew cautiously predicted then, 'It's nonsense really to talk about money. After we've paid taxes I think we'll be lucky to finish with £25,000 each.' But David Land expressed disbelief: 'It's much more. I predict they'll both [Tim and Andrew] be sterling millionaires within four or five years.'

After the London launch of the show, even Andrew had to admit that the money was rolling in. By November 1974 he was estimated to have earned £400,000 before tax from *Superstar* alone. And after *Evita*, four years later, he was comparing himself, though deprecatingly, with Beatle Paul McCartney and popstar Elton John. 'Everyone always thinks one has done well, but by international standards I don't really think one has. I have the house [Sydmonton] and enough funds to take off when I want to, but nothing else.'

By early 1982 Andrew was no longer able to deny wealth. His bid of £1,350,000 for the Aldwych Theatre was backed by considerable loans, but confirmed his personal millionaire status. When both this and his offer for the Old Vic failed he was left with funds which were increasing nightly with the box office returns from the triumphant *Cats* in London, and were soon augmented by *Song and Dance*. By the time *Cats* opened in New York (in October that year) with some five-and-a-half million dollars' worth of advance bookings assured, it needed an accountant to tell Andrew himself what he was worth.

Yet *Cats* in London had cost £470,000 to launch and only half that amount was actually in the kitty when it opened. Those who turned down Andrew's offer to invest are still biting envious nails. In June 1982 he announced that he had 'paid off all my mortgages' and felt more confident. At the same time he confessed to being 'not very good at investing' and having 'seldom thought about money'.

There was no pressing need for him to do so. By December 1982 John Huxley in the *Sunday Times* was reporting 'anyone with a £1,000 stake in *Evita* would have made about £4,000 already and now be pulling in an estimated £135 a week.' Andrew's returns were several times that amount. The following summer cheques were going out to the fortunate backers of *Song and Dance*. And

Daisy, the show his company had shrewdly backed and brought to the West End, was said to have broken even. When Andrew went to Budapest in July for the opening there of *Cats* (with runs planned in Los Angeles for the Olympic Games, and in Tokyo and Vienna) there were mutterings that royalty payments, which were reaching backers from Cameron Mackintosh's office every six weeks, could well have been increased. Andrew accepts this philosophically, knowing that by that time all the original 'angels' – those who had courageously taken up units of £750 in the original London production and who had seen the show prosper on Broadway – were more than satisfied.

'It's true we'd trebled our original investment by last summer [1983],' a retired solicitor, Colin McFadyean, admits, 'and we're told that the "cream is a long way from curdling" still. Sadly, though, one has to pay *unearned* income-tax on the royalties, which, in my case and I should have thought most other investors', is a hefty 75 per cent, or three-quarters of everything.'

Even so, each unit of £750 in February 1981, when McFadyean invested at the suggestion of a firm of stockbrokers, had seen a complete return of that sum within the same year. And by the summer of 1983, profits on the show had amounted to 240 per cent more.   The figures Mackintosh sent to McFadyean and others show that by then the show had grossed £1,725,433 in box-office takings without reckoning advance bookings. Broadway had provided £102,606 of that sum, and nearly a million and a half had been distributed, presumably to all backers including Andrew.

At a guess, his portion may well have been 25 per cent or more (recalling Robert Stigwood's previous interest). From this one show, which he had had such difficulty in raising the cash for, he was probably earning at that time close to half a million a year. However, he too must pay taxes.

Clive Barnes in New York remembers how Andrew and Tim Rice had scoffed at the money they were suddenly seeing for *Superstar* all those years ago. 'They said they felt almost immoral at making so much so young,' the critic recalls. Andrew still feels a sense of obligation if not guilt on this score.

'What it comes back to at the end of the day,' he says, 'and I don't quite know how to put this . . . is my fundamental feeling about the quality of life; in the sense that if I ever get passionate about anything it is that. And of course it is the most difficult thing to get passionate about. I mean the liberal democratic way of life, with a small "l". It's the hardest thing in the world to defend, I know that. Especially when everything is or seems to be going all right. But it is what counts for me every time. There is something extraordinary about this country which makes it possible to do things that are genuinely for the good. I'm talking about the moral commitment of one's own talent. How one uses it. The one thing my father particularly brought me up to believe is that everybody is responsible in the end for the positive use of his or her best qualities.'

He adds with a smile, 'I keep talking like some sort of evangelist, and in fact I am – in a somewhat confused sense – quite deeply religious myself. But what I'm trying to say is that there are certain things which have absolutely guided my life, ever since I was young. One is belief in a free society such as we have in Britain. And this is something which deep-down I believe I share with Tim, an appreciation of that remarkable fact. So we have a moral duty to defend its tradition. Not by taking up weapons, I don't mean, but by recognizing and respecting the liberal and democratic tradition for what it is; a great privilege.'

In the week before Andrew's father died, on 29 October 1982, he and Dr Billy Lloyd Webber discussed plans for setting up a chair in musical theatre in his father's college, the London College of Music. Andrew has since started a fund to that end in his father's memory. His own future will, he believes, increasingly be devoted towards work for its fulfilment, for a school which one day may produce, who knows, a composer like himself.

As his friend, the man whose critical eye and ear have seen him from the prep-school production of *Joseph* at Central Hall, Westminster to the present day, *Sunday Times* writer Derek Jewell, expresses it, 'Andrew Lloyd Webber has done more for the status of the musical in this country than anyone in history, without the slightest doubt. It may be debatable whether he is the most significant composer of pop music after Ellington in this century. I think he may well be. But at thirty-five or so it's still early days. He hasn't got a corpus of work yet as large as Cole Porter or Richard Rodgers. I suspect he will have, and I don't think any composer of popular music in history – certainly not of stage musicals – can possibly have started off so unbelievably brilliantly in the first ten years of his career.'

Indeed, he *is* quite remarkable. And although his singlemindedness may make him difficult to work with – he demands, he demands, he demands – the result, in terms of what has gone on the stage, is as Jewell has said, 'absolutely stunning, a justification in itself'. If there is an argument that the price of genius should not be at the cost of human feelings, all one can say is that it would be a very poor life without geniuses. In Andrew's case there is not much for which he would not be forgiven by those who work with him.

'His music is undoubtedly derivative, but whose music is not?' a rival composer has said. 'Andrew's gift is that he has listened to the music of his age, and to the music of many ages before it. He has taken, with genius, the essence of them all and put them together with his own magic.'

The result is a cocktail of daringly different forms and styles, but is it recognizably Andrew Lloyd Webber music? To those who empathize with it, there is no questioning its marvellous, light-hearted gaiety and warmth. To those who do not, or who rate his work as over-praised and his success as largely due to luck, the continuing acceptance of it by an increasingly large universal audience makes him a child of fortune. They wait with foreboding and envy to see what future years will bring.

19

The Way Ahead

AND well he knows it. The Andrew Lloyd Webber we see today is unsure of his emotional path, worried about every decision – he even on one occasion urged Robert Stigwood not to stage *Superstar,* or bring *Evita* to the West End of London – and troubled by doubts and insecurity about the future of the world and his own finances. But of one thing he is sure: the talent he has to create music for the theatre, for the stage, whether at operatic or semi-operatic level or commercial popular show business, is running at flood tide.

One has only to listen to him. Between the occasional moods of gloom and testiness it carries him along with bounding force. To be with him on these occasions in the patio garden of his London flat or in his comfortable den at Sydmonton with its array of electronic aids to musical reproduction, is to feel the power of wings.

'I have two huge ingredients,' he says without vanity, 'fundamentally different, both of them, from what, say, Richard Rodgers or most of the pop writers have. One is that I have an understanding of a-tonalism and dissonance – which frankly Prokofiev had, only I go farther than that. The other is that I have no fear about where I will make harmony go, so long as I can make melody take it there naturally. My main concern is to make sure that the tunes basically exist for themselves. I can't stand the tune that puts in a sort of dissonant note just for the sake of doing it, just for effect – because somebody's trying to say "Hey, aren't I clever?" And there are plenty of examples of that by people whose work, I think, is silly.

'For instance, I love the idea that "The Jellicle Ball" in *Cats* does in fact go . . . does actually take us through [he sings]: der-di-der der . . . di-der . . . der-di-der-di-der der . . . I mean, which is going through four separate, possible harmonic solutions before we get to the fifth.'

Andrew the composer says he has always been 'obsessed by melody'. He goes on to explain this, still in the same tone of assurance that refutes any suggestion of complacency or conceit. 'There are two things needed to make musical theatre work. One is construction, one is melody. Construction is vital, because you can have your key tune, say "Some Enchanted Evening" in the wrong place, on the wrong night, in the wrong show and it would be lost. It just would not work. I mean you'd say "Hmm, fine. Great tune." But you wouldn't remember it. *But*, if you've got it set up in the *right* place, then it happens.'

The luminous, dark eyes widen in wonder. 'You can push forward melody quite a long way, of course. I mean, I believe that I am pushing it forward quite a bit. I am going quite far. Some of the things I do in *Cats* are really quite dissonant, quite a-tonal, quite definitely about a type of melody that normal pop music does not encompass.

'The trouble is that the moment you give people a lot of melody in one evening it's awfully difficult for them to take in. Their normal view would be that it's either "unmelodic" or "derivative" or whatever. They will *not* take a vast amount of melodic invention in an evening. And also it's quite difficult because melodic invention is, by necessity, original and unique. It has to be, which is why I try to move forward all the time.

'I mean with bits of *Cats* and *Starlight Express* and some of my new pieces which are still to come out you'll see that they now adopt my style, but with original dissonances. It isn't easy, because you are basically listening to things that follow along well-worn paths. Not always, but often. What I've done is I've absorbed into my vocabulary something that is quite different.'

He muses, then adds thoughtfully, 'There is, of course, a mathematical concept to music, which I can't analyse – and I know Prokofiev was supposed to be the greatest chess player and one of the greatest mathematicians that ever lived! I just accept that it is there, somewhere, like an underlying set of rules which in my case I follow purely instinctively.'

With the public, it is not easy to argue that his instinct in this direction has misled him, yet there are those who try. The veteran musical arranger Stan Butcher finds Andrew's music 'lacking its own stamp'. After forty years of working in and with leading British and American pop groups, Butcher can read a composer's signature in his music as easily as his own handwriting. 'All the great popular song-writers – Gershwin, Cole Porter, Jerome Kern, Richard Rodgers – used recognizable tunes, whether they did so consciously or unconsciously. *They* were derivative. But what they did was give them an individual twist, so that everthing they wrote had their stamp on it. Andrew still has to find his, in my opinion.'

Butcher finds it hard to explain exactly how the Lloyd Webber songs such as 'Memory' and 'Don't Cry For Me, Argentina' and the great *Song and Dance* cycle of 'Tell Me On A Sunday' and others fail to register with him. To him, they are 'too reminiscent, too harking back to classical melodies'. As he declares, 'Andrew has been wonderfully successful, but I'd say he doesn't yet have an identifiable individual style. He's drawn to the operatic on the one hand, yet with jazz-rock overtones. And his jazz is in the old classical mould. In other words, I don't think he has much originality, but that doesn't mean I don't like what he's doing. It's great.'

Among those who disagree fundamentally with Butcher's personal viewpoint – and bearing in mind that an arranger is not an originator – Andrew's brother Julian, the cellist, has perhaps the most right to be heard. 'When I first played through "Variations" I knew that, especially in the slow variation, it was essentially *his* music. *His* voice,' he says. 'I think it's very easy for people to say a composer is derivative, but if that is all he is he just couldn't survive.'

Julian's position in an altogether different area of music adds weight to his comments. Although, as he says, 'The one person classical musicians will never discuss with me, in terms of what they think of his music, is, of course, Andrew. But I have to say that they are always asking him to arrange his pieces for a full orchestra, which so far he has never done.'

He has his own views on this. 'I would like to see Andrew write expressly *for* an orchestra,' he says, 'because it would be very interesting to see what he did to alter the normal symphonic line, by bringing in new instruments and so on.'

Having grown up together and shared, however distantly, their musical development, Julian and Andrew have a bond which few brothers know. 'I played in the original Colet Court performance of *Joseph*,' Julian recalls. 'Does he have a tape of it? I'd be very surprised if Andrew hadn't taped everything he ever did.' He laughs. 'I have some tapes of him which he doesn't know about, done very early on, shall we say. He's singing!'

About Andrew's future progress – where he goes from here – Julian gives a relaxed and comforting projection. 'He says he wants to write an opera, a traditional one,' he says. 'Well, I personally think he shouldn't. I also think that if he'd wanted to write one he would have done it by now. But if he turned his hand to it now I think he might find it quite restrictive, and that would be a pity. He's so exceptionally gifted in other ways.'

In particular, Julian believes, Andrew's great talent for, as he puts it, 'sending up' other musicians should not be dimmed. 'In the Prokofiev part of "Variations", for instance, he does a remarkably clever pastiche of the composer. He's always doing it. In *Evita*, the Elvis number is a satirical take-off. The point is that he tends to imitate only people he is very fond of.'

Also in *Evita*, as Julian points out, Andrew scored a section for a solo guitarist in the style of another of his favourites, Hank Marvin, lead guitarist of The Shadows. 'Hank played it in the show,' Julian explains, 'but if he hadn't been available, I'm sure Andrew would have found someone who could play like him.'

As he says: 'What's wrong with that? Through the ages composers have been very strongly influenced by people they have had a great respect for. Prokofiev, certainly. Puccini, too, who has also influenced Andrew.'

And he can be provoked to an unaccustomed testiness about the critics who sneer at Andrew's music as 'derivative'. 'Wasn't Rachmaninov derivative?' he asks shortly. 'He's one of my favourite composers. So what can you say to that? Why shouldn't people have absorbed what went before them? Andrew will never take from anyone whom he does not respect, that I can assure you.'

When they meet now, Julian and Andrew seldom discuss music. 'No, funnily enough, we talk mostly about football. Or we might just be meeting socially, as we did when the Everly Brothers came over in September 1983 and we went to hear them, having been among their greatest fans in the past. We had our picture taken with them, and that was the greatest picture of all time in my opinion.

'But Andrew and I, now that our careers have gone in such very different ways, very rarely talk about "What should I do with this, or that?" Music isn't something we talk about much.'

At the same time it is obvious that Andrew's instinct is guided by dreams. He sees a world in which music blooms like flowers, matching the seasons of feeling, joy and suffering, as fully as it corresponds to the deeper passions. What of his immediate future? 'I should like,' he says, 'to see "Tell Me On A Sunday" done one more time, but by a girl closer in age to the girl it is written about. After all, it is supposed to be about the sort of girls who hang around Los Angeles, about twenty-seven or twenty-eight. You know, getting a bit disillusioned. It's much more an amalgamation of people Don [Black] and I had met – British types who think America is going to be a panacea for all ills, drifting from bloke to bloke, then writing home to mum. That's exactly what they do. And I think something would have to be done to make that part work for America.'

So he is still undecided about taking *Song and Dance* to the States. 'It needs something for over there. One further incarnation to the first part, perhaps. As it is it would be a great crowd-pleaser for middle-America, but I don't think it would get past the New York critics.'

He's worried, too, about the 'Britishness' of it. 'Quite a few American artists – Shirley Maclaine and others – have wanted to do it, somewhat re-written and adapted for themselves. But there's a certain integrity about doing it with an English girl. I don't know. Again, I'm a little bit of a stick in the mud about this sort of thing, and I'm not a great advocate of changing something unless there are very good reasons for doing so.

'I do feel that the girl, at the end of the day, ought more firmly to come to terms with her situation. There's a marvellous lyric to be written, or song to be written, which would be about the girl going from the idea of a married man saying "You're the one for me" to her saying "You'll absolutely do, and this is terrific". Then from "Yes, we did live together" to her telling him his wife ". . . can get along fine – after all she's young enough to do so, just like me". Then to the girl saying "I can't stand the fellow. Really! Phoning his wife every minute!" to the last verse "I'm young enough to get on perfectly well on my own, so out you go!"

'I mean, that's an interesting set of lyrics which we haven't even touched on. I'd like to see that done. But it would only be moving if the girl was young. And there is a way of bringing her back into the show at the end of the [Wayne Sleep, second half] dance which would be quite sensational. The trouble is that then you limit it to very few performers, because it would need dancing as well.'

Sarah Brightman, perhaps? Andrew returns to depression when he recalls the media coverage of his love affair before his divorce from the first Sarah. 'I can't possibly use Sarah B. now in any of my shows for at least a year,' he says mournfully. 'It would be ruinous for her career if it appeared that I was only putting her in because of my feelings for her.'

Whereas in fact he values her quite separately as an artist. His adaptation of the popular Hubert Parry hymn tune 'Dear Lord And Father Of Mankind' which Sarah has recorded shows more than devotion to her as a person. In it he uses her unusual double vocal range to the full. Sarah's voice, though still forming and being trained, possesses a dual capacity, he says, 'of what is called "chest voice" – this is the sort of voice associated with say Elaine Paige or Barbra Streisand – and a much larger voice which goes right up to top C. A chest voice has only a range of about fourteen notes.' He finds her, therefore, much more interesting to write for.

Hardly fair, perhaps, to compare him with Professor Higgins in *My Fair Lady* when he talks about her in this way, but the comparison is hard to avoid. Andrew is shaping Sarah's voice as he might tune a fine instrument. His interest in this aspect of her is purely aesthetic and detached. If she has been fortunate in gaining his love, she has been no less so in winning his regard and professional guidance.

There is no doubt she is a large part of his future, a sustaining and delightful force. He stands on the threshold of the second half of a life which has so far lasted no more than thirty-six years. Will it, like his *Song and Dance*, now offer a radical change from all that went before, beginning in Westminster in 1948 and leading through his 'bohemian' childhood to the placid comforts of Sydmonton and the first Sarah? Or will it now move into the creative pattern which seems to be settling on his life-style to accommodate the profusion of music and work pouring from his talented mind?

We must wait and see, as he must himself. 'The thing,' he says, 'that has always sustained my desire to write has been a total enthusiasm for what I do in the musical theatre. And the joy sometimes of feeling – as at my Festival, or as I had hoped to do with the Old Vic, and which has not yet happened, but which I hope will do so now that I have my own theatre, because I'm still young enough to look pretty far ahead – that what I am doing may have some use in encouraging other people to come into an area that I very strongly believe in.'

Others offer a more specific forecast. Around Andrew now is a formidable team. Trevor Nunn would welcome any prospect of working with him. Cameron Mackintosh (though he is said to find Andrew an uncomfortable partner in business affairs) must relish the memory of their first unpromising meeting and of all that it has led to. He would hardly be likely to decline another production of Andrew's.

Who else? Richard Stilgoe, the witty television performer and personality, was first involved with the

Broadway production of *Cats*. He has since made his mark
with both Andrew and Trevor Nunn. As the director says
of him: 'Richard is *incredibly* fertile. I mean, unlike anyone
I've ever come across. Richard can deliver you a complete,
formed, inter-related, internally-rhyming and cross-refer-
encing lyric in half an hour.'

It was Stilgoe whom Andrew and Trevor Nunn worked
with on the production of *Starlight Express* which opened
triumphantly in London in March 1984. In Nunn's view he
was an ideal recruit, perfectly tuned to the Lloyd Webber
musical philosophy. 'Whatever else you care to say about
it, *Starlight* pushes back frontiers,' Nunn declares. 'It could
only be happening *now*, not possibly even ten years ago.
Andrew's music in it reflects what has been happening very,
very recently – the social changes, the disco revolution, the
birth and growth of the robotic age and so on. It is *hugely*
in advance of the technology you find in most theatres.'

To Nunn, Andrew Lloyd Webber is a composer with
unique powers of observation. 'Musically,' he declares,
'what is so marvellous about him is that he writes scores
which acknowledge his age. He *accepts* that Elvis Presley
has been born and died in recent years. And that Rock and
Roll has actually happened in this century. At present, in
the Broadway theatre, you've absolutely no notion of that.
No idea that anything has changed in popular music since
the 'forties and 'fifties.'

Can he say what this enlightened ear will accomplish for
his hero, and those around him, in the future? Trevor
Nunn is personally unsure of his place in the Lloyd Webber
team of the future, but fully optimistic about its success.
He is back now (in 1984) with the RSC. His contract,
signed in 1978, was for seven years with one year's
sabbatical leave (which ended in May 1984) intervening. He
must therefore undertake full administrative, if not
directorial, responsibilities for both the Barbican and
Stratford theatres. Thus he admitted, towards the end of

1983: 'I don't think I'm at the point of being able to decide how my future with Andrew will go. I also don't think I'm at the point where I *need* to decide it.'

What he means is that the future and the demands it puts on him will make the decision for him. Between Nunn and Andrew there has never been a formal involvement. As the director says: 'We have no ongoing arrangement, formally described. It is unnecessary.' Nevertheless, the likelihood of them not getting together on future shows seems unbelievably remote.

Already, the planning and some of the writing of *Aspects of Love* has fallen to Nunn. This is no guarantee that it will succeed as *Starlight Express* has in the Andrew Lloyd Webber catalogue but it shows how keen they both are to see it staged. 'We've certainly done a lot of work on it,' Nunn agrees, 'and I do still think that it would make a wonderful show for Tim and Andrew to do together, whether or not I'm involved.'

Behind this comment is another curiously unfulfilled passage of arms between Tim and Andrew, as Nunn – before he rejoined the RSC – went on to explain. 'You see, I dropped each of them a note to that effect after I'd read the book,' he said. 'I confess I wanted my own enthusiasm to be registered, but the important thing to me was that, historically, Andrew and Tim should get back together, and on a project they both wanted to do.'

Yet Nunn heard that Tim Rice had subsequently declined to take any part in *Aspects*' development. Had he expressed any feelings about Trevor Nunn's direction of it? All Nunn knows is that Rice refused to come in at that time. As the director says: 'If Andrew had written back to me to say that they were starting on it together, with Hal Prince directing, I'd have been thrilled.' Perhaps Rice had misread his intention.

The question of how deeply hurt Tim Rice had been by Andrew's acceptance of Trevor Nunn's lyric for the song

'Memory' in *Cats* can hardly be ignored in this connection. Nunn's account of their most recent contacts makes this abundantly clear.

'I didn't refer to it again,' he explains. 'But then, for some reason, Andrew asked me to have dinner with them both to discuss it. He said that he and Tim had spent a week together in France and he'd played over some of the tunes for *Aspects* which he'd already written. Though Tim had apparently told him at the time that he didn't see much future, if any at all, in the project, Andrew wanted us to have another go at persuading him.'

Nunn was surprised by the invitation but delighted to accept. As he goes on to say: 'That was several months later. Andrew asked me to "enthuse" about the show to Tim, and I could see that my role was to be "chairmonical", by which I mean helping them to keep to limited targets and so on in a sort of administrative way.

'Well, we had a good dinner and discussion. And Tim did agree to spend another three days with us some three weeks later – after we were back from the New York opening of *Cats*, it must have been.

'At the end of those three days, I'd have said that the future was absolutely crystal clear. He and Andrew were going back together! And this piece of work, *Aspects of Love*, was definitely going to happen. I felt sure that Tim's enthusiasm was genuine. There were even plans for us to spend three weeks working on the show, getting down an exact form for the production and the book. Tim said he'd have come up with some lyric angles by then. I really believed we were moving.'

Instead of which Rice pulled out of the show altogether. Nunn says apologetically: 'I'm sure he did so for very good reasons. Tim actually said he'd continued to think about it and felt he'd been "urged up to it" and "pushed to feel excited about it". When he left us, he said, he had had to admit to himself that he didn't feel *that* excited.'

Nunn says that he hasn't talked to Tim Rice about this since, though they have often met. 'All I know is that the message came to me,' he says, 'that Tim would prefer for there not to be any directorial involvement (by me) until the completion of whatever he did next. So that, once he was free, he could then see who would be the best and most ideal person to direct.'

It is hard not to think that Tim Rice may have been acting under a grudge over Trevor Nunn's preferred *Cats* lyric at that point. But Nunn continues: 'I went to see him after I'd seen his show *Blondel* late in 1983. There was no suspicion of strain then. And though I'm sure there must have been a lot of disappointment – that's natural – I really can't believe that what happened over "Memory" included me in Tim's eyes. He must know that all that was born of desperation.'

No doubt Tim Rice does know. But his change of heart over *Aspects of Love* makes it far less likely that he and Andrew will work together for some time. To those, like Trevor Nunn, Richard Stilgoe and Cameron Mackintosh, who see *Aspects of Love* (based on a sophisticated love-story novel of several inter-twined relationships) as ideally suited to Andrew's talents and liable to add one more hit to his repertoire of success, Rice's indifference may lack judgement. But his and Andrew's attitudes to emotional relationships can be very different.

Where *Starlight Express* pushes back musical frontiers, *Aspects* – despite the fact that its author was nearly sixty-five when he published it in 1955 – expresses almost daringly modern views on love-making and sexuality. In Nunn's view it is 'wickedly brilliant, posing aspects of romantic love which are more and more difficult to remain sympathetic with.

'For instance, a 14-year-old girl goes off with a much

ANDREW LLOYD WEBBER

older man who meanwhile keeps on his mistress – and after the girl has fallen in-love-at-first-sight with a boy her own age, who then plunges into destructive obsession. Finally, two women fall in what they describe as love with each other. And all these affairs are pushed a little bit further than we like our comfortable notions of love to be.'

Tim Rice apparently saw nothing in all this to excite the warmth and brilliance of his lyrical genius. As Nunn says, with more than a hint of sadness: 'Because of the subject matter, and because of its modernity – morally, that is – and because it would allow the discussion of manners and mores which rarely find their way on to the musical stage, I thought *Aspects of Love* was a wonderful thing for those two to do together.'

Perhaps he underestimated the widening gulf between two exceptionally gifted and individually creative men who had met as youths.

Samuel Butler once described genius as 'a supreme capacity for getting its possessors into trouble'. And Butler knew something about music and those who compose it. Whether or not Tim Rice feels pique at having been supplanted in one desperate moment by Trevor Nunn's magnificent post-mortem recreation of Eliot's magic, Andrew can take comfort from the satirical poet's further words on the subject.

'The history of art,' Butler wrote in his *Handel and Music*, 'is the history of revivals.'

Is there still time, then, for Andrew Lloyd Webber and Tim Rice to mend any broken fences between them? To 'revive' what they both have in large measure, the capacity for artistic achievement of the very highest order?

No doubt there is. But, with or without his old partner, the way ahead for 'bouncer' Lloyd Webber seems indelibly marked.

Chronology

1913 25 August   William Charles Henry Webber (26)
                     marries Mary Winifred Gittins
                     (24) in Chelsea, London
1914 11 March   William Southcombe Lloyd Webber
                     (Andrew's father) born
1916   Webbers move to Lloyd Square,
                     London WC1
1922   Jean Hermione Johnstone
                     (Andrew's mother) born
1933   William Lloyd Webber elected
                     Fellow of the Royal College of
                     Organists
1938   William Lloyd Webber created
                     Doctor of Music (London) and
                     appointed organist of All Saints,
                     Marylebone
1942 3 October   William Lloyd Webber marries Jean
                     Johnstone in All Saints Church,
                     Marylebone
1944 10 November   Tim Rice born
1946   William Lloyd Webber appointed
                     Professor of Theory &
                     Composition, Royal College of
                     Music
1948 22 March   Andrew Lloyd Webber born, West-
                     minster Hospital

1949	2 October	William Webber (grandfather) sings in Radio Gala with Kentucky Minstrels at London Palladium
1950	13 November	William Webber in Royal Variety Performance at London Palladium with George Mitchell Glee Club
1951		Andrew enters Wetherby School, South Kensington
	26 January	William Webber's photograph in *Radio Times* with George Mitchell Choir 'Calling All Forces'
	14 April	Julian Lloyd Webber born
1953	15 June	Sarah Hugill (Andrew's first wife) born
1956		Andrew enters Westminster Under-school
1958		William Lloyd Webber appointed Musical Director, Central Hall, Westminster, and organist
1959		Andrew's first work, a set of six short pieces entitled 'The Toy Theatre Suite', published
1960		Andrew enters Rigaud's House, Westminster School, as dayboy
1962		Andrew wins Challenge scholarship to College House as Queen's Scholar
1963		William Lloyd Webber elected Fellow of the Royal College of Music and Fellow of the London College of Music
1964		William Lloyd Webber appointed Director of London College of Music

	9 December	Andrew interviewed at Magdalen College, Oxford, for Exhibition
1965	21 April	Tim Rice writes to Andrew offering lyrics
		Andrew leaves Westminster for Oxford
	11 October	Andrew enters Magdalen College, Oxford, reading history
	5 December	Andrew leaves Oxford
		Andrew and Tim write musical on life of Dr Barnardo (*The Likes of Us*)
		Andrew sees Maria Callas perform Tosca
1965–6		Andrew takes one-year course in orchestration at Guildhall School of Music
1966		Andrew takes short course at Royal College of Music
1967		William Lloyd Webber created Honorary Academician, Royal Academy of Music
		Andrew and Tim have two songs recorded by singer Ross Hanniman
1968	1 March	*Joseph and the Amazing Technicolor Dreamcoat* performed by Colet Court choir and pop group
	May	*Joseph* (enlarged) performed at Central Hall, Westminster
	July	*Joseph* recorded
	9 November	*Joseph* performed in St Paul's Cathedral
1969	1 January	*Joseph* album released

	October	*Superstar* single recorded
	November	*Joseph* single released
		Sefton Myers signs Tim and Andrew to 3-year contract (10 years with options)
	7 November	*Come Back, Richard* recorded on RCA-Victor label
	20 December	Andrew and Tim write *Jesus Christ Superstar* in Herefordshire hotel
1970	January	Andrew meets Sarah Hugill at Oxford party
	May	*Superstar* single released in UK
	June	Andrew and Tim on David Frost show in UK
		Sefton Myers dies
		Andrew and Tim sail to New York on QEII
	October	*Superstar* album released in UK
	November	*Superstar* album released in USA
1971	6 February	*Superstar* No. 1 in the American charts
	June	Sarah takes her A-levels
	24 July	Andrew marries Sarah at Ashton Keynes
	12 October	*Superstar* opens at Mark Hellinger Theatre, Broadway
	November	Andrew and Tim appear on David Frost TV show, nationally syndicated throughout USA
	December	*Superstar* film in preparation
		During year: Andrew composes music for *Gumshoe* and studies trains as a forerunner to *Starlight Express*
1972	9 August	*Superstar* opens at Palace Theatre, London

	20 August	Shooting begins in Israel of *Superstar* film
	September	*Joseph* – first professional performance at Edinburgh Festival, and re-written for Broadway
	16 November	*Joseph* performed at Round House, London
	December	*Superstar* filming completed
1973	14 February	*Joseph* opens at Albery Theatre, London
		Andrew acquires Eaton Place West house, London
		Alan Doggett dies
		Andrew buys Sydmonton Court
	10 June	*Superstar* performed at Lancing College
	October	Tim Rice joins Capital Radio as DJ – hears radio programme on Eva Peron
		Superstar film released
1974		Andrew, with Julian, writes music for film *Odessa File*
		Julian Lloyd Webber marries
		Tim Rice backs out of *Jeeves* and Alan Ayckbourn takes over
	19 August	Tim Rice marries Jane McIntosh in London
		Tim and Andrew (sporadically) start writing *Evita*
1975	22 April	*Jeeves* opens at Her Majesty's Theatre, London
	24 May	*Jeeves* closes
	30 December	*Joseph* staged at Brooklyn Academy of Music, NY
1976	July	Andrew holds first Sydmonton Festival

		Daughter, Imogen, born to Sarah and Andrew
	November	*Evita* recorded by MCA
1977	9 January	*Joseph* ends limited run at Brooklyn Academy
	July	Second Sydmonton Festival (Andrew plays music for 'Variations' and score of *Cats*)
		Andrew invites John Hiseman and his group to form his regular 'sessions' musicians
1978	14 January	'Variations' performed on TV in LWT's 'South Bank Show'
	February	'Variations' at No. 3 in charts
	21 June	*Evita* opens at Prince Edward Theatre, London
	10 August	Andrew and Tim featured on TV (BBC 1) 'The Songwriters'
	3 October	*Superstar* achieves longest UK musical run
1979	July	Son, Nicholas, born to Sarah and Andrew
		Stigwood contract ends; Andrew becomes independent
	25 September	*Evita* opens at Broadway Theater, New York
	November	'Tell Me On A Sunday' album recorded
		Conservative victory in the General Election prevents Andrew's emigration to USA
1980	January	Andrew and Cameron Mackintosh lunch at Savile Club and plan *Cats* and *Song and Dance*
		Evita opens at Shubert Theatre, Los Angeles

	12 February	BBC-TV broadcast Marti Webb singing 'Tell Me On A Sunday'
	9 March	BBC-TV repeat Marti Webb show
	July	*Cats* performed at Sydmonton Festival with Trevor Nunn present
	4 November	Andrew featured on Thames-TV *This is Your Life*
	5 November	*Evita* achieves 1,000th performance
1981	11 May	*Cats* opens at New London Theatre, London
1982	27 January	*Joseph* opens on Broadway
	7 April	*Song and Dance* opens at Palace Theatre, London
	July	*Starlight Express* tried out at Sydmonton Festival
	7 October	*Cats* opens at Winter Garden Theater, New York
	29 October	William Lloyd Webber dies
1983	19 April	Andrew announces separation from wife Sarah and intention to marry dancer Sarah Brightman
	June	*Evita* closes on Broadway
	7 June	*Cats* wins seven 'Tony' Awards in New York, including 'Best Score'
	26 July	Andrew and Sarah Lloyd Webber divorced
	23 August	Andrew buys Palace Theatre, London for £1,300,000
	September	Sydmonton Festival performers stage *Aspects of Love*
		Cats opens in Vienna – first proscenium production
	29 October	Tim Rice's *Blondel* opens at London's Old Vic

1984	22 March	Andrew and Sarah Brightman marry, on his 36th birthday; and are presented to the Queen at a preview of *Starlight Express*
	27 March	*Starlight Express* opens at Apollo Victoria, London
	31 March	*Song and Dance* closes at Palace Theatre, London

Discography

Catalogue Number	Release Date	Record Co. and Label	Show	Artists and Titles	Length S=Single SA=Single Album DA=Double Album EP=Extra Play
1969					
SKL 4973	1 Jan	Decca (UK)	Joseph and the Amazing Technicolor Dreamcoat	'The Joseph Consortium'	S
RCA 1895	7 Nov	RCA Victor	(a) Come Back, Richard (Your country needs you) (b) Roll On Over the Atlantic	Tim Rice and the Webber Group	S
MKS 5019	Nov	MCA-UK	Jesus Christ Superstar	Murray Head (Judas)	S

Catalogue No.	Date	Label	Title	Contents	Code
DCL 79 178-79	Dec	(Decca-UK distributed)	*Jesus Christ Superstar*	(a) *Jesus Christ, Superstar* (b) 'John Nineteen Forty-one'	S
		MCA-US (Decca label)	*Jesus Christ Superstar*	(a) *Jesus Christ Superstar* (b) No B-side	
1970	May	MCA-US (Decca Label)	*Jesus Christ Superstar*	Murray Head (Judas) 'Heaven On Their Minds'	S
Original No. MKPS 2011/2 (MAPS 2075/6) New No: MCF 2503	Oct	(Decca-UK distributed) MCA	*Jesus Christ Superstar*	Studio recording (Murray Head, Ian Gillan, Nancy Elliman, Barry Dennen, Mike D'Abo, Victor Brox, Joe Cocker's Grease Band, Juicy Lucy)	SA
MCX 501 Originally DXSA 7206 6-6000 (C73-6000)	Nov	MCA-US (Decca label)	*Jesus Christ Superstar*	Studio recording (see above)	DA

Cat. no.	Date	Label	Title	Artist / Notes	Code
1971					
MKS 5063		Decca distributed – MCA-UK	*Jesus Christ Superstar*	Yvonne Elliman (a) 'I Don't Know How To Love Him' (b) The Overture (off London cast recording)	S
MCA 5000	Nov	MCA-US (Decca label)	*Jesus Christ Superstar*	Original Broadway cast	SA
1972					
MFP 5280	July	Music for Pleasure	*Jesus Christ Superstar*	No artist credits	SA
MDKS 8008	Oct (recorded August)	Decca UK	*Jesus Christ Superstar*	Original London cast	SA
1973					
MCX 502		Decca distributed – MCA-UK	*Jesus Christ Superstar*	Original motion picture sound track	DA
MCA2-11000		MCA-US (Decca label)	*Jesus Christ Superstar*	Original motion picture sound track	DA
1974					
MCF 2544	May	MCA-UK	*Joseph and the Amazing*	Various artists	SA

			Technicolor Dreamcoat		
(Cover changed early 1982)					
MCA 399	May	MCA-USA (Decca label)	*Joseph and the Amazing Technicolor Dreamcoat*	Various artists	SA
MCF 2503		MCA-UK	*Jesus Christ Superstar*	Original London cast	SA
MCA 2084	Late	MCA-USA (Decca label)	*The Odessa File*	Julian Lloyd Webber & Orchestra	SA
1975					
MCF 2591 (Maps 7735)	Jan	MCA-UK	*The Odessa File*	Julian Lloyd Webber & Orchestra (Vocal by Perry Como)	SA
MCF 2726	Oct	MCA-UK	*Jeeves*		SA
1976					
MCA 260	Oct	MCA-UK	*Evita*	Julie Covington (a) 'Don't Cry For Me, Argentina' (b) 'Rainbow High'	S
MCA 266	Dec	MCA-UK	*Evita*	Barbara Dickson (a) 'Another Suitcase, Another Hell' (b) 'Requiem For Evita'	S

MCX 503	Dec	MCA-UK	*Evita*	Julie Covington, Paul Jones, C.T. Williams, Barbara Dickson (Studio recording)	DA

1978

MCF 2824	Jan 3	MCA-USA	*Variations*	Julian Lloyd Webber	SA
MCA 2332	Jan	MCA-UK	*Variations*	Julian Lloyd Webber	SA
MCA 345	Jan	MCA-UK	*Variations*	Julian Lloyd Webber (a) Theme & Variations 1-4 (b) Variation 16	S
MCA 360	Feb	MCA-UK	*Variations*	Julian Lloyd Webber (a) Variation 5 (b) Variation 23	SA
MCA 376	June	MCA-UK	*Variations*	Julian Lloyd Webber (a) Variation 23 (b) Variation 5	SA
PSR 423	June	MCA-UK	*Variations*	Julian Lloyd Webber (one side only) Variation 23	S

Catalogue	Date	Label	Title	Performers	
PSR 429	July	MCA-UK	*Evita*	London Theatre audience applause (one side only)	S
MCG 3527	Sep	MCA-UK	*Evita*	Original London cast (Elaine Paige, Joss Acland, David Essex)	SA
1979					
MCA2 11007	Aug	MCA-USA (Decca label)	*Evita*	Patti Lupone & Broadway cast	DA
MCDW 453	Late	MCA-UK	*Evita*	Patti Lupone & Broadway cast	DA
MFP 50455	Nov 5	Music for Pleasure	*Joseph and the Amazing Technicolor Dreamcoat*	Paul Jones, Tim Rice, Gordon Waller, The Mike Sammes Singers, Geoff Love and His Orchestra	SA

POLD 5031 (2442-170) (Equivalent Cassette POLDC 5031)	Dec 10	Polydor	*Tell Me On A Sunday*	Marti Webb	SA

1980

2442 186	Oct 1	Polydor	*Evita* (etc.)	Marti Webb	SA

'Won't Change Places' (Marti Webb)
(a) Title Song (Andrew Lloyd Webber & Don Black)
'All I Am'
'Your Ears Should Be Burning Now'
'Angry And Sore' (Rod Argent)
'Don't Cry for Me, Argentina'
(b) 'I've Been in Love Too Long' (Andrew Lloyd Webber & Don Black) 'What You Gonna Do With Your Freedom?'
'Don't'
'I Guess I'll Miss The Man'

Catalogue	Date	Label	Show/Title	Artist / Tracks	
POSP 193 (2059 292)	Oct 7	Polydor	(a) 'I've Been In Love Too Long' (Andrew Lloyd Webber & Don Black) (b) 'I Won't Change Places' (Andrew Lloyd Webber & Don Black)	Marti Webb	S
POSP 204 (2059 301)	Oct 21	Polydor	Cats	Paul Nicholas (a) 'Musical Mr Mistoffelees' (b) 'Old Deuteronomy'	S
1981					
MCA 698	March	MCA-UK	Cats	(a) Instrumental version of 'Memory', (b) 'The Lost Variation'	S
POSP 279 (2059 364)	11 May	Polydor	Cats	(a) Elaine Paige 'Memory', (b) The Overture	S
1982					
M-BOX 1	Early –since deleted	MCA-UK	Boxed set of Joseph... Jesus Christ Superstar Evita		N/A

POSP 425 (2059 484)	10 Mar	Polydor	*Song & Dance*	Marti Webb (a) 'The Last Man In My Life' (b) 'Come Back With The Same Look In Your Eyes'	S
PODV4 (2478 160 and 161) (Equivalent Cassette: PODVC4)	8 June	Polydor	*Tell Me On A Sunday*	(I) Marti Webb (a) Overture, etc. (b) 'Come Back With The Same Look In Your Eyes', etc. (II) (a) Variations 1-16 (b) Variations 13 & 14, 17-20, 5 and 22-23	DA
1983					
SPELP 6 (813 584-1)	19 May	Polydor	*Joseph and the Amazing Technicolor Dreamcoat*	Original cast of Young Vic production	SA
POSP 625 (813779-7)	2 June	Polydor	'Him'	Sarah Brightman & Royal Philharmonic Orchestra (a) 'Him' (b) 'Memory'	S

Index

Note: Titles of Andrew Lloyd Webber's works appear under
'Lloyd Webber, Andrew'